Key Themes
in Philosophy

ROYAL INSTITUTE OF PHILOSOPHY LECTURE SERIES: 24
SUPPLEMENT TO *PHILOSOPHY* 1988

EDITED BY

A. Phillips Griffiths

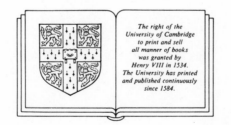

*The right of the
University of Cambridge
to print and sell
all manner of books
was granted by
Henry VIII in 1534.
The University has printed
and published continuously
since 1584.*

CAMBRIDGE UNIVERSITY PRESS

CAMBRIDGE
NEW YORK   PORT CHESTER   MELBOURNE   SYDNEY

Published by the Press Syndicate of the University of Cambridge
The Pitt Building, Trumpington Street, Cambridge, CB2 1RP
40 West 20th Street, New York, NY 10011, USA
10 Stamford Road, Oakleigh, Melbourne 3166, Australia

British Library Cataloguing in Publication Data

Key themes in philosophy.—(Royal Institute of
Philosophy; 24).
1. Philosophy
I. Griffiths, A. Phillips (Allen Phillips), *1927*–100
ISBN 0-521-37579-7

Library of Congress Cataloguing in Publication Data

Key themes in philosophy—edited by A. Phillips
Griffiths p. cm. — (Royal Institute of Philosophy
lecture series; 24)
ISBN 0-521-37579-7
1. Philosophy. I. Griffiths, A. Phillips. II.
Philosophy (London, England). III. Series:
Royal Institute of Philosophy lectures: v. 24.
829.K388 1989   89-36878
100—dc20   CIP

Origination by PPC Limited, Leatherhead, Surrey
Printed in Great Britain by the University Press, Cambridge

Contents

Preface

The Royal Institute of Philosophy lectures of 1985–6, *Philosophers Ancient and Modern,* arranged and edited by Godfrey Vesey, dealt with the classical philosophical texts prescribed by the two examining boards for the General Certificate of Education. In his preface to that volume—of lectures intended to exemplify the highest standards of analysis and evaluation, but expressed in such a manner as to make them accessible to sixth-formers without previous acquaintance with philosophy—Professor Vesey wrote 'Aiming at one, fairly well-defined audience, the lectures in fact attracted a considerably wider one. I hope this volume does the same.' In the event, it did.

The other part of the General Certificate of Education examination in philosophy centres on key philosophical themes rather than texts. The lectures in this volume attempt to do a correlative service with regard to these themes for an equally wide audience. It must, however, be a quite different kind of book from one dealing with specific philosophical texts. Questions on these topics invite the respondent not only to show a knowledge and understanding of philosophy, but to practise it. (Though it is doubtful how far one may press this distinction: one cannot get far in one, without the other.)

The philosophers who have contributed their thoughts on these topics in these lectures have done so while placing them in the context of philosophical thinking to which they belong, and to that extent are informative and instructive. But they are all also essentially argumentative, and their value will be in stimulating an argumentative response.

The Problem of the External World

I: D. W. HAMLYN

Heidegger[1] says concerning the question of the possibility of a proof of the existence of an external world that 'the "scandal of philosophy" (Kant's words) is not that this proof has yet to be given, but that *such proofs are expected and attempted again and again*'. Heidegger thinks this because our being (*Dasein*) is in the world, and this is something which Descartes for one failed to appreciate. I am not concerned here to answer the question whether Heidegger's own views on these matters will do, though I think that they will not. Indeed they might well be said to beg the question at issue, in that Heidegger starts from the *presumption* that we are actually in the world, even if we are not in it in the way in which the tree in the garden is (and does not this last point make a great difference to the situation?). Another way of reacting to Heidegger would be to say that he does not treat the fact and force of scepticism seriously enough when he makes that presumption. After all, it is possible for us to raise sceptical doubts about the existence of a world apart from ourselves, while it is not possible for the tree in the garden to act similarly. Hence, even if we make the presumption that we are in the world, as Heidegger insists, we are in it in a way that leaves untouched the possibility of sceptical doubts about what that world and our being in it are like. It might, logically, be the case, for example, that the world consists of just me and that my being in the world is no more than for me just to exist. In other words, my being in the world does not directly entail that there exists a world apart from me.

Nevertheless, raising or having doubts about the existence of a world apart from myself is not *ipso facto* to raise or have doubts about an *external* world. If someone professed doubts about the existence of anything apart from himself, others might reasonably ask (apart from thinking him mad) what he supposed to be the case. Would he not have to say something to the effect that all of his supposed perceptions must really be figments of his own imagination, however that came about, and that he has for that reason no grounds for belief in the existence of anything for which we should normally think the senses provided evidence? For such a person would have to disbelieve the 'evidence of his senses' in a systematic way. Even this, however, would not give adequate sense to the thought that what he doubts is the existence of an *external world*.

1

Aristotle says in one passage in his *De Anima*, II.5, that sense-perception requires the existence of an external object. But what Aristotle meant by that last phrase was an object external to the body. It is far from clear what the person whom I was trying to describe earlier must believe about his body. Can he, for example, believe anything about his body without believing that it stands in actual or potential spatial relations to other things, or at least that it occupies space? And if he believes that, does he still believe that nothing exists apart from himself? Or is his body also part of that world apart from himself?

It is notorious that Descartes, and at least some of those who followed him, did believe just that. For in asking in *Meditation* 2 'What am I?' Descartes answers 'A thinking thing', and the body is held by him not to be part of that thinking thing. Of course, Descartes came to maintain in *Meditation* 6 that some of the ideas which he had were in fact dependent on the body and would not have existed but for what he elsewhere described as the quasi-substantial union between the soul and the body. These ideas, those involved in sensation, were, he said, *modes* of thinking, not pure thoughts; that is to say that they depend for their existence on the existence of a thinking soul, but equally they depend on the union of that thinking thing with the body. Nevertheless, the answer to the question 'What am I?' remains 'A thinking thing', and the body is no part of that.

We are still not quite at the point at which we can give a natural interpretation to the suggestion that everything apart from myself, including my own body, is part of an *external* world. I do not think that that phrase was ever used by Descartes himself (although that remark is not based upon anything like a complete and exhaustive survey of Descartes' writings.) Nor do I know who was the first philosopher to use it. Hume undoubtedly did in his *Treatise* I.4.2, and Berkeley speaks often of external things. Locke (*Essay III.1*) opposes 'sensible objects without' to the 'inward workings of our own spirits'. Spinoza, on the other hand, seems to speak of external bodies only in such a way as to contrast other bodies with one's own. It looks almost as if the internal/external contrast which is implicit in the idea of an external world, as it has come to be used, is something of a British notion, even if its ancestry lies in Descartes. It is perhaps noteworthy that it is in Berkeley's writings that the notion becomes really explicit; for Berkeley was an idealist, as the philosophers who preceded him were not. As I have indicated elsewhere, following a suggestion put forward by Myles Burnyeat,[2] Berkeley's idealism would not have been possible without the background provided by Descartes' claim that I have a clear and distinct idea of my mind in a way in which I do not of my body. But Descartes himself was not an idealist; he fully accepted the existence of matter and material bodies, although he thought that, in the light of the conclusions to be drawn from the 'method of doubt', argument for their existence was required. After all, God might have been a deceiver, even if he is not so in fact. The situation is quite different with Berkeley, who seems little concerned with that possibility, being more concerned to show that nothing exists 'without the mind'.

That phrase might be thought to be ambiguous, and the claim that nothing exists without the mind might be taken to mean either that nothing exists unless the mind does (in which case some explanation of the fact is called for) or that nothing exists outside the mind (in which case there is a definite implication that some sense can be given to the idea that whatever is mental is in some way inner). Could Berkeley be guilty of trading on such an ambiguity? And if so, why? It may be that in order to answer that question we need to go back to Descartes. We need to do that, not because there is any suggestion of such an ambiguity in his way of stating his problem or because there is any suggestion in him of idealism, but simply because, as I have in effect already indicated, there is in what he has to say the germs of that way of thinking which emerges in Berkeley.

Descartes' central thought in this respect is that, unless we can show to the contrary, those ideas which we have of a material world and of material things might be produced in us by a malignant demon or arch-deceiver. In which case we should be confined, as far as concerns what we can know, to the contents of our own minds. The question is exactly what that means. Any answer to that question depends on the answer to a prior question or set of questions—what is the mind and what sort of thing comprises its contents? If you had asked Aristotle, for example, that question, either he would have failed to understand what he was being asked or he would have interpreted it as a request for an elucidation of the idea of the intellect. In the latter case he would have said that its contents consist of the intelligible forms of things. None of that gives any support to the idea that in being confined to the contents of our own minds we are being confined to something which makes the world external in any sense apart from that of its being external to our bodies. I believe that the same or similar things could be said of other philosophers who lived before Descartes. What then is the new way of thinking on these matters which Descartes introduced and what is its basis?

It is often said on this point that it is the radical character of Descartes' method of doubt which led to the result which we are now considering and the reason for which we are trying to diagnose. In a way, so it is, but it is not enough to say that without some further attempt to make clear the exact nature of what is radical in all this. Let me ask again what Aristotle would have said if you put before him the suggestion that God or a malignant demon might be systematically deceiving us (a suggestion which, it is worth noting, would be quite foreign to his nature, since Aristotle, I believe, was not much moved by sceptical considerations, preferring to point to the standard cases and situations in which correctness is to be expected). He might have thought that you were suggesting that our beliefs are systematically false either because there is something systematically wrong about our powers of judgment or because there is something systematically wrong about our faculties of sense-perception or intellect so that they do not in fact receive the actual forms of things. It would not have occurred to him to think that in all this sea of error there is one thing that must necessarily stay afloat—that I cannot be in error over the thought that 'I think' or that 'I exist'. Why not?

One reason is that Aristotle's approach to the issues is not likely to have been so autobiographical, as one might put it, as that. To follow Descartes' method of doubt to its conclusions I would have to consider what *I* would think in these circumstances, not simply what might be concluded from the hypothesis of our being subject to systematic deceit. To follow Descartes I have to consider, given that hypothesis, what I can and what I cannot (preferably logically cannot) suppose to be false. I do not myself think that Descartes is right to conclude that I cannot suppose it to be false that I think or that I exist. What he is right about is that if I am thinking I cannot rationally be in doubt as to the fact that I am thinking or that I exist. That is because of what thinking is—a necessarily self-conscious activity, so that if I engage in it I must *ipso facto* be conscious of doing so (and my consciousness of my own existence follows *a fortiori*). Hence the certainty of the truth in question is, so to speak, a conditional one; its necessity is what Aristotle called 'hypothetical', not absolute.

Nevertheless, the place at which Descartes finds such certainty is of manifest interest for the question why there emerges from all this the distinction between the inner and the external world. For, to find the certainty which he requires Descartes has to look into himself. That is an intelligible exercise because of self-consciousness—of which the thinking to which I have made reference is an instance. It is notable, however, how natural it is to use the expression 'look into himself' in connection with the appeal to self-consciousness which Descartes wishes to make. If we take that expression seriously we are on the edge of thinking of mental processes, or some of them, as constituting an inner realm. Nevertheless, granted that they might be inner from the perspective of others (they do not manifest themselves on the periphery of the human being), why are they inner to the person whose mental processes they are? Why, more particularly, might that person's self be thought to be inner?

William James once suggested that, as an aspect of what might justifiably be called phenomenology, it was natural to think of oneself as located some short distance behind the centre of one's forehead. Yet the Greeks showed no inclination to think in that way. Perhaps in any case only a philosopher or similar intellectual would be tempted to think in that way; those who are concerned more consistently with some aspect of the body might well think otherwise. Once again the connection between the idea of the self and the phenomenon of thinking is noteworthy, but the supposition that the self itself is inner—an inner 'I'—could be thought to follow only if it was also thought that thinking itself is inner, and only if the self was supposed to be, as Descartes conceived it, a thinking thing. When Descartes answered the question 'What am I?' by saying that he was a thinking thing, he purported to derive this conclusion from the 'Cogito'. But, as has often been said about the 'Cogito', all that follows from the method of doubt as a certainty is the existence of thinking, and as I have insisted all that is really valid in that connection is the conclusion that one cannot be in doubt as to the occurrence of thinking if one is engaged in thinking. One can move from that to the indubitability of the self, the 'I', only if thinking presupposes the existence of a thinking thing, and the 'I' is the only sort of thing that can be that. That is presupposed by the 'Cogito', not a conclusion to be derived from it.

The idea of an external world presupposes the thought that we, each 'I' of us, are inner and the world outside. Given what I have said, it is no good answering the question 'Inside and outside what?' by answering 'Inside and outside the body'. For, apart from the question whether the body itself is part of the external world, the inside that seems to be involved in all these considerations is, despite the suggestion of William James which I referred to and which is at the best phenomenology, not that sort of inside. Rather, it is one to which sense can be given only via the suggestion that self-consciousness either is or makes possible a kind of inward looking. If one engages in active self-consciousness in the sense presupposed in, for example, thinking about one's thinking, one clearly does not look outwards. But the source of the conception that one looks inwards still remains somewhat puzzling in that it does not gain a complete purchase on what is at issue. According to Descartes the constituents of the mind of which thinking is composed and which are revealed to self-consciousness are ideas, and by the time we come to Berkeley those ideas are conceived as inner by contrast with 'external things'. In this way the inner/outer or internal/external distinction becomes full-blown.

I have made something of an issue of this because, if one can give sense to the internal/external distinction in the way that it is made and used by at any rate Berkeley and Hume, there appears to emerge a gap

5

between those inner or internal states and so-called external objects, and a problem about how one can get from the one to the other. According to Hume, for example, one cannot do so, although the vulgar, ordinary people, simply confuse them, making no distinction between objects and what Hume calls perceptions or impressions; the philosopher, if he follows Hume, knows better and equally knows that, while one can explain why one believes in an external world, one cannot provide any rational justification for doing so. So scepticism about such a world reigns supreme. But even Hume, as is well known, found that unsatisfactory, seeking the relief provided by a good dinner and a game of backgammon. Many other philosophers, starting similarly from impressions, ideas or sense-data, have tried, despite Hume, to provide a justification of belief in an external world by a variety of means, such as, for example, phenomenalism (i.e. the view that objects just are bundles of actual and possible sense-data, or, as it has been put, logical constructions out of these). But such attempts are doomed to failure if that gap between the internal and the external remains.

Whether or not Descartes embraced the idea of an external world and with that the internal/external distinction, he did accept both the representative or representational theory of perception and the theory that the ideas which we have in perception and which are in some sense representations of physical objects are caused by those physical objects. Thus, to perceive an object in the physical world is to have an idea of that physical object which is caused to exist in our minds by that object. That perception involves causal processes seems obvious; for we know something about the physics and physiology of vision, hearing and so on, and the story that these involve is an essentially causal one. But these accounts provide no warrant for the thesis that the end-product of the causal processes are ideas or what have you which function as representatives, however adequate, of the objects which are the initial cause of the perception. Modern causal theories of perception of the kind put forward by H.P. Grice[3] are in effect attempts to spell out the meaning of perceptual statements in terms of truth-conditions which include a reference to causality. Whether or not any theories of this kind are adequate to provide an account of the meaning of statements of the form 'X perceives M' (and my own view is that they are not and cannot be), they do not of themselves presuppose any reference to states of mind which are simple representations of the object M. Nor does Grice think otherwise, since although he invokes the notion of sense-data he defines that notion in terms of things looking or appearing such and such.

Things in the world may rightly be said sometimes to cause us to perceive them as such and such or to cause it to be the case that they appear such and such, whether or not it is the case that whenever we perceive things as such and such this is *always* caused by those things. (And it is reasonably obvious that sometimes how we see things is a function, at least in part, of something about *us*, rather than a function of how those things are.) But to say this is not to say that they bring about certain inner states which are representational of them. Of course, in being caused to see things in a certain way our experience is changed and we gain an experience which we did not formerly have. Once again, however, to say that is not to imply the coming about of new experiences akin to Humean impressions or Berkeleyan ideas. The term 'experience' is no doubt ambiguous. I believe with Christopher Peacocke[4] that there is an aspect of perception which is, so to speak, sensational. Indeed I think that the total perceptual experience is, as it were, 'coloured' by the sensations which are a constituent part of the whole thing, such that it would not count as perception if this were not the case. To say this, however, is not in any way to side with Humean impressions or Berkeleyan ideas; for the sensations which I take to be involved in perception are not *of* anything.

It follows from all this that a causal theory or account of perception by no means entails the existence of inner, representational states. *A fortiori* it gives no credence to the idea of an external world in any other sense than that of a world which is outside one's body. The thought that we are provided with inner states to which we have direct access and which constitute the epistemic basis for knowledge, if that is possible, of an external world, must have an independent ground, and is not to be found in any appeal to the causal processes which undoubtedly take place in perception. Given all the other things which I have said, it is far from clear what that ground could possibly be. If that is so it is best to say that there is no such thing as an external world in the sense which makes Heidegger say that the 'scandal of philosophy' is that a demand for the proof of its existence is made again and again. There is only the world, most of which is external to our bodies and in which we plainly exist, and there is no reason for doubt as to its existence simply on the ground that it is external.

I said at the beginning, however, that in leaving the matter at that Heidegger does not treat the fact and force of scepticism seriously enough. It is possible for the sceptic to ask, without any appeal to the idea of an external world, how we know that we are not dreaming or that all our supposed perceptions are not really figments of our imagination. These are ancient sceptical questions. The former, the one about dreaming was not only raised by Descartes in the course of his argument following out the 'method of doubt'; it was mentioned by Plato in his *Theaetetus*[5] in the course of an argument attributed to Protagoras, which is in fact sceptical, being a version of what has become known as the 'argument from illusion'. That is to say that it is an argument which seeks to cast general doubt on the reliability of perception by arguing that there is nothing to distinguish cases of veridical perception from cases which are admittedly instances of illusion. The sceptical question 'How do we know that we are not dreaming' is an example of that, since it suggests that there is nothing to choose between dream and ordinary perceptual experience, so that, for all we know there may be no veridical perceptual experience and we may be dreaming now.

The suggestion that what we suppose to be veridical perception may be merely figments of our imagination is an easier one to deal with than the one about dreams. The straight answer to the suggestion that it is all a product of our imagination is that there is absolutely no reason for thinking that that is the case. There are, of course, examples of people a large part of whose experience is coloured by what is in some sense or other a product of their imagination; their experience is the product of delusion and they may not be aware of that. The sceptic wants to suggest that our individual experience may be like that for all we know to the contrary. But if I am asked whether I may not be in that position I can reply only that there is absolutely no reason to think that that is the case, and the fact that the insane may conceivably react similarly has nothing to do with it. It might, logically, be as it is with them, but there is no reason whatever for thinking that it is so in fact. And there a rational argument ought to end.

The attraction of the dream argument is that the experience of dreaming is so common and most of us have been in the position of not knowing whether we are dreaming or waking. Moreover, the experience of the dream is even more a passive one, so to speak, than that of being subject to flights of fancy. It does not appear in any sense up to us whether we dream and if so what form the dream takes. (I say 'appear', because there are plenty of theories, including Freud's, which suggest that the dream is more up to us than appears at first sight.) As Schopenhauer suggested[6] the only empirical criterion for distinguishing dreaming from reality is that provided by waking up. The radical sceptic wishes to suggest that waking up itself might be a dream waking up. If this is suggested (a dream suggestion?) to the person waking up, the only rational response is to say again that there is absolutely no reason for supposing this to be the case, and the fact that a sequence of dream experiences may be exactly like a sequence of veridical waking experiences has nothing to do with it. Life might, logically, be exactly like a dream and it might, logically *be* a dream, but there is no reason at all for thinking that it is.

I do not suggest that what I have said on these matters is in any way the final reply to and refutation of the sceptic. He can always come back with fresh arguments, and if he does they have to be answered. As I have suggested elsewhere,[7] the forms of argument that must go on between the defender of the possibility of knowledge of the world and the sceptic are dialectical; the appropriate response to the sceptic depends on what he has to say. It follows from this that arguments in reply to the sceptic, even if not, perhaps, a proof of the existence of an external world in the terms presupposed by Heidegger, *will* be required again and again.

If we grant that knowledge of the world is possible, that it is mediated by perception, and that the only viable sense in which that world may be said to be external is that it consists of objects which lie outside one's body, then we must admit that when we perceive the world we normally perceive objects with an identity and properties and which stand in a web of causal relations in which we, via our bodies, also stand. Moreover, despite the fact that perception depends on causal processes which mediate between ourselves and other objects, there are no grounds for thinking that perception is *epistemologically* indirect. That is to say that there are no grounds for thinking that we directly perceive such things as sense-data and perceive physical objects only indirectly via them. Nor is there any other sense in which our normal perception of the world may be said to be indirect, although there are of course special circumstances in which we are forced to see things indirectly, as when we have to rely on a mirror. To repeat and emphasize the point— the fact that in perception we are linked to objects only via certain causal processes, such as those involved in the reflection of light from objects, the passage of light between them and us, and the consequent stimulation of our sense-organs, has no bearing on the question whether we perceive those objects directly or indirectly from an epistemological point of view. Something is epistemologically indirect only when it is known only indirectly by, for example, inference from other things; and that is not how our normal perception of objects works.

Of course, we not only perceive objects *simpliciter*, we perceive them as such and such's. What such and such's we are capable of seeing them *as* depends on what concepts we have. Perception is certainly concept dependent. That thought should give no comfort to the sceptic in general, nor to that particular brand of scepticism which is particularly prevalent among sociologists and which sees the world as some kind of construction on our part, perhaps a social construction.[8] The thought that the world is in some sense a construction on our part is sometimes ascribed to Kant, because of what he has to say about bringing concepts and categories to bear on intuitions in judgment. The suggestion that we employ concepts in judgments about the world (even given the fact that for Kant as a so-called transcendental idealist the only world to which such concepts could be applied were appearances) says nothing, however, for any view that the world thereby becomes our *construction*. There is a distinction between that which objectively falls under a given concept and that which does not, and what is objectively so is not up to us to construct; it is independent of us.

Concepts are not simply frames of reference which we bring to the world. Concepts are, after all, acquired, either through or at least in the course of experience. To have the concept of X is to know what it is for something to be X, whatever is exactly involved in that. That knowledge has to be acquired; it is a function of learning.[9] To learn what it is for something to be X is a matter of coming to know what sort of thing really falls under the concept X and what does not; and that presupposes that there is a question of what really falls under a given concept and what does not. Hence, although perception is concept dependent, what is there in the world to perceive is independent of how we perceive it at a given time, even though our concepts of what is there in general do depend on perception. The growth of our understanding of the world is a function of the interplay between concepts and the use of our senses in this way. None of that suggests, however, that we in any sense construct our world or that what we perceive is other than independently existing objects, the character of which determines whether they are properly and objectively to be perceived and conceived as we do.

Nevertheless, *how* we perceive things depends in part on what concepts we have. Clearly it also depends on what and what kinds of senses we have; equally it depends on whether our senses function in the way that they can be expected normally to do. It is an obvious and elementary point that the colour-blind cannot see things in quite the way the normal sighted can. Hence what colours we are capable of discriminating depends on the degree of sensibility that our senses make possible. It does not follow from that that colours (and so-called secondary qualities of things in general) are in any important sense subjective. The colour scheme which we have is anthropocentric in the sense that it is one which presupposes normal human sensibility, normal human sense-organs with normal powers of discrimination, and normal human powers of understanding involving normal human conceptual apparatus.

Alternatives to these are of course conceivable, as is the possibility of creatures who have a different colour sensibility and a different colour scheme from ours, or who have none at all. Up to a point we might be able to explain why these differences existed by reference to differences in the structure of their sense-organs or differences in their ways of thinking about colour (as, for example, it has sometimes been suggested that the ancient Greeks paid more attention to the intensity of colour than to hue, something that might explain Homer's otherwise improbable reference to the wine-dark sea!). For such creatures an orange might not be that colour, or might not be coloured at all. None of this affects the fact that a ripe orange *is* orange coloured. Questions

10

about what is so and not so presuppose for their answer the satisfaction of the terms of reference within which the questions are raised. Questions asked by us about the colour of things presuppose terms of reference which are anthropocentric, in that they take for granted normal human colour vision and normal human ways of thinking about colour. The fact that the questions might have quite different terms of reference if they were asked by different creatures is something which we can recognize as a possibility without that affecting the validity of answers to such questions raised with our normal terms of reference.

The distinction between primary and secondary qualities has, historically, been made for a number of different reasons, e.g. that there are differences between qualities directly detectable by one sense and qualities detectable by more than one sense, and that there are differences between qualities which admit of intensive variation, such as colour saturation, and qualities which are extensive, such as size or weight, the former kind of quality not admitting of extensive measurement. The connection between these two considerations, and with others that might conceivably be adduced, is an interesting and complicated one, but not one into which I can go now. The British Empiricists tended to assimilate secondary qualities to sensations on the grounds of supposed similarities between the two. Locke, for example, asserted the likeness of extreme heat to pain. But there are differences too between secondary qualities and sensations. For example, there can be agreement and standards of agreement on what colour a thing is, so that failure to recognize it for what it is is a defect, whereas it is not normally thought a defect of the same kind if someone does not recognize something as painful in the way that may be generally agreed. The main ground adduced, however, for worrying about the objectivity of judgments such as those about colour is, in effect, that properties such as colour are anthropocentric, and that, as we have seen, is no real ground. Questions about the objectivity or otherwise of something arise only within a scheme of concepts and with the presupposition of whatever makes judgments involving those concepts possible.

Of course, someone who can make more, or more refined, discriminations between colours, as, for example, the normal sighted can do in comparison with the colour-blind, must be considered the expert on colour. That is a point on which Aristotle rightly insisted. If someone appeared to make more distinctions than the normal sighted can, we, if we are in the latter category, might not be able to comprehend fully what he was up to. In some cases a suitable scepticism might be appropriate. But the proof of the pudding is in the eating. Can he make such distinctions systematically in a way that makes the application of the ideas of correctness and incorrectness possible and plausible? Can he achieve things which turn on such distinctions in a systematic way?

D. W. Hamlyn

And so on. The question at issue is whether or not there are differences between the objects so discriminated which, given an understanding of the phenomenon of colour, can be put in terms of colour differences. And that is an objective matter.

Another point which Locke, for example, appealed to is the fact that colours disappear in the dark; that is to say that colour vision depends on the satisfaction of conditions about light. Do objects have colours in the dark? Of course they do, but the fact that a condition of their perceptibility is not satisfied because there is no light means that they cannot be perceived in those circumstances. There is no need to follow Aristotle in this context and make a distinction between actual and potential colours. Perception always requires the satisfaction of certain conditions if it is to take place. That fact does not rob objects of possible perception of objectivity when the conditions are not satisfied.

What I have been trying to argue for in the latter part of this paper is that certain facts about perception—its concept-dependedness, its presupposition of specific perceptual apparatus and the satisfaction of the conditions for the effectiveness of that—are in no case grist for the sceptic's mill. There is reason for scepticism only when specific considerations pointing in that direction are relevant and not because perception is subject to certain general conditions. Of course, when there is reason to expect the satisfaction of those conditions, and they are not satisfied, one has reason to doubt the perceptual claims of the person concerned. But that is clearly no reason for general scepticism about the objectivity of perceptual claims made under these conditions, and no reason for general doubt about the objectivity of such things as colour.

Berkeley ended his *Three Dialogues*[10] by making Philonus (his protagonist) say, 'My endeavours tend to unite, and place in a clearer light, that truth which was before shared between the vulgar and the philosophers: the former being of the opinion, that *those things they immediately perceive are the real things*; and the latter, that *the things immediately perceived are ideas, which exist only in the mind*. Which two notions put together, do, in effect, constitute the substance of what I advance.' Berkeley was right in the characterization of his own philosophy. But I doubt whether the vulgar have ever believed that the real things are merely those which are the objects of immediate perception. For one thing, the notion of immediate perception—perception of such objects as allow perception of them to be inference-free—is problematical and is certainly not one to be taken for granted in the ordinary man. The vulgar may have generally believed, and rightly, that what we perceive normally exists (and the use of 'normally' here admits of plenty of exceptions in special cases). Berkeley would not have claimed that the things immediately perceived are ideas unless Descartes had, as a result of his use of the 'method of doubt', claimed that it is the contents of the mind of which we have primary and privileged access. But, as we have seen, none of this is, in general, a reason for doubting that what we perceive includes ordinary physical objects, although, it has to be said, much more besides.[11]

Notes

[1] M. Heidegger, *Being and Time*, trans. J. Macquarrie and E. Robinson (Oxford: Blackwell, 1962), 249.

[2] See my *Metaphysics* (Cambridge University Press, 1984), Ch. 2, and the reference to the work of Myles Burnyeat given there.

[3] H. P. Grice, 'The Causal Theory of Perception', *PAS* Suppl. Vol. (1966), 121ff., reprinted in G. J. Warnock (ed.), *The Philosophy of Perception* (London: Oxford University Press, 1967), 85ff.

[4] Christopher Peacocke, *Sense and Content* (Oxford: Clarendon Press, 1983), Ch. 1. See also my 'Unconscious Inference and Judgment in Perception' in my *Perception, Learning and the Self* (London: Routledge and Kegan Paul, 1983), 11–29. I do not agree, however, with Peacocke's way of characterizing the sensational element involved. The whole idea of perception involving sensation goes back to Thomas Reid.

[5] Plato, *Theaetetus*, 158bff.

[6] A. Schopenhauer, *The World as Will and Representation*, trans. by E. F. J. Payne (New York: Dover, 1969), I.5.

[7] D. W. Hamlyn, *The Theory of Knowledge* (London and Basingstoke: Macmillan, 1971), 50–52.

[8] See, for example, P. L. Berger and T. Luckmann, *The Social Construction of Reality* (London: Allen Lane, 1967), and a critique on my part, 'The Concept of Social Reality' in Paul F. Secord (ed.), *Explaining Human Behavior* (Beverly Hills, Cal.: Sage Publications, 1982), 189–209.

[9] There are admittedly problems about that, in that, as Aristotle pointed out at the opening of his *Posterior Analytics*, learning presupposes prior knowledge. Hence, if a regress is to be avoided, there must be ways of coming to know things which are not learning. I have tried to say something about this issue in my *Experience and the Growth of Understanding* (London: Routledge and Kegan Paul, 1978) and in 'What Exactly is Social About the Origins of Understanding?' in my *Perception, Learning and the Self* (London: Routledge and Kegan Paul, 1983), 162–177.

[10] G. Berkeley, *Principles of Human Knowledge* and *Three Dialogues of Hylas and Philonous*, G. J. Warnock (ed.) (London: Collins, 1962)

[11] It is one of the great virtues of Fred Dretske's *Seeing and Knowing* (London: Routledge and Kegan Paul, 1969) that it emphasizes the great range of things which we can rightly be said to see, and the great range of facts of which we can rightly say that we see that they obtain, including, for example, facts about molecular structure. We cannot see these things unaided, but that is not a reason for saying we cannot perceive them.

II: J. E. TILES

Our Perception of the External World

The phenomena of perception have been used by philosophers to kindle and fuel doubts about the reality of 'the external world', a phrase which points roughly in the direction of our natural environment. After grappling with problems, which trade under this title, one often discovers that the issues have less to do with the reality of anything which might be called 'the external world' and more to do with the reality of the problems themselves. In this paper I propose to examine three approaches to what might deserve to be labelled, 'problems about the external world'.

The worry reached by the first approach often tempts those who reflect for the first time on the causal mechanisms which underlie human perception. Following this approach we will turn up serious oversights and confusions in the way people are prone to think about perception, but the approach will not be seen to generate any real difficulty about the 'external world'.

What will become clear, as we think carefully about perception and the mistakes which we sometimes commit, or feel ourselves tempted to commit, is the importance of the inferences, which we are led to make as we perceive things. A second approach which raises problems about 'the external world' is to inquire about our right to make such (in most cases automatic) inferences. It will turn out that this is not a real problem, for it is simply not coherent to imagine ourselves in a position where we could ask for a justification for doing this.

A third approach, which raises problems about the external world, is to consider the possibility that what we base our inferences on has been tampered with on a grand scale. Whether this third way of attempting to raise a problem about the 'external world' succeeds in raising a real problem will turn out to depend not on the facts of perception, but on what it is for our thoughts and words to have a meaning. This is where issues, which deserve the title 'problems about the external world', are seen to fall not directly on questions about perception, but, as with many other contemporary philosophical problems, on questions having to do with meaning.

We begin, however, with the natural history of perception, the facts of physics and physiology, which suggest to people that we have some kind of problem in relating to 'the external world'. Take a very simple fact about the eyes. The cornea acts as a lens distributing light reflected from objects in the environment on to the retina, which is a layer of light sensitive cells on the back of the eyeball. The basic effect is studied in elementary optics. In fact it does not require a lens. Imagine some prisoners kept in a dark cell with one barred window covered by a blackout shutter which has a pin hole in it, and on bright days, their cell becomes a camera obscura: an image of the view from the window is projected, upside down, on the wall of the cell opposite the window. Now there is a sense in which they can 'see' what is outside the window of their cell but only by means of what they see on the wall at the back of the cell, which is part of the world internal to the prison.

Once people learn to think of their eyes as governed by principles very like those that produce the camera obscura effect, some of them become strongly tempted to treat what they 'see' as what happens at the back of their eyeballs and they regard themselves like the prisoners, who only see what is external to the prison by means (of seeing) what is internal to it, viz. the inverted image on the wall. Because one can artificially produce similar effects (on the backs of people's eyeballs as well as on prison walls) they entertain the philosophic worry that what they 'see' may not be good evidence of the way things are in the world outside their bodies.

The retinal image, like that of the camera obscura, is inverted on the retina. Asked why they do not see the world 'upside down', these people will reply that either the image is reversed at some point further along the chain of causes of visual perception (the chain which links the optic nerves to the visual centres of the brain), or people have just become used to using an inverted image, in the way that people, who wear spectacles which invert what they see for long enough, eventually fail to notice this.[1] For a similar reason, we do not see two images, although we have two eyes with two retinas. And as a clinching proof that we see the world outside our bodies mediated by what we 'see' at the backs of our eyeballs, these people will point to the double image, which is experienced when one eye is dislocated by pushing on it with a finger.

There are three observations to make about this train of thought. The first is that if our interest was in a scientific or 'causal' account of perception, we have become side-tracked. What we have taken up is a form of account suitable for explaining how information is brought to a perceiver, but not what happens when that information is taken in perceptually. The account we are using, when we compare the eye to a camera obscura, is formally similar to the more complicated story which has to be told when one explains how the image on a television screen originates in a studio many miles away; in other words, how light is converted to electronic impulses, transmitted, received and reconverted to light by bombarding a phosphorescent screen with electrons.

It is formally similar in that there is a perceiver at the receiving end of a shorter or longer chain of cause and effect. Even when we trace the causal chain inside the perceiver's body, we are not giving a causal account of perception, but an account of how causal influences can be linked together to join the point where perception takes place with a point some distance away from the perceiver. And this is not to explain perception.

But is it not an important first step in explaining perception? It is a first step, and it may very well be important, but if so, only because it is a step precisely 180° in the wrong direction. Our next step in this direction will be to ask how we make use of the images on our retinas, and if we continue using this pattern of explanation, we will soon find ourselves tracing the nerve impulses from the retina through the optic nerves to the visual centres of the brain. But as long as we continue to use this pattern of explanation we will have a perceiver at the end of a chain of causal influences.

And this leads to the second observation which needs to be made about this line of thought, which is that it initiates a process of pushing the perceiver out of the natural world. As we trace the chain of causal influences further back into the nervous system, we push the perceiver further into the depths of the nervous system, until there is nowhere to locate the perceiver. In other words there is nowhere in the physical world to locate the point at which the information conveyed along the causal chain is taken in perceptually. Eventually, if we persist along this line we will have to place or 'posit' our perceiver in some way outside the limits of physical reality. We may not be as brazen as Descartes and speak of two distinct substances (two distinct realities) represented by our bodies and our minds, but we will have reached dualism, nevertheless. We will have pushed perceptual experience, and that which has such experience, out beyond the margins of physical reality.

This is not a consequence which everyone finds distasteful. Some take comfort in being able to secure the possibility of human freedom, or of an immortal soul, along with conscious experience, somewhere, somehow beyond the clutches of the natural necessity, which will eventually destroy any individual human body. But whatever the attractions of dualism reached from this direction, they should not be mistaken for its inevitability.

We reached dualism by repeating a step which, it was suggested above, was in a direction diametrically opposed to that in which we should move. That suggestion contains the third observation on this way of drawing the line between the internal and the external world. The step we took was to concentrate on events in the body by means of which (or which could be said to constitute) perception of things outside the body and, moreover, those events inside the body were regarded as perceived, i.e. 'seen' in the way our prisoners see the images cast on the back wall of their cell. Now it has to be acknowledged even by those setting out the case for this move that, when we perceive, our thought fixes on what it outside the body, not on what mediates that perception, not on the events taking place in the retinas of our eyes or the visual centres of our brains. In a sense we see *through* the events in our retinas.

This seeing 'through' also takes place in objects and events outside the body. The prisoners following the image cast on their cell wall could come to see what is outside the cell window *through* that image, but this does not on the whole happen automatically. If an object moves parallel to the wall, say from east to west, the image it casts will move west to east and one is strongly tempted to assume that is the direction in which the object travelled. (A gap at the top of the curtain in my bedroom turns the ceiling into a fuzzy camera obscura on sunny mornings. It is extremely difficult not to assume the postman is passing west to east, as his image moves in that direction across the ceiling.) If one stops and thinks, one can correct the judgment, which one is tempted to make about the direction the object has gone, but as long as one has to stop and think, one is not seeing *through* the image in the required senses. But with the right sort of experience one can form the correct expectation unreflectively.

The right sort of experience is probably not available to our prisoners. One sort of experience which will lead a person to see *through* an image on the wall is having to act in response to the image in such a way that the success of the act depends on where the object is (e.g. treating it as a target to be hit). Now this sort of experience *is* available to many people who use many other kinds of images and instruments. The first time one tries to modify something while monitoring one's performance in a mirror, one's left and right expectations are, commonly, wrong. With practice, one comes to see *through* the mirror in the required sense, and the operations on the object, which are reflected in the mirror, come to be performed smoothly, accurately; without having to think, for example, 'to move this way, I have to make what I see move this way', etc. With practice, blind people come to feel things at the end of their canes, to feel them *through* the canes in the required sense.[2] Skilled operators of any piece of machinery receive information about what is happening well away from where their own bodies are located. It does not matter if the information comes by means of vibrations reaching the seats of their pants; the objects which they perceive are not vibrations in the seats of their pants, but events happening in the bowels of their machine or out at its cutting edge.

So the step made above, as a consequence of considering causal chains underlying perception, was in the wrong direction because it moved the object of perception inside the body and identified it with objects *through which* perception normally takes place. To understand perception one should turn around and ask how a thing which is normally the object of perception comes to be something a person can perceive—can see or hear or feel—*through*. If we can explain how people come in effect to extend their bodies, if we can explain how people come to respond to things as though they stood directly in front of them, when in fact they stand at the end of a long and convoluted path along which light or other causal influences travel, then we will have come to grips with the phenomena of perception. We will not simply be saying, in effect, 'people perceive A, because A causes B and B causes C and . . . and Y causes Z and Z is perceived', where we no more understand what it is to percive Z than we know what it is to perceive A. And where, moreover, it is far from clear that we can even be properly said to perceive Z.

If we count as 'internal' for a person anything *through which* that person perceives, then the boundary of the 'external world' will sometimes be well outside the person's body. Now it happens that the boundaries of some people's bodies shrink and their 'internal worlds' in the sense just indicated do not immediately shrink to coincide with this new boundary. People who have had limbs amputated experience something known as a 'phantom limb'. They will feel cold or pain in the limb which they no longer have. (Some who feel cold in feet, which they no longer have, can be comforted if a hot water bottle is placed where the foot used to be.) A physiological explanation of what is going on will possibly refer to nerves which used to connect to the lost limb, nerves which are still alive and sending signals, through which the amputee is feeling (falsely) cold or pain in the lost limb.

People who are prone to 'explain' perception by tacking a perceiver on to the end of a chain of causes and effects will use this as evidence that we do not experience cold or pain in our extremities. As a first step towards moving the locus of our experience up the nervous system and out into some non-physical limbo, it will be pointed out that the experience of pain or cold can be generated by stimuli in nerves well away from, for example, the foot. But although this is true, the policy we are considering now is to resist the conclusion that it is the stimulus, for example, in the thigh, which is felt by us, or by an amputee, or by any person who is being artificially stimulated in the nerves of the thigh to feel cold in the foot. The neural activity is simply something *through which* people normally feel cold in the foot.

But the amputee is under an illusion. There is no foot and *a fortiori* there is no cold to be felt there. Yes, there certainly is no cold there, but should that prevent a person from *feeling* cold there? For something outside of the body, e.g. an image on a wall, to become an object *through which* some further object is perceived, the image has to lead to the formation of certain immediate attitudes, which include anticipations or expectations. There is never any guarantee that the anticipations which one is led to form, are infallible and indeed such anticipation may continue to be experienced when it is known by the person, who has formed them, that they are wrong. We cannot help ourselves; this is why we continue to experience the 'perceptual illusions' which psychologists catalogue and study, even after we learn how they arise. And it is because we see *through* certain qualities and combinations, in our environment, that these qualities and configurations can be manipulated to produce illusions. Lines can be arranged on a canvas to give the illusion of looking through a hole in the wall into a courtyard and on to a field beyond. Shadows and reflections can be imitated to give the illusion that the back of a stage is lavishly furnished with books, curtains and carved panels.

It must be stressed that the experience of illusions includes considerable variety. We are in some cases 'taken in'. We do not realize that we have formed the wrong anticipation. In some cases we are perfectly aware of what we should expect and still experience a contrary expectation. In some cases we put aside our awareness of what we should expect, and surrender to the illusion—make it perhaps the basis of an evening's entertainment. That we experience illusions in all these ways is a fact of our psychology and it points to the need for the distinction which has been marked here as that between 'an object *which* we perceive' and 'an object *through which* we perceive'. The latter, the objects through which we perceive include most of the neural impulses travelling toward the centres of the nervous system, as well as qualities and configurations of the environment which produce modifications in the patterns of those impulses. The objects which one perceives include some events in the body, some of what takes place in the immediate and remote environment, as well as the contents of illusions.

The distinction between the two is fluid. Some things which at one time were objects *which* one perceived become at a later stage objects *through which* one perceives, as when what is happening in an image or an instrument leads one to form immediate unreflective expectations. Some things which were objects through which one perceived can come to be objects which one perceives, as when a painter becomes aware of the shadows, reflections, saturations, hues and lines which people ordinarily see through when they experience a particular scene.

Illusions establish that people do not always perceive what they take themselves to perceive and for this reason provide philosophers with a convenient way to introduce problems regarding the 'external world'. It is not uncommon, however, to find certain threadbare examples used in a way which sows confusion about what it is that we 'really perceive'. A pole or the shaft of an oar will appear to bend at the place where it enters the water. Many people would agree that such an object appears to be bent, but that what they *really* see is a straight pole. If, on the other hand, people are invited to look at some coins lying on a table some distance in front of them, they will agree that what they appear to see are a number of circular objects. If one traces the outline of those objects on a piece of glass put between the table and the onlookers, one will trace an elliptical plane figure. It is not uncommon to find philosophers urging us to conclude that what we really see in this second case are elliptically shaped objects.

These two ways of using the word 'really' face in opposite directions. Compare these two cases to that of people who, because they spend a great deal of time at the water's edge working on objects partly below the surface, no longer notice the apparent bends. If we treat these people in the way in which we are urged to treat our perception of the coins, we will have to say that they really see objects that bend at the water line and like us when we look at the coins just do not notice what they really see. But in that case we should not have said that what we really see is a straight object which appears to bend at the water line— not if 'really see' is to be used in the same sense.

In the first sense, 'really see' is linked to what we will experience if we take the pole out of the water or handle the coins and trace their outlines on a piece of paper. In a similar sense amputees, who feel cold or pain in amputated feet, do not *really* feel something in their feet, for this involves the anticipation that they (still) have the feet in question, an anticipation which will not be borne out when they try to stand on them. In the second sense what is 'really seen' is being attached to the objects *through which* we normally perceive. We normally pay no attention to what is known as the visual shape of coins, and the people who work a great deal at the water's edge have come to overlook the effect which water has on light reflected from beneath its surface. These are features which are *seen through*. They are really involved in perception, because they enter into the story which traces the causes and effects which make perception possible. But it is somewhat misleading to say they are 'really seen' or 'really perceived'. Of course they are things which are perceived by a person trying to draw the table 'in perspective' or trying to paint a 'realistic' picture of the scene at the water's edge. But turning objects *through which* we perceive into objects *which* we perceive takes a certain amount of training.

Since it will only generate confusion to use phrases like 'what we really perceive' in two such different ways, it would be best to leave 'really' tied to the correctness or otherwise of the anticipations embodied in our perceptions. For the task of indicating the features *through which* we normally perceive, there is a common philosopher's phrase, 'what is given in perception', and there is a Latin participle, *datum* (plural *data*—from *do*, *dare*, meaning what is given) which allows a convenient shortening of the phrase to 'the data of perception'. The data of perception, causal factors located both inside and outside our bodies, lead us to form anticipations. These anticipations embody judgments and constitute the content of what we take ourselves to perceive; they can be discovered to be correct or incorrect (and if incorrect we can say that the people in question do not *really* perceive what they take themselves to perceive). It is the slack between the data (objects *through which* we normally perceive) and the things we take ourselves to perceive, which artists of illusion manipulate in order to produce in us anticipations constituting for us objects of perception which we do not *really* perceive.

If the consequencs of having been taken in by an illusion are unwelcome rather than entertaining, we will be on our guard, we will become sceptical, we will suspend, if we can, any action on our anticipations until we have a better idea of what we are *really* perceiving. It is in situations like this that we discover the objects *through which* we normally perceive, the data of perception, and turn them into objects *which* we perceive. We can, moreover, under philosophic motivation force ourselves to hold this sceptical frame of mind, where otherwise we would not trouble ourselves. An analogy is often used to give this sort of exercise a point and to show what sort of mental discipline is required:

Every time we form an immediate anticipation, a psychological event takes place which has important similarities to conscious inference. In each case we end up holding a belief. The difference is that in the case of conscious inference we are aware of what prompted us to form that belief, whereas in the case of what we might call 'subconscious inference', it usually takes the exercise of 'critical reflection' to discern what prompted the inference. What we are invited to undertake as a philosophic exercise is the application of 'the solvent influence of critical reflection'[3] to all our beliefs, particularly those which we hold about our environment in an effort to find what premises we actually have and whether they logically (i.e. deductively) support our beliefs.

The project is not unlike that of tracing causal chains though the portals of the senses and along our neural pathways. We are in each case turning our attention from the objects which we normally perceive toward objects *through which* we normally perceive. However, as we proceed in the case of tracing the causal story we find ourselves needing (or assuming we can get) an increasingly sophisticated scientific story, but as we proceed in the case of applying 'critical reflection' we find ourselves having to divest ourselves of such sophistication. Science is based on precisely the sort of non-deductive inferences which must be put aside under this project of applying critical reflection.

What we must increasingly do is to strip our perceptions of those anticipations which point beyond immediate experience. That means we will be interested only in a very restricted range of what might count as the data of perception. We may be given (in the sense of exposed to) all manner of causal influences, but the identification of them is too dependent on non-deductive inference to count as 'critical reflection'. And along with the objects discovered by physics and physiology go a number of more familiar objects. We may experience grey-green spikey shapes, a smooth slightly waxy feeling over our fingers and a smell which is characteristic of rosemary, but to say we are perceiving a rosemary bush is to infer more than we are given. Even to locate the smooth slightly waxy feeling in our fingers is to infer something, viz. that we have fingers, which will not survive 'the solvent influence of critical reflection'. We find thus, as we did when we traced the causal story behind perception in the wrong way, that we are being backed out of thinking of ourselves as among the bodies which inhabit the natural world. Only in this case a good deal more of the natural world is being called into question.

In this project of applying critical reflection, as in the project of tracing the chains of cause and effect up through the nervous system, we are being encouraged to overlook something important about human perception. When the world frustrates our anticipations in ways we do not welcome, we do not just retreat to more cautious judgments. We look for something else among the data, which will indicate better what we should expect. Hardly any adult is completely taken in by the appearance of a bend at the waterline. The presence of the waterline is itself an obvious counter-indication. And if the stage appears to be lavishly furnished, we look closer to see where the props end and the backdrop begins.

All perception relies on what is given, but all perception also involves a selection from what is given. Between the giving and the anticipating there is a taking, a taking which may need to be reconsidered. And if what is given is inadequate to form anticipations, we often have scope to ask that more be given, until we can take what we need to form correct anticipations. We can change our position, use instruments which aid observation, experiment on the object of perception. Rational people do not retreat in the face of uncertainty, they act to reduce the uncertainty. The project of applying 'critical reflection' on the other hand tries to carry the policy of retreat as far as it can be taken.

There is, nevertheless, something to be gained from this project, or rather from considering the route which we would have to travel to undertake it. What we are asked to do is to turn our attention away from the objects which normally concern us in perception, objects which are bound up in an essential way with our anticipations, our inferences, and turn our attention toward objects which may have occasioned those anticipations, but which do not appear[4] to require the same sorts of anticipation. To perceive a table is to anticipate a certain possibly painful experience, if one walks into it rather than around it; it is to anticipate being able to leave a book on its surface and not have to bend down to recover the book from the floor; it is to anticipate certain exertions, if one wants to clear the space which the table occupies. To perceive the *colour* of its mock teak top, the *smoothness* of its plastic laminated surface, the *cold* of its tubular steel legs, we do not appear to require anticipation. We can just behold these qualities and can then ponder at our leisure our right to infer from them the existence of the table and our right to form all of the anticipations which that entails. To apply the 'solvent influence of critical reflection' is to select from the data those which appear to involve us in no anticipation, no inference, nothing beyond the bare experience of perceiving.

Russell referred to the data, which we select on this basis as 'hard data', while such facts as that we are given solid light reflecting objects or that we are given eyes, ears and fingertips, were all 'soft data'. He took the problem of the external world to be, 'Can we infer the existence of anything other than our own hard data from the existence of those data?' (OKEW, p. 61). We do of course infer on the basis of such data, the existence of a great many things other than those data, but what Russell was questioning was our justification for doing this and if in order to be justified in doing this we have to be able to infer by valid deductive steps, then the answer is 'no'. Hard data remain hard only when they are actually being experienced. If I anticipate a hard datum, e.g. a pain (from brushing against stinging nettle) the pain is not (yet) a hard datum. All that is hard is green jagged-edged nettle-leaf shapes. And there is no deductive step that will take me from hard data experienced at one time to hard data experienced at another (past or future) time. So the answer to the question 'Can we infer the existence of anything other than our own hard data?' is 'No, we cannot even infer the existence of hard data at times other than now'.

But before we accept this as the last word, it is worth examining the question; for there are difficulties involved in posing it which suggest that we may be able to appeal to a different kind of justification[5] for making the inferences, which Russell called into question, and hence for our belief in an external world (if that is what such a belief amounts to). For if we do not infer at least the existence of data at times other than when we experience them, it is not clear that our experience of our hard data one after another can even count as an experience. If one datum succeeds another without being anticipated and the succeeded datum vanishes without leaving a memory trace, we do not have anything which we can call 'experience'; we have nothing above the level of the wind pressing at irregular intervals against a stone wall.

To have experience we at least have to experience a succession of data and a succession of experiences of data is not the experience of a succession of data. To experience a succession we must experience the successive data with memory and anticipation and as these are inferences to the existence of something other than our own hard data, we can answer Russell's question in this vein: Yes, we must make these inferences if experience is to be possible. To ask us for a justification is to ask for our justification for having experience at all. To suggest we might not be justified is to suggest we might not be in a position to ask for justification. Since, therefore, to answer the question 'no we cannot', would be to call into question its own intelligibility, it must be answered 'yes, we can'. And if being able to answer 'yes' is having a justified belief in the (an) external world, then we have settled that problem in favour of the external world.

It might, however, be felt that this quick resolution depends on a perverse interpretation of Russell's question. Russell himself was prepared to interpret 'hard data' 'with a certain latitude' (OKEW, p. 61). He included limited spatial relations (our immediate visual fields are spatially structured), limited temporal relations (based on short-term memory) (ibid.) and correlations between, for example, muscular and visual sensations (OKEW, p. 65).[6] Surely his problem is not were there, or will there be, hard data at times other than now, but are there at any times things other than our own hard data—furniture, garden plants and summer showers in addition to colours, scents and tactile sensations? Russell himself suggests his question is equivalent to: Can we 'know that objects of sense, or any other objects not our own thoughts and feelings, exist at times when we are not perceiving them?' (OKEW, p. 63).

But asking about objects other than our thoughts and feelings puts a somewhat different light on the problem and on the question which asked about our right to make (non-deductive) inferences. What we have in this new question, which we do not have in the earlier question, is an explicit reference to our own thoughts and feelings. Recall the conclusion, which we reached after considering the question about our right to make inferences: to count as experience our hard data must include anticipations and recollections of hard data not immediately experienced. Now to anticipate is to have certain thoughts and feelings which represent a succession, in this case of hard data. The succession which is represented must be regarded as independent of thought or feeling. That does not mean it has to be a succession of things not accessible to thought or feeling, merely that its occurrence in a certain order at a certain time is not something that is determined by thought or feeling. But Russell's second question presupposes that we can represent ourselves as possessing thoughts and feelings. These thoughts and feelings necessarily involved anticipations and anticipations necessarily involve the representation of something that will take place independently of our perceiving it. Something that is independent of our perceiving it is something that could take place at a time when we are not perceiving it.

As a general objection to this way of responding to Russell's problem, it might be pointed out that all we are establishing is how we have to think, viz. to count as having experience we have to anticipate in our perceptions and to represent ourselves as anticipating, we have to represent a world independent of our perceptions. But this does not prove that there is an external world, merely that we have to think there is one.

But is it not enough in order to justify a certain belief that we establish that we cannot think, cannot have experience, without holding this belief? Not at all, comes the reply. However much comfort we take from this conclusion about how we have to think of our situation, we are not taking radical scepticism seriously enough. We are not addressing the possibility that we are labouring under a massive illusion. But if we cannot think coherently about the possibility of such an illusion, why should we take this radical scepticism seriously? No, comes the reply, the possibility of massive illusion can be demonstrated. It simply requires the consideration of the kind of science fiction horror stories which have been discussed in the recent past by philosophers at Harvard.[7]

These stories start with the fact that we perceive through events in our bodies and that these events, like qualities and configurations in the environment, make us liable to illusion. We are invited to imagine an alien race of super-technologists, who have studied human neurophysiology so minutely that they are not merely able to produce in people effects like the phantom limbs; they can generate a whole phantom body, complete with a coherent experience of a phantom environment, by stimulating various parts of the central nervous system. To make the story vivid, if somewhat macabre, we are further invited to imagine a human being, who has suffered a complete amputation of the body and of whom all that remains is a brain, and spinal cord kept on a life support machine. This brain is provided with a neural input as rich and detailed as anything which passes into our own central nervous system over an extended period of time. Human beings, of course, are not passive in perception, their perceptual input occasions motor responses, but we assume our alien neuroscientists are clever enough to monitor the motor nerve output of their captive brain and provide further sensory input as coherent as anything occasioned by our environment.

The neural input of this brain, being sufficiently similar to, say, that of a citizen of London, there seems no reason to think the brain will not believe itself to be a Londoner and to have experiences of the South Bank, crowded rush-hour tubes and grey wet streets. This, however, is illusion on a truly massive scale; what actually produces this experience bears, it seems, no relation to its content. But although that may be true, this fantasy example does not save Russell's question from the answer 'yes, there is an external world, there has to be'. For the brain is not mistaken in thinking that there are objects which exist independently of its perceptions, it is mistaken only in what it assumes to be the nature of the ultimate causes of those perceptions.

But if this fantasy example cannot be used to breath further life into Russell's problem, it does appear to challenge us in a different way. Both challenges arise from the fact that our perceptual experience is based on inference. Russell raised his problem by trying to isolate within experience a portion not based on inference and asking whether any inference could legitimately be based on it. The challenge presented by the science fantasy horror story is not whether we are justified in making any inferences, but whether we can be assured of getting right any except the most general of our inferences (any that is except, 'There is *something* independent of our thoughts and feelings'). Russell's challenge turned out not to raise a real problem; does this new challenge raise a real problem?

There are two possibilities covered by the science fantasy story, which give the challenge two possible forms. The first is, 'Are we liable one day to discover that our beliefs about our environment are nothing more than massive illusion similar to that experienced by the captive brain?' The answer here has to be that no philosophic argument can be advanced to prove that the world has in store for us no really big surprises. The experience, which our ancestors had of the immovable earth beneath their feet and ceiling of the heavens above their heads, turned out to be an illusion on a massive scale and nothing can prove that we will not discover that we still hold more such illusory beliefs. The case of the brain without a body raises, however, acute and insufficiently examined difficulties in saying what would be (i.e. what *should* count as) sufficient evidence to persuade a brain in that position of the truth of its situation. What evidence could it be shown that would lead it inexorably to the conclusion that what sustained its existence was not a human body but a life support machine, etc.?[8]

But if this is a difficulty, then the second version of the challenge seems more pressing. What if we (each of us, anyone of us) are actually in the position of this brain and can never discover it? Here, it has been suggested by Hilary Putnam,[9] we can mount an attack on the question and reassure ourselves by the realization that we are posing an incoherent question and hence have no real problem. Putnam's argument proceeds by considering the meanings of words or thoughts in the experience of the captive brain. It thinks of, and speaks of, say, 'crowded rush hour tubes', but it cannot mean what *we* mean by such a phrase, for its experience of such things cannot make the right connections to what we call 'real underground trains'. Its phrase connects only to past, present and future neural imputs, which generate its experience of crowded tube trains. Consequently it cannot ask itself if it is in a situation in which it is cut off from what we would call 'real underground trains', because its thoughts and words simply cannot refer to what we would call 'real underground trains'. Thus although we might imagine it raising a question which looks like, 'Am I nothing but a captive brain which has never really experienced the underground train I take myself to travel on to and from work everyday?' its question cannot mean what it appears to us to mean. Now if we ask a question like this, our words can likewise only refer to our past, present and future experience of what we call tube trains, not to anything which might lie behind or beyond that experience. So in spite of its looking as if we have a problem, we are in fact not equipped to raise it because our words cannot possess the meanings which are required actually to formulate the problem.

Putnam's argument leaves a certain amount of dissatisfaction in its wake. It says in effect that we do not understand a question, which seems perfectly clear to us. If we, outside the experience of the captive brain, can coherently consider its situation, why can we not, as it were, put ourselves in its situation? Why can we not imagine within its experience the fantasy of the captive brain and thus being led to conceive of itself as we are conceiving of it, viz. as under massive illusion. And why then can we not, Putnam's argument not withstanding, imagine ourselves to be in its situation? What is being used here is a pattern of argument, known in other contexts (the 'problem of other minds') as the argument from analogy. If Putnam's general approach to meaning is correct, such arguments are worthless. But if his approach is mistaken, then there is a real problem about the external world. That is pretty much how the problem stands at the moment in contemporary philosophy. Which way we decide certain central issues in the theory of meaning determines how we will settle questions like that of whether there is a problem about 'the external world'.

Notes

[1] See R. L. Gregory, *Eye and Brain* (London: World University Library, 1966), 203–206.

[2] See Michael Polanyi, *Personal Knowledge* (London: Routledge, 1958), 55–56.

[3] This phrase and this notion of 'critical reflection' come from Bertrand Russell, *Our Knowledge of the External World*, 2nd edn (New York: Mentor Paperbacks, 1929), 60. References to this book will hereafter be given in the text and marked by the abbreviation 'OKEW' followed by the page number.

[4] The reason I say 'appear' here and below is that it has been argued that *no* perceptual experience is without expectation. C. S. Peirce considering the following challenge presented by the suggestion that simple colour experiences provide a counter-example: 'I lay down a wafer before me. I look at it, and say to myself that wafer looks red. What element of expectation is there in the belief that the wafer looks red at this moment?' But judgment (or the act of asserting) takes time, and its reference is to the state of the percept at the time it begins to be made. By the time the judgment (or assertion) has been made, it is already about the past. 'The judgment, then, can only mean so far as the character of the percept can ever be ascertained, it will be ascertained that the wafer looked red.' *The Collected Papers of C. S. Peirce*, Charles Hartshorne and Paul Weiss (eds), 8 vols (Harvard University Press, 1931–35), 5. paras 542–544.

[5] The alternative kind of justification is what Kant would have called 'a transcendental deduction'. See *Immanuel Kant's Critique of Pure Reason*, trans. by Norman Kemp Smith (London: Macmillan, 1933, second impression), 120, for this use of 'deduction' to label the demonstration of a right. The argument, which will be used here in response to Russell's problem, is clearly inspired by Kant, although it does not draw directly on the arguments which Kant himself sets out.

[6] That Russell allows himself particularly these correlations between different sensory modes was regarded by at least one of his critics, John Dewey, as begging the question in favour of the inferences, which the question was supposed to challenge. And if we are going to assume this much of an external world, then the only question remaining is what are we justified in believing about the world. What Russell assumed, 'may not be a very big external world, but having begged a small external world, I do not see why one should be too squeamish about extending it over the edges'. John Dewey, *Essays in Experimental Logic* (New York: Dover, no date, original 1916), 292.

[7] See Hilary Putnam, *Reason, Truth and History* (Cambridge University Press, 1981), ch. 1, and Robert Nozick, *Philosophical Explanations* (Oxford: Clarendon Press, 1981), ch. 3.

[8] There is a similar insufficiently explored difficulty with the temporal version of the problem of the external world, viz. is there any reality to our beliefs about history? Russell formulated a version of this problem by means of the hypothesis (sometimes known as 'Russell's Five Minute Hypothesis') that God created the world five minutes ago complete with all the apparent evidence of possessing a lengthy past, including our memories, historical documents and archaeological and geological phenomena. What evidence could we ever have that this was the case and why, if we had any evidence should we take it seriously? What would make it convincing evidence? On the five minute hypothesis, see Bertrand Russell, *The Analysis of Mind* (London: George Allen and Unwin, 1921), Lecture IX.

[9] Op. cit. above note 7, 14ff.

Scientific Method

I: MARY TILES

Method and the Authority of Science

The thought that it might be possible to develop a method of scientific discovery, a procedure of investigation and reasoning which, so long as its principles were studiously followed, would be guaranteed to result in scientific knowledge, has long been recognized to be a mere philosophers' dream, with no more possibility of fulfilment than the alchemists' dream of producing a philosophers' stone which would turn base metals into gold. Yet it remains the case that the authority of science (the deference given to scientific experts, the credence given to their theories) rests on claims made on behalf of its methods; they are regarded as somehow superior to, or more reliable than, any other means of acquiring beliefs about the world around us. To say that there is no scientific evidence that any of the food additives currently permitted in Britain have any harmful effects is a way of dismissing as groundless and irrational the fears of those who think that such additives do have harmful effects. Whereas to say that it is scientifically established that smoking causes lung cancer is a way of saying that this is something a smoker ought to worry about.

Here one continues to find a reflection of the ideal which was expressed by the seventeenth-century seekers after a universal scientific method, those such as Bacon, Descartes, or Leibniz. This method was to be a way of making scientific discoveries, of acquiring essentially new knowledge which would be such that the route of discovery would itself provide the justification for thinking that this really did constitute an increase in knowledge and thus a way of legitimating claims to have made scientific progress.[1] Bacon's vision was of science as a product of methods of *reasoning* from experience, methods which present scientific claims as conclusions rationally drawn from empirical data and thus as rationally justified conclusions. The novelty of his aim, as he saw it, was the combining of reason and experience:

> Those who have handled science have either been men of experiment or men of dogmas. The men of experiment are like the ant, they only collect and use: the reasoners resemble spiders, who make cobwebs out of their own substance. But the bee takes the middle course: it gathers its material from the flowers of the garden and of the field,

but transforms and digests it by a power of its own. Not unlike this is the true business of philosophy;[2] for it neither relies solely or chiefly on the powers of the mind, nor does it take the matter which it gathers from natural history and mechanical experiments and lay it up in the memory whole, as it finds it, but lays it up in the understanding altered and digested. Therefore from a closer and purer league between these two faculties, the experimental and rational (such as has never yet been made), much may be hoped.[3]

But are there any methods which can perform this function of certifying claims based on them as scientifically justified, as scientific discoveries? Is there anything which characterizes all the many and various ways in which the different branches of the natural sciences conduct their enquiries in virtue of which they can legitimately claim the status which goes with the title 'science'? Is it possible to say why we should give more credence to the pronouncements of scientists than of astrologers? Is there a way of distinguishing between genuine science and that which tries to pass itself off as science, but is not the genuine article? This was the question to which Popper, who has been perhaps the most influential modern philosopher of science, addressed himself. His answer was that genuine science proceeds by making bold conjectures, then strenuously attempting to test them by finding and observing situations in which they might very well fail to be correct. Scientific theories are empirically falsifiable and the scientific approach, is characterized by the non-dogmatic postulation of bold conjectures.[4] This is Popper's answer to the question of how reason and experience are combined to produce scientific progress.

But should Popper's answer to his own question be accepted? Should we even accept his question—should we expect to find some criterion which will enable us infallibly to distinguish science from non-science? I shall return to this second query later. For the time being let us accept Popper's question and attempt to understand and then assess his response to it. There are two subquestions that can be asked here: (1) Has Popper isolated a feature which is an important factor in the methods of science? (2) If so, has he captured something which is unique to science, and which would justify the elevation of science to a special position of respect? I want to answer with a qualified 'Yes' to the first question and a qualified 'No' to the second.

As Popper himself says, the idea that understanding is advanced by critically rational enquiry and debate can be traced back at least to the Socratic dialogues of Plato. It is a conception which is constitutive of the ideal of a liberal education and which leads to its valuation over a process of indoctrination. It is an ideal to which the majority of academic disciplines, and philosophy in particular, are expected to conform. The justification for academic freedom is not the same as that for religious freedom—it is not a matter of the individual's liberty to follow the dictates of his own conscience—but of a diversity of opinions being necessary to the furtherance of understanding, the development of knowledge. This is because critical debate is necessary for the exposure and correction of errors, inconsistencies and inadequacies. What is pursued is not individual opinion but objective knowledge, a form of knowledge and understanding which can command the respect of, and prove valuable to, a wider community. The public funding of academic research could hardly be justified if some sort of objective or universal value were not built into the conception of its goals. The elimination of individual biases and shortcomings may never be wholly possible, but can only be started by discussion with others, by critical examination from viewpoints other than one's own.

So far then we have not distinguished between scientific knowledge and the forms of understanding sought in arts faculties in universities. Popper's idea must be that it is a particular form of critical rationality which distinguishes the natural sciences from all other academic disciplines. It is the idea that scientific theories are criticized not merely, or even primarily, by confrontation with other people's opinions and theories, but by the world itself. The standard in this case is objective in a strong sense—it is set by the very world of which we seek knowledge. The natural sciences then, are special because their critical dialogue is conducted with a world which exists independently of men, their perceptions, opinions and thought processes, a world which sets an absolute standard which is not available to other disciplines. (This is Popper's realism.) Thus Popper says 'It is through falsification of our suppositions that we actually get in touch with "reality"'.[5]

The term falsification derives from Popper's model of the nature of the dialogue between the scientists and the world. He assumes that scientific theories take the form of universal statements 'All A's are B's'—'All metals expand when heated' and that observations must always be of the form 'Sample a of metal A expanded when heated' or 'Sample b of metal B did not expand when heated'. No accumulation of observations in agreement with a generalization can establish it beyond all possible doubt (the 'Problem of Induction'), but a single observation disagreeing with it is sufficient to falsify the universal statement. Our observations of the world can thus never provide rational certification for any universal claims but can provide the basis for rational criticism and rejection of universal claims. It is in this way that Popper claims to have solved the problem of induction—how can science justifiably claim to be based on and to learn from experience when observation can never serve to establish any universal laws? Popper's answer is that science learns from experience only about where it has gone wrong.

This does not justify claiming any scientific laws as conclusively established.

Here Popper is opposing the inductivist view of scientific knowledge as positive knowledge accumulated on the basis of experience. Inductivists acknowledge that experience can never establish the truth of any universal law beyond all doubt, but take it that the appropriate response is to provide a logical characterization of the most reliable ways of generalizing from experience. They look for ways of assessing the degree of support that the evidence gives to a proposed generalization, or of calculating the probability that a given claim is true given the available evidence. Here there would be a general presumption that the more evidence available which agrees with a generalization, the more likely it is to be true, or the more reasonable it is to believe it.

But Popper claims that this cannot be the way to make real scientific progress, because if one is looking only to make those generalizations that are best supported by the available evidence then there will be no adventurous hypotheses made. To demand that observation precede reasoning, and that this be followed by the formulation of hypotheses which are best supported by those observations is to insist that science stick to being strictly empirical with there being no scope for the proposal of exciting, fundamentally new theories. Popper therefore insists that hypotheses and conjectures should come first and should go well beyond the available evidence. Observations should then be made to test the hypotheses. In this case theory actively guides and determines the observations to be made.

Popper is, I think, correct to stress the importance of critical rationality and the use of theory directed empirical testing as a critical tool characteristic of empirical sciences as distinct from mathematics or philosophy, but his characterization of this in terms of falsification is unhelpful. It is easy to see why he should have formulated it in this way, given that he was conducting a debate with inductivist philosophers of science from the logical positivist stable.[6] It was they who picked on the procedure of induction as presenting the central problem of scientific method and saw the challenge as that of providing rules of inductive logic that might serve as a canon of scientific method. These philosophers reinstated the problems Hume raised about how we can ever claim to have knowledge of casual laws, laws of nature, when all experience comes in the form of individual perceptions each one of which is independent of every other (the sequence is radically contingent). It is assumed here that all knowledge and all ideas must have their foundation in sense experience.

Now Popper himself argues, that even if this were a correct account of the problem of how individual people form beliefs and habits on the basis of sense perception, it is not thereby a correct account of the situation in science. For in science observations, not sense perceptions, form the point at which experience enters. Part of what is important about science is precisely the contrast between scientific data and the sense perceptions of ordinary individuals. 'Scientific method'—the procedures in virtue of which science is accorded special status extends to the collection and recording of data. This is not the random accumulation of perceptions, but organized observation, frequently employing measuring instruments. It requires training to learn how to make observations, as anyone who has tried to do either laboratory or field work will know. One has to learn what sort of measurements to take and how, that is how to take samples, what to look out for, what to record, etc. There are many skills involved here, different ones for the various difference sciences. But what is common is the requirement that there be standard procedures which are meticulously followed, that the observations are made as precisely and unambiguously as possible. The importance of standard procedure here is again the elimination of peculiarities of the individual observer. If what we are after are observations which reveal as much as possible about a specific aspect of the natural world, then information should be dependent to the minimum degree possible on the characteristics and idiosyncracies of the individual observer. Scientific observations are required in principle to be repeatable, checkable by other scientists who, following the same procedures should be able to confirm the observations (reproduce the results). (This is merely an extension of the demand that measuring instruments should be cross-calibrated and referred back to a common standard.) Cases where experimental results are reported but fail to be reproducible by other scientists tend to be discounted and disregarded as unreliable. It is just too easy for the individual to see what he wants, expects, or hopes to see, for mistakes in measurement or failure of equipment to occur, to be able to take every particular but non-reproducible observation on board. In this very requirement of repeatability we see (a) that the problem of induction, if it is the problem of passing from individual experiences to generalizations, has been bypassed, and (b) that scientific observation hardly represents a direct and unmediated contact with reality.

(a) The data on which scientists work are already in an implicitly generalized form. If the problem of induction is a problem, it is one which is encountered long before we get to doing science (e.g. in arriving at belief in the existence of an external world) and is not a special problem for the acquisition of *scientific* knowledge—it is more a problem for the acquisition of any empirical knowledge at all. This is not to say that the question of how or in what circumstances it is legitimate to extrapolate from given observational data is not a real one for science: it is indeed quite crucial; but the forms extrapolation might take are many and cannot be captured in a simple logical scheme of transition from the particular to the universal (as we shall shortly see).

(b) Since the process of data collection, the making, recording and processing of observations is, in any scientific discipline, governed by standardized procedures, these procedures themselves contribute to the form and the content of the observations. But they embody socially established and enforced standards: they are not dictated directly by nature, but by people's beliefs about the best way to go about getting information of a given sort, given the technological and other resources available to them, and given their very general beliefs about the nature of the field concerning which they want further information. This means that the methods of making observations are not themselves beyond the reach of critical appraisal. When theories, available technologies or other resources change, there may be debate about what are the best, or even the legitimate, methods of data collection, recording and interpretation. These are the sorts of points which have been emphasized in the philosophy of science of the last twenty years by those such as Kuhn and Feyerabend.

While Popper notes the distinction between observation and perception, he sees this merely as the distinction between a random perceptual input and the selective recording of what is perceived in observation reports (which means that observations enter in the form of asserted sentences). He does not really get to grips with the specific practical requirements which are made on scientific data or with the view, which is inherent in claims about whether there does or does not exist *scientific* evidence for, for example, the harmful effects of food additives, that there is a difference in kind between scientific evidence and non-scientific evidence—the view that scientific evidence is of a special, and specially reliable kind. Indeed, Popper claims that science is merely common sense writ large and that there is an essential continuity between the role of experience in everyday life and its role in science. His picture of the role of experience in science owes much to his opposition to what he calls 'the bucket theory of the mind'. He calls his own view 'the searchlight theory of the mind'. According to the bucket view, the mind resembles a container in which perceptions and knowledge accumulate (which is very much the view of empiricists such as Locke, Berkeley and Hume). According to the searchlight view, all observation is selective and is determined by our interests. We start with questions which we want answered, problems we want solved; and it is this directed interest which picks out particular features of the environment as relevant.

Popper can plausibly maintain the continuity between science and common sense only by using 'theory' in a very broad sense. Any practical interest which prompts a question 'Is this so?' has to count as a theoretical conjecture.[7] But then he is unable to give any account of what is distinctive about *scientific* theories. Yet some distinctions must be made here both between scientific theories and other interests which may prompt requests for information and between scientific and non-scientific observations. My observation of the cloud patterns thrown into relief by the setting sun as I ask myself whether it is likely to rain tomorrow would hardly qualify as a scientific observation. Nor would my eminently falsifiable conjecture that it will not rain tomorrow be a very good example of a scientific theory. We can readily accept that observation is a matter in which those making the observations play an active, and not a passive role. Scientific observation is a matter of selecting and organizing, of conducting a systematic programmes of observation. But it does not follow that it is always scientific theorizing which guides this activity. Once the above distinctions are made, it becomes clear that it is not the case that the sole point of making scientific observations is, or should be, the testing of bold scientific conjectures.

To take but one example. In 1946 the British government commissioned a National Survey of Health and Development. This was to collect data on a variety of aspects of the physical and intellectual development of British children. This was not done with the aim of testing a theory, but had more to do with simply getting information on the basis of which to assess the effect of the setting up of the National Health Service and the 1944 Education Act. Since this was the first survey of its kind it had to form the baseline for future comparison and could not hope to present a before and after picture. A later survey was started in the 1960s for purposes of comparison. The aims here were much more practical and political than scientific. But the data bank built up is widely acknowledged as a uniquely valuable resource for those with pure theoretical concerns, because it is the sort of information that simply cannot be gathered by the individual theorist, and because it was collected methodically.

How can one get a picture of the health and development of a nation's children? It is clearly out of the question (especially before the advent of electronic data processing) to monitor every child. Here we have one of those real questions of what evidential base will serve for a legitimate extrapolation to the whole of a generation of children. How does one get a representative sample? One can suggest strategies to be avoided—the sample should not be drawn from a single region, or from a single stratem of society, it should not be restricted to hospital as opposed to home births, and so on. In the end the sample was selected by simply taking all those children born within a given two-week period in 1946. (And even this would be unsuitable if one of one's questions was whether there was any difference between the health in the first year of children born in the summer as against those born in the winter or whether a difference of birth sign is really correlated in any way with character, career, etc.) These people have then been monitored, as far as possible, for the rest of their lives with a particular concentration on early years. But here again there had inevitably to be selection. It is clearly quite impractical to consider recording every aspect of a child's physiological and psychological development. There could only be a concentration on certain aspects and they would have to be aspects which it was felt could be recorded in an unambiguous, precise way by the army of educationalists, health visitors, district nurses, etc. required to collect it. So, for example, at a time when much more value was placed on IQ scores than now, regular IQ tests were part of the monitoring programme as were tests for reading and arithmetic ability. Given that opinions about IQ testing have changed there might well be debate over the interpretation of the results of these tests. Similarly, the health data collected reflect the concerns of the time. Questions were not asked about amounts of fat or fibre in the diet, but careful records were kept of height and weight gain in a climate of opinion still very much concerned with the problem of how to rear strong, physically well-developed children. Special attention was also paid to the occurrence of respiratory diseases.

It is not merely its scale which makes this a scientific survey but that the way in which it was carried out was thought out in advance with attention being paid to the question of what must be done to make the actual observation programme serve the end required—giving as accurate a picture as possible of the health and development of a generation of British children. The problem of selecting a representative sample, of getting standardization between different data collectors by careful design of questionnaire and data recording forms, and so on were explicitly addressed and the programme designed to overcome, as far as was possible given the resources available, the problems that were foreseen. Of course there were problems that were not foreseen and which provide the basis for criticism and cautions about the interpretation of the data (such as the greater tendency for middle class families to co-operate as against working class families, which, as the years passed put an increasing bias on the sample).

Here we see that, and how, it is possible to discuss the scientific status of observational evidence, something which is omitted by Popper with his concentration purely on classifying *theories* as scientific or otherwise. We also see that a programme of data collection whose methods can claim scientific respectability may be conducted for reasons and be shaped by concerns other than those of pure scientific research. There is frequently a need for factual information. Where this information cannot be obtained by direct methods, there has to be a strategy thought out about the best way to obtain it. This will be the case whether it is a scientist wanting the information to test a conjecture, a politician wanting information on the basis of which to shape future legislation, or a civil engineer wanting to construct a bridge over a river. Critical rationality enters into the process of gathering factual information when there are problems about obtaining it directly; it demands that the problems be explicitly addressed and that methods be developed and evaluated. Whether the techniques are those of conducting surveys or of instrumental measurement they will never deliver a set of definitive (hard) facts. There will always be caveats about margins of error, possible distortions etc. These will have been estimated by evaluating the techniques used. It is not the observation report in itself which is of scientific value, but the report together with information about how it was arrive at—the information which makes possible an assessment of its reliability.

By way of illustrating the process of evaluating the kind of information that can be gained by using a given set of techniques, we can consider the question of food additives. How could it be shown (scientifically) that they do, or do not, have harmful effects? The general area to which this question belongs is that of toxicology. And the topic has been discussed very fully by Eric Millstone.[8]

First, what is it that we would like to know? We would like to know of each of the range of over 3,500 permitted food additives whether they have any harmful effects on human beings. More specifically, those who claim that, for example, certain food colourings (the azo dyes, such as E102 tartrazine and E123 amaranth) can trigger the hyperactivity syndrome in children, need to establish that there is a causal connection between ingestion of these substances and a particular type of behavioural disorder in children (a conjecture which is still not very theoretical). One way of doing this would be get an account of the effect that these substances have on the body's biochemistry and in particular on that of the parts of the nervous system which affects activity levels: in other words, by giving an explanation of why and how ingesting these dyes produces hyperactivity in some children. But we are in no position at present to trace such a causal chain; it would require a much greater knowledge of human biochemistry and its links with behaviour than is currently possessed. We might here make a bold conjecture, but it would be unlikely to be so bold as to go beyond the bounds of current testability and hence to be of little immediate utility, even though it were in principle falsifiable and might have a place in a pure research programme. It is more likely that finding out about the effects of certain chemicals will teach us something about human biochemistry. The approach then, cannot be by *theoretical* conjecture and refutation.

The more directly empirical approach would be to take two groups of children, feed food containing azo dyes to one group and feed the other, the control group, with exactly the same diet minus the azo dyes. If a significant number of the first group became hyperactive, but none, or very few in the control group did, and this result was repeated over a number of different trials we might conclude that since the *only* difference between the groups is consumption of the dye, this must be causally responsible for hyperactivity (Mill's method of Difference).[9] But what if we got no such clear-cut outcome, would this mean that there was no causal connection? Because there are many problems about conducting such tests we could not draw either conclusion definitively. The first problem is that unless the groups are kept in strictly controlled conditions, requiring presence in an institution of some kind, the results will always be disputable; there will inevitably be differences other than those of consumption of azo dyes both between the two groups and between individual children, thus one could never be sure that the only relevant difference is consumption of the dyes. Any confinement of children in strictly controlled conditions would be regarded as an infringement on human rights and for this reason, as well as that of any medical risks involved, there are ethical restrictions on the extent to which tests can be carried out on human subjects. If, on the other hand, trials are run on people in institutions already (for some other reason) then it may be argued that such people may well not be typical of the population at large. Moreover, the claim is only that these dyes trigger the syndrome in children already genetically predisposed, not that they produce it in all children. So we would really need to know how to tell which children has this genetic predisposition and conduct trials just on them. In addition it is allowed that the dyes are just one of several triggers. To find out what the various triggers might be and what might be indications of genetic predisposition one would need to collect data on hyperactive children to see if there are common factors in their environment and physiology. (Mill's method of Agreement.)

Here one moves to the field of epidemiology (of which the national survey for health and development provides an example) where variation in patterns of illness and death can be compared between different groups of the population. Studies of the effects of changes in the dietary regimes of penal institutions, ships' crews, and boarding schools have played a significant role in obtaining recognition of the importance of factors such as vitamin C in the diet by establishing a connection between vitamin C deficiency and scurvy.[10] Epidemiological studies are also good ways of detecting occupational health hazards. What such studies can pick up are dramatic, acute effects, which become manifest pretty quickly in groups which are well defined. They do not pick up the less dramatic, long-term or chronic effects of factors to which ill-defined groups within the population are exposed. In the case of food additives—where the population is exposed, to varying degrees dependent on individual choice, to an endless variety of combinations of additives present in very small quantities—such studies can never yield conclusive evidence of lack of harmful effects. They can provide assurance that none of the currently permitted additives is acutely poisonous in the quantities permitted.

The alternative to trials on human subjects are (1) trials on animals and (2) *in vitro* tests. With both of these there are very real problems about how, if at all, extrapolations can be made to the case of whole human beings. (1) In running animal tests one has to consider questions about the dose level, the laboratory environment, the length of trial, obtaining a suitably healthy and representative animal population, and so on (laboratory mice tend to show little genetic variation and to be very susceptible to disease and to cancers in particular). Even if the animal tests do yield unequivocal results, there are still questions about the extent to which this can be extended to human beings. The question here is neither one of logic, nor of sampling methods, but of detailed comparative biochemistry and physiology. (2) *In vitro* tests are tests involving tissue and bacteriological cultures kept on glass dishes. They have mostly been used for detecting for possible carcinogenicity, because they are tests for genetic mutations in the culture cells. There have been problems about these tests in that they do not all give the same results and they do not always correlate well with animal feeding trials. They can test only for the likelihood of cancers resulting from damaged genetic material, and there are other cancer-triggering mechanisms. Thus substances which pass all these tests cannot thereby be certified as non-carcinogenic.

What do we learn from this? First, that, if we applied Popper's falsifiability criterion to the statement 'All currently permitted food additives are safe' it would be unscientific because unfalsifiable, as also are lower level generalizations which might refute it such as 'Azo dyes trigger hyperactivity in sensitive children'. Such claims are not unfalsifiable in principle, but they are so in practice given the limitations on the kinds of methods currently available. To demand conclusive scientific evidence in this area is therefore unreasonable because it cannot currently be met. We have to choose between assuming something safe until shown to be otherwise, or potentially hazardous until shown to be otherwise. So even in what look like straightforward factual matters the demand for scientific evidence cannot always be met. To determine this requires critical assessment of the effectiveness of methods available as well as creative thinking about what sorts of new methods might be introduced.

Secondly, we see that there is a distinction, not reflected in Popper's treatment of all conjectures or theories as merely universal laws, between conjectures which take the form of low level empirical generalizations, which one might expect to have a fairly direct relation to observations; and conjectures which take the form of theories about the details of mechanisms, or detailed causal chains, which would serve to explain, clarify and qualify the lower level empirical generalizations. These have a more complicated relation to those observations which bear directly on the question we want to settle.

This contrast can be brought out more strongly by considering a final example. Let us start with Hooke's law. Hooke noted that materials, and metals in particular, stretch when they are subject to a force, as when a weight is suspended from a spring or when a cable is being used to pull a heavy load, and that they return to their original shape when the force is removed (elastic behaviour). By conducting systematic observation on samples of various materials one can plot, for each sample, a graph of the force applied against the amount the sample has stretched. What Hooke found he got was something approximating to a straight line. On this basis he proposed the law: the extension (amount the material stretched) is proportional to the applied force. Here we have already examples of extrapolations of more than one kind: (i) to the intermediate forces which one has not actually applied (all the points on the line in between the dots) and to values of the force which go beyond those applied. In practice one cannot extend the line indefinitely because the material will either break or become plastic—start to flow, like plasticine, in such a way that it will not return to its original shape even when the load is removed; (ii) drawing a straight line, even when the points recording observations do not lie exactly on one, presumes that this scatter is due to the inevitable imprecision in measurement and thus discounts it, so extrapolating from observed values to values approximated by measurement; (iii) to all samples of the same kind as that studied; and (iv) to samples of substances in general.

All of these represent low-level empirical generalizations of differing kinds. They can be tested by making further observations of the same sort. In particular one will soon notice that the shape of the sample effects the amount that it stretches under a given load. A thin steel bar will stretch more under a given load than a fatter one. This raises the query of whether there is a way of characterizing the elastic behaviour of a given material which is independent of the dimensions of the particular sample (which is assumed to have a uniform cross-section). If stress, S, is defined as load per unit area (pounds per square inch) and strain, L, as amount of stretch (under load) per unit length, then Hooke's law can be expressed by 'Strain is proportional to stress' or '$L \propto S$'. If we now focus on the material rather than the changes in shape of a particular sample this can be rewritten as stress/strain = constant, $S/L = e$. Thomas Young conjectured that this constant (now called Young's modulus) was characteristically different for each chemical substance. This constant expresses the elastic flexibility of a material as such, whereas the flexibility of a given object will depend both on its geometrical shape and on the Young's modulus of the material of which it is made. Until recently it has not been possible to test materials at strains of much over 1 per cent—they either broke or flowed beyond that. But more recently it has been possible to take very strong 'whisker crystals' up to strains between 3 and 6 per cent, and here measurements show that Hooke's law is not strictly true; the curve does not remain straight but starts to bend.

Now it is also possible to characterize materials in terms of the strains at which they break (their tensile strength). Knowledge of tensile strengths and elasticity characteristics is essential to most practical construction crafts from shipbuilding to violin making. But traditional craft knowledge does not take the form of a numerical classification of materials based on a series of tests—it is built up from years of experience of handling materials passed on from master to apprentice. Newer, inherently more dangerous and adventurous engineering technology (steam engines, wide-span metal bridges, suspension bridges, etc.) requires a basis for calculation at the design stage, if disasters are to have any chance of being avoided. In this case one needs a systematic and scientific programme of testing and characterizing the various kinds of construction materials. This is detailed, scientific work, but still observational and strictly empirical. One does have to work out how to conduct, for example, tests for tensile strength and to develop testing machines which can be as automatic and reliable as possible. The requirements of the engineer are consistency in materials; he would thus be attracted to the idea that each material has a characteristic strength which one could determine accurately, once and for all, providing enough tests were done. His requirement was not for an understanding of the why's and wherefore's of the engineering characteristics of a material, merely an accurate specification of those characteristics.

With the advance of theoretical chemical and physical knowledge of the composition of substances, knowledge of the strength of chemical bonds and interatomic forces became available. The theoretical question could then be raised as to whether, or how, these forces within a substance relate to and determine its strength. Here we shift from the engineering approach to building houses and bridges, to an engineering approach to building materials out of which to make further artifacts, and at the same time enter what might seem to be the domain of pure research science with its quest for theoretical explanations of the data obtained from years of material testing in engineering laboratories.

It was known that the strength of chemical bonds was not related in any very systematic way to the strength of a material: that it is easy to make a weak material from strong chemical bonds, but not possible to make a very strong material from weak bonds. It was Griffiths, who asked the questions 'Why are there large variations between the strengths of different solids? Why don't they all have the same strength? How strong should they be anyway? What would theoretical physics and chemistry predict?' Griffiths found a way of calculating theoretical strengths for materials. His calculation for steel gave a value of something on the order of five million pounds per square inch, whereas the tested strength for commercial steels is more like 60,000 pounds per square inch and that of some very strong wires about 400,000 pounds per square inch. Is this then a case of an empirically falsified theoretical prediction or a fact calling for explanation? Griffiths took it to be the latter and looked for a further physical theory to bridge this gap between theory and practice. But he did not do this in isolation from empirical work. He also experimented with glass fibres and found that they got stronger as they got thinner and by persisting in this route was able at least to approximate to his theoretically predicted strength for glass. So he had demonstrated, experimentally, that the theoretical strength could be approximated and thus that the real task was to explain why in normal cases there was such a vast discrepancy between theoretical and actual strength.[11]

Here we have a pattern of the role of experimental work in science which is quite other than that given to it by Popper. It is the important role of showing that something, which is theoretically predicted as possible, really is possible. This serves as confirming evidence for a theory and can serve to make continued work on it sensible in spite of apparent conflicts with other observations. It also shows the distinctive way in which the development of explanatory theories guides empirical work—it is not just a matter of making systematic observations, creating the right test or observation conditions and methods—all of which have a classificatory and descriptive aim, but of conducting experiments, in which the aim is to try to create new situations and realize new possibilities. Griffiths's work marked the beginning of the science of strong materials, which has been one of the success stories of post-war scientific research.

> At the present time the new materials . . . and the new methods of making them offer possibilities for new technologies almost without limit. We can say this because we understand the limits to strength, stiffness and toughness of materials of widely different kinds and how these limits arise in terms of interatomic forces and the microstructure of the solid. From this we can go on both to predict and to make materials with hitherto unknown combinations of properties and at the same time we can devise new methods of manufacturing

both the materials and the articles made from them. To take simple examples, both a boat and a bicycle may be made from light alloy, plastic or ceramic and so can an aeroplane wing or a kettle. Now, and increasingly in the future, the designer will choose his materials so that consideration of final properties and the method of making an article are not separate processes but are one and the same. The distinction between materials science and engineering with materials will have disappeared' (p. 129).[12]

Amongst the startling new effects now possible are springs made of cement, glassy metals, plastics as strong as steel, crystals that are liquid, and fibrous tough ceramics.

And what has made this sort of development possible? What were the methods which used to bring it about? These are listed as (i) the identification of crystal boundaries, defects, and the way that the properties of these depend on interatomic and intermolecular forces—the theoretical work of Griffiths and those who followed him; (ii) the development of tools for observing these defects, such as electron and ion microscopes, together with very sophisticated means of determining chemical composition on a minute scale; (iii) the development of new techniques for processing materials, involving rapid quenching and the attainment of very high pressures; (iv) an understanding of how to combine materials from the different classes into composite materials and the development of techniques for doing so. This sort of programme depends on much more than the making of bold theoretical conjectures (although Griffiths's conjecture about the possible strengths of materials was certainly bold). It requires the development of instruments and technological process in the light of theory as well as with a view to testing theories.

In the course of considering our three examples Popper's characterization of the distinction between science and non-science has been found wanting on several counts. (1) He presents the problem of scientific method as a logical problem derived from the problem of induction, characterized as that of making inferences from particular observations to universal generalizations, whereas the real problems are those of extrapolating from data, which is already implicitly generalized, extrapolation which takes many different forms and which resists logical formalization. (2) Although he distinguishes between perception and observation, he does not distinguish between scientific and everyday observation. His concern seems to have been to distinguish between empirical knowledge and metaphysics, rather than to distinguish between science and everyday empirical knowledge. He thus provides no clear basis on which science could claim superiority over everyday knowledge. In particular he does not pay attention to the role of systematic methods and their critical scrutiny in scientific observation. This leads him to underplay the social component in the objectivity claims made on behalf of scientific observation. (3) He does not distinguish low level empirical generalization from scientific theorising which has an explanatory goal. His falsification model may bear some resemblance to the former but does not at all fit the logic of the latter, where experimental realizations of theoretical claims about what is possible or about what exists provide evidence directly supportive of theories.

But can we expect to find a criterion which will effect a sharp division between science and non-science? Well, in so far as we are concerned with *empirical* sciences, sciences which claim to yield knowledge of contingent truths about the world around us, we can say, with Popper, that these must be responsive in some way or other to observational findings. This would rule out as non-science any body of knowledge which is maintain purely by tradition, which is handed down from mother to daughter, from master to apprentice, in the form of procedures to be followed, rites to be performed, of stories to be told but whose authority stems from its traditional origin, an origin which places it beyond question and beyond modification in the light of the experience of subsequent generations. Galenic medicine, based on the theory of humours had very much this status until the sixteenth century. Practices such as bleeding were continued because they were in accord with theory in spite of their lack of effectiveness as cures. There was a theoretical framework within which the phenomena of disease could be conceptualized, and in that sense understood, but the effectiveness or otherwise of treatments based on that theory had little or no impact on the theoretical framework. (In the terms of Bacon's metaphor this would be a web spun by reason.) It is this idea of criticism of a theory or theoretical tradition by reference to empirical observation which lies behind Popper's falsifiability criterion. But the very acceptance of this as a standard indicates a certain attitude toward the function of scientific theorizing; only if theorizing is supposed to provide the basis for practical success can practical successes and failures be made to count for or against the theory.

But we can still ask (a) is all science empirical science? and (b) is all empirical knowledge scientific? (a) Is mathematics, for example, to be counted a science? It is not empirical, but for a long time Euclid's geometry was held up as the model of what a true science should be. It might be argued that the birth of modern science in the sixteenth and seventeenth centuries marks the demise of that ideal, one which was replaced by some, not altogether clear, ideal of an empirical or experimental science, although I think it would be more plausible to say that an attempt was made to marry mathematical and empirical ideals. To debate the matter further would be to go into a discussion of the requirements which might be made on the purely theoretical parts of science. There is a very wide scope for debate about the relation between mathematics and the natural sciences, about mathematical methods and the authority attaching to them which cannot be entered into here.

(b) We do not count all empirical knowledge as scientific. It is now being recognized that there was much genuine empirical knowledge embodied in traditional herbal medicine. Teams are sent to scour the fast-diminishing rain forests for native populations in order to record their law and collect specimens of the plants they use in a search for new organic chemicals with medical potential. But this does not amount to a withdrawal of the judgment that such traditional medicine is unscientific. Bacon was also critical of 'men of experiment', those who like the ant only collect and use; their methods may work, but they have no real idea about how or why, or how to improve them. The incorporation of such lore into scientific medicine involves carrying out tests on plant materials for medical effectiveness, subjecting them to chemical analyses, isolating what are thought to be the active ingredients, possibly synthesizing them artificially and retesting pure forms. Again in Bacon's words 'the bee gathers its material from the flowers of the garden and of the field, but transforms and digests it by a power of its own'. But is there any sharp line, drawn by a single criterion which will make it possible to distinguish between scientific and non-scientific ways of allowing observation to have a bearing on theoretical claims?

This is really what we have been discussing, and we have found that the answer is that there may be no single characterization of the distinction between scientific and non-scientific methods. Methods which provide scientific evidence in some cases (acute poisoning) may fail to provide it in apparently closely related ones (slowly cumulative, long term, or chronic toxic effects). We could only suppose that there was a simple characterization to be found if we were to assume, as Popper seems to, that in all empirical investigation the relation between theory and observation is constant and that the only issue to be addressed is whether the observer is passive in observation, with observation preceding theory, or whether the observer is active, with theory preceding and directing observation.[13] But we have seen that even if the active role of the observer is acknowledged, (a) it may not mean that it is theory which precedes observation and dictates its direction—it may be purposes more generally and (b) questions of method involve means–end reasoning. To the extent that the kinds of empirical knowledge wanted are different the empirical methods appropriate to obtaining and checking it will be different; and kinds of knowledge sought may differ precisely in their presuppositions about the relation between the knower and the object of his knowledge, relations which crucially affect the sort of evidence that is going to be available or relevant, the sorts of experiments that will constitute tests of theoretical success or failure. Besides the form of knowledge sought, background conceptions of the kind of thing to be investigated and of the means available in principle and in practice for getting observational evidence relating to it are also important. These of course can change with the advance either in the instrumentation available or with theoretical advances.

For example, the engineering approach to theoretical explanation is asking for an understanding which would enable the theoretician to imagine himself in the role of engineer constructing and bringing about that which he wants to understand. Theories of this kind can only be empirically checked by engaging in some engineering, even if understanding is the primary aim. By way of contrast, it may be that what we are after is, as in meteorology, a predictive science. Here we need lots of continually updated data and detailed records provided by weather stations, satellite pictures, and so on from which to detect patterns in climatic conditions, their changes and the patterns of their change. The requirement is to be able to get data into a form from which extrapolations into the near future can be made. This may include the computer modelling of weather systems, and the models will then have to be tested by running them to see how well they would have predicted weather of which we have past records. The meteorologist is not trying to create the weather—he seeks understanding from a more passive perspective, wanting to get some conceptual mastery of a large and immensely complex system, where intellectual mastery is manifest in an ability to predict accurately. Again, it may be that we are after ways of maintaining a maximally healthy human (or animal) population. Here there is an ideal at which we are aiming, an ideal which itself has to be characterized (a far from uncontentious task) and we need observations which reveal departures from that ideal, their causes and the effects of attempts to prevent such departures and restore health. Here the mastery sought is a mastery of conditions, not in the sense of being able to create new things, so much as in the sense of being able to maintain a desired *status quo* through a wide variety of conditions which threaten to disrupt it.

The way in which the critically rational dialogue with nature is conducted depends on the form of understanding, explanation, or theory sought, for it is this which determines the imagined ideal standpoint from which the theoretician will look at that aspect of the world which is the object of his study; it determines the way in which the theoretician must conceive of his engagement with the world even when his aim may be purely theoretical (when he is doing pure research science). If theories are to be empirical in the sense of being responsive to experience, then the theoretician must conceive his knowledge from the standpoint of some kind of engagement with the world of which he seeks knowledge, for only then can he test his theories by reference to success or failure in this engagement, whether it be from the point of view of the master-builder, forecaster, conserver, or whatever.

Now which of these standpoints can be adopted (what kind of knowledge or understanding can be sought) depends to some extent on the kind of thing or range of phenomena under study and on our observational and other powers in relation to them. Our relation to metals is very different from both our relation to the weather systems of our planet and to dogs and other living creatures. These in turn are all different from our relations to other human beings and to the society in which we live. Controversies over genetic engineering suggest that although, in terms of knowledge and power we have reached a point where we have some, albeit limited, engineering type knowledge of life forms, it is not unambiguously legitimate to pursue this route. It may be argued that unless this is placed in the context of a quite different kind of understanding of complex of environmental interdependencies, it is not knowledge at all but a dangerous ignorance. Conversely the forms of understanding appropriate to living things would be inappropriate to metals. There are no normative concepts such as health or life relative to which or around which enquires concerning steel can be focused. Once we take into account the variety of standpoints from which we may want empirical knowledge and the variety of the objects of which we want this knowledge, we can see that it would be irrational to imagine that the same rules of engagement between theory and experience will be applicable in all cases. There may be no one scientific method other than the insistence that enquiry should be methodical, the insistence that there be standardized procedures which can be made explicit and are available for scrutiny.

What has been suggested is that the authority of empirical science has a double grounding in manifest practical power, on the one hand, and on the exercise of critical scrutiny at all levels of observation and theory, on the other. Neither of these can confer an absolute authority, can justify a claim to have a direct line to *the* truth. It should also be emphasized what actually goes under the name of science does not always live up to these ideals, and to the extent that it does not, is not entitled to claim authority.[14]

Notes

[1] Thus the conception of a scientific method as a method of discovery cuts across the distinction of which much has been made in the literature of analytic philosophy of science between the context of justification and the context of discovery. Here it should be noted that there is a distinction to be drawn

between a scientific discovery (something which is recognized by the community of scientists as a discovery) and the original occurrence of an idea or the original making of an observation by an individual scientist. Even if Newton did first get the idea for his gravitational theory as a result of an apple falling on his head (which is itself doubtful), this would not be the point from which his gravitational theory can be ranked as a scientific discovery. Even Newton did not at that point believe it to be correct, but merely an hypothesis which was worth working out and testing. As *Principia* shows, there was a lot of work involved in thinking through the mathematical shape of the theory then comparing this with the available data on planetary motions. Only then was Newton sufficiently confident to present the whole to the public for critical scrutiny (and there was plenty of criticism). It is here, if anywhere, that method enters: it enters in the transformation of what may be no more than a daydream, a speculation, into a precisely articulated theory which has been tested against some observations and which thus can begin to claim for itself the status of a scientific discovery. An integral part of being judged and accepted as a discovery is being judged to have been a justified claim, not merely a true one.

[2] Note that Bacon here means natural philosophy or what we now call science.

[3] Francis Bacon *Novum Organum*, trans. J. Spedding and R. L. Ellis (1857), reprint F. H. Anderson (New York: Bobbs-Merrill, 1960), Book I, xcv.

[4] Popper's answer is slightly paradoxical. He is saying that we should have most confidence in those theories which have been most severely tested and have survived, whilst at the same time insisting that the scientific attitude must be that we are not entitled dogmatically to assert the correctness of those theories (they do not constitute knowledge but are merely well-tested conjectures). The scientific approach consists precisely in being critical, in being prepared continually to subject theories to further tests and to think up better theories. Science is the product of critical rationality which compels us to recognize that no series of tests can establish the correctness of a theory beyond all doubt. Our so-called scientific knowledge is fallible. On Popper's account then, the very strength of science's claim to respect rests on its own recognition of its fallibility. It is just to the extent that the scientist is prepared to challenge his own pet theories, or is prepared to consider seriously the challenges presented by others, rather than to defend it at all costs, that we should respect his opinions. But it would then be paradoxical in the extreme to elevate the scientist to the position of guru, according to his pronouncements an absolute authority, treating them as dogma, for we would then be failing to recognize the inherent fallibility of all scientific knowledge claims, recognition of which is, if Popper is right, crucial to the progress and development of science.

[5] K. R. Popper, *Objective Knowledge* (Oxford University Press, 1972), 360.

[6] That is, those philosophers of science who were either members of or were influenced by the Vienna circle. This includes philosophers such as Carnap, Russell, Hempel, Schlick and Ayer.

[7] *Objective Knowledge*, 342–3 (see 5).

[8] Erik Millstone, *Food Additives* (Penguin, 1986).

[9] Mill's Four Experimental Methods are set out in his *System of Logic*, Bk III, Ch. VIII. They owe much to Bacon's Tables of Induction set out in the second book of the *Novum Organum*.

[10] See K. J. Carpenter, *The History of Scurvy and Vitamin C* (Cambridge University Press, 1986), which contains material providing nice examples both of the application of systematic methods of investigation and of failure to apply them in the search for means of preventing scurvy.

[11] This story is told in J. E. Gordon, *The New Science of Strong Materials* (Penguin, 1968), which is a fascinating and very readable book.

[12] A. Kelly, 'The New Materials' in *Science and Public Affairs* No. 1 (Royal Society, 1986).

[13] This assumption goes hand in hand with the idea that what science aims at is Truth and that the Truth is one—it consists in a non-distorted mirroring of the world. To reject this conception of the unitary aim of science is not to abandon all hope of objectivity—non-distorting mirrors within the world only ever present an image of a situation or an object viewed from a certain perspective.

[14] The exercise of critical scrutiny has, for example, become very limited in areas related to research which is regarded a sensitive for one reason or another, toxicology and some areas of information technology provide cases in point.

Realism, Reference and Theory

The claim of this paper is that only by adopting an approach to the analysis of theorizing based on the highlighting of analogy relations, that is on an analysis of the content of theories, can a defensible form of realism be found.

Varieties of Realism

In this section two versions òf realism are set out. Truth-realism is based on the principle of bivalence; that in a realist reading of a theory its statements are taken as true or false by virtue of the way the world is. Referential-realism is based on the principle of denotation; that in a realist reading of a theory its terms are taken to denote real beings. There are two versions or varieties of referential-realism. In the stronger version it is held that the terms in plausible theories do denote real beings, while in the modest form, to be called 'policy realism' it is only required that the terms of a plausible theory be taken as possibly denoting real beings, thus making possible a policy of looking for examplars of such beings.

In recent years the form of the debate between realists and anti-realists has been set by the particular version of realism espoused by one group of defenders. It is based on the Principle of Bivalence. Realism is the doctrine that the statements found in a scientific theory are, generally, true or false by virtue of the way the world is, whether or not we can know this. The principle lies behind such popular but well criticized ideas as the argument to the best explanation. The best explanation of the success of science is that scientific statements do obey the bivalence requirement, just as the best explanation of the success of a particular theory, for instance as a basis for making predictions, is that it is true.

This line of argument is based upon two assumptions, neither of which is easily defended. The first is that the true/false distinction can be applied to the generality of scientific statements. Given that *all* claims made by scientists must be revisable (and I will provide a detailed argument to that effect below) it is surely paradoxical to base the most central and far-reaching claims about the nature of scientific theorizing on a principle which cannot be applied in practice. If we can never claim with surety that what we believe about the natural world *is* true or false, realism conceived in terms of bivalence is surely indefensible. At best one might argue that scientific statements of whatever level of generality enshrine the most useful conventions for thinking about nature. But there is another assumption involved in bivalence realism that is equally vulnerable to criticism but has hardly had the attention it deserves from many philosophers of science. This is the assumption that doing science is statement-making. So both experimenting and theorizing are discussed by philosophers in terms of the statements that issue from those activities—observation statements and theoretical statements (and laws) and their concatenation into discourses. But it has been clearly demonstrated by historians and sociologists of science that scientific texts are constructed in such a way as to present a certain kind of face whose lineaments can best be understood by reference to certain social and literary requirements of the scientific community. For instance research results are presented as success stories, and the overall structure of scientific thought in some domain is set out as a logically ordered, deductive structure of statements, preferably having the scope and modality of laws, that is being both universal in application and necessary: they could not be otherwise.

But the realities of scientific activity are not fully expressed in the format of the scientific paper or textbook. So the true form of that activity is not captured in the analysis of such texts. Since the texts enshrine the principle of bivalence and its associated rhetorical convention of adherence to the orderliness of deductive logic, one way of disabusing ourselves of these illusions is to try to discover what lies behind texts. And this we can do in studying the conditions that the content of the whole of a thought pattern or cognitive structure which lies behind and is only partially expressed as a written out theory.

There is another way of conceiving realism in science, and this is through the principle that in a scientific discourse terms denote real things and can be used in picking them out. Within this apparently simple suggestion lie two deep problems: what is the nature of denotation, the word/thing relation achieved by acts of reference, and what do we mean by a 'real thing'? Ironically it was long ago pointed out by P. F. Strawson that the bivalence principle could not be applied at all unless reference had already been secured to beings to whom this or that property could be correctly or incorrectly ascribed. So even if we accepted the bivalence idea it would depend on another idea of realism, that of denotation or reference. In this paper I shall not even try to defend any particular account of reality. Suffice it to say that I shall be assuming that a being is taken to be real if it has a location in space-time and if it has causal powers. This leave space-time itself in an equivocal ontological status. Is space-time a 'container' independent of matter, or are spatiotemporal relations just one among the possible sets of relations in which material things can stand to one another? But that problem cannot be resolved here. However it will be necessary to make clear what notion of reference will be required to set up a scientific realism that makes essential use of it.

Before I turn to a closer look at reference, the kind of realism that is defensible must be sketched in outline. Defenders of bivalence would like to be able to justify their claim that the statements of science are probably true or false, and to do that on the basis of the pragmatic successes of theory. But theory is more often wrong than right, and even when right endlessly open to revision. Suppose instead of claiming that the statements of theory are true or false we claimed instead that it pays to read them as if the terms in them might denote real things, that is we should be defending a realist *reading* of theory under certain conditions summed up in a requirement yet to be spelled out, that the theory in question be plausible. But what would this achieve? It would allow for a well controlled and ontologically well defined search programme to be mounted, not to try to prove this or that statement true or false, but to try to locate and capture specimens of the kinds of beings to which the theory, read realistically, refers. This version of referential realism, I shall call 'policy realism'. And there is a final twist of the greatest importance in dealing with certain kinds of anti-realism, for instance that offered by Laudan. A real world search is scientifically successful whether it succeeds or fails. So the failure of such research programmes is as much support for policy realism as their success. It was reasonable to give the theory a realist reading. The policy of so doing paid off.

Varieties of Reference

In this section I will show that there are two main varieties of reference. An act of reference is successful if a defining set of predicates is satisfied, that is certain statements are found to be true of the being in question. The other idea is that an act of reference is successful when a physical relationship exists between the *user* of a word and what it denotes. This relationship still exists even when all the our original beliefs about an object have to be revised because they are apparently false. This idea of reference (denotation) fits with policy realism Theory guides us in the search for such beings as we can use its terms to try to pick out.

We must now turn to the problem that was set aside in the first section, namely how the idea of a term referring to a real thing is to be understood. Once again there are two main points of view. There is that which reflects that fact that the current focus of attention in philosophy of science is on texts expressing scientific theories.

I will call this variety of reference the 'satisfaction' conception since it is based on the principle that we know something of a certain kind exists if we can find a being that satisfies certain requirements, that is certain predicates can truly be ascribed to it. The fact that a term picks out something in the world is expressed as the fact that the object referred to has certain properties, necessary and sufficient to individuate it. This comes down to a question of the satisfaction of a set of simple open sentences. Let us say that the term in question is 'the AIDS virus'. Reference for that generic term is achieved if we can pick out an entity 'X' of which is it true that 'X is disruptive of T-cell function', 'X is sexually transmitted', etc. Thus the question of the reference of terms is transformed into the question of the truth or falsity of certain statements about individuals representative of the class of beings we refer to by the use of those terms. So bivalence turns out to be the nub of the matter even when realism is expressed as a matter of terms referring. The claim that a theory is realist if its terms typically refer to real things, becomes the logicist demand that only if its terms satisfy certain propositional functions, that is if certain statements are true or false, do its terms denote real beings.

But the problem with this treatment has long been understood. We do still accept that a term denoted something if we did manage to pick out a thing with the help of the predicates tied in with the term, even though it turned out that what we believed about it, even what was semantically implicated in the term itself, happens to be false. 'The man driving the BMW' may have been used successfully to pick out the man who was actually driving the Jaguar.[1] One has to admit that every claim about a putative entity is revisable. Of course revisability is a hierarchical notion, with attributions of accidental properties the most vulnerable to revision, that of natural kind the next most vulnerable and finally that of ontological category the least. That the AIDS virus has a certain protein which is characteristic of it, is revisable without our losing confidence in its reality. That it is a virus (rather than a bacterium, say) could be revised without loss of confidence in its existence, but there would be problems for a realist if it were finally agreed (as it was in the case of 'June bug fever') that the AIDS epidemic is a special case of hysteria triggered by depression.

Can anything be saved of the idea of achieving reference? Reflection on the problems of the satisfaction idea suggests that there is an aspect of the matter that is not brought out by that treatment. That is that if any part of the above procedure is to be applied there must be a robust *physical* relationship between the being in question and the scientist him or herself as an embodied being, who is a user of the term. When the exemplary instance of the AIDS virus presented itself via electron microscopy to the knowledgeable scientist the instrument linked scientist as embodied being with virus particle physically, by a stream of wavicles. Linking in this fashion someone who does not know the word does not allow that person to achieve an act of reference and so it does not show that the term does denote something real. How is this relationship tested? Not by looking for further predicate-functions to try to satisfy, but by setting about manipulating something by 'interfering' (as Ian Hacking has put it) with the virus/itself. This is not an original idea, but is set out by Robert Boyle in *The Origin of Forms and Qualities* when he argues for corpuscularian realism by trying to show that mechanical manipulations of the invisible particles brings about visible changes in properties of materials.

We can now sum up the new point of view: a term denotes a real thing if an embodied scientist as a user of the term can, with or without the help of instruments, set up a physical relationship between him or herself, sufficient to separate the being in question as a figure from a ground, and in the central cases by manipulation. The progress of science consists in a critical accumulation of specimens of the natural kinds which theoretical discourse has described. But how can theoretical discourse describe kinds of beings prior to their discovery? How does a theoretician know what to say and what the terms in a theory mean? To solve that problem we must turn to a study of the activity of theorizing, resisting the temptation to take the traditional shortcut by confining our studies to the textual presentation of a moment in the flow of theoretical activity, the logically organized written papers produced by a scientific community.

I must first explain why the study of the logic of scientific discourse has proved to be a blind alley in the attempt to understand science as the process of the production of trustworthy knowledge of nature.

Varieties of Theory

In this section I distinguish two ideas of what a theory is. One is based on the analysis of the logical structure of scientific discourse, the other on the analysis of the content of theories. The former presents a static picture, the latter a dynamic one. A theory family is an evolving structure organized around three models: an analytical model used to abstract patterns from phenomena; an explanatory model of the unknown causal mechanism which produces those patterns; and a source model which controls the way the explanatory model can be imagined. We can say a theory derived from a theory family is plausible by reference to relationships between these models. A plausible theory can guide a search for things denoted by the terms in that theory because they specify ontological type (through the source model) and natural kind (through the explanatory model).

Rom Harré

(i) *A Logicist Analysis of Theories*

The way of understanding that has had such an influence on our view of science we could call 'logicism'. According to that point of view there is a logical core, a kind of 'armature' around which the structures of scientific thought are built. To understand and in the end to account for the power of science (and sometimes it is thought almost any human activity to which standards can be applied), we must reveal the logical core. Thus logic becomes both a tool for analysis and a means of justification.

The idea that there is a logical core to science is an ancient one, and can certainly be found clearly articulated in Aristotle's Posterior Analytics. There it is associated with his idea that part of the explanatory task for a scientist is to develop an account of the essence of a substance or process in such a way that this essence is incorporated as a definition or premise within a syllogism or sorites that has the phenomenon to be explained as a premise. One proceeds as follows:

All rabbits are herbivores

can be taken for this example as an observational generalization. By adding the concept 'rodent' to express the essence of rabbithood as a 'middle term' it is possible to construct a syllogism in Barbara as follows:

All rodents are herbivores
All rabbits are rodents

therefore

All rabbits are herbivores.

But another source was equally potent in the almost ubiquitous assumption of the logicist conception of scientific activity. This was the influence both on actual method and on the rhetoric of the presentation of science of the style of Euclid's geometry. A clear parallel was thought to exist between

Axioms and definitions yield theorems

and

Principles and definitions yield laws.

So potent was this model that by the time of Newton it had become customary to lay out a scientific text under headings like 'axiom', 'theorem', 'corollary' and so on.

The final step in the logicist conception of a scientific project was the use of the same structure to tie the results of experiment and observation to laws. Thus:

Laws
Experiment set-up (conditions)

therefore

Description of expected result

A startling consequence, much discussed in recent philosophy of science, is that a mere change of date can change an explanation into a prediction and vice versa. The above schema presents a prediction before the experiment has been done or the observation made, and it presents an explanation if the experimental result has already been obtained or the observation made.

The fact that this story of science as applied logic is daily contradicted in the actual practices of scientists has led some people to try to remove the philosophy of science from intimate contact with science itself. This protective strategy is labelled 'rational reconstruction' and amounts to the claim that to bring out a logical essence as the core of a discourse or a practice is to reveal that practice or that discourse in ideal form.

(ii) *The Paradoxes of Logicism*

From time to time a scientific community finds itself with a plethora of theories each of which seems, from a logicist point of view, an adequate explanation of a common set of phenomena. This is particularly so if the adequacy is determined by how accurately each theory predicts phenomena of the kind in question. In the sixteenth century there were at least seven cosmological theories, comprehending the structure of the solar system, that were adequate in this sense. How to decide between them? In particular how could one decide which one was true? By taking a simplified model of this situation Clavius showed that there was no determinate answer to that question. His argument runs as follows: Consider the above example of the herbivorous rabbits. The general form of that explanation could be expressed in the following syllogism:

All Ms are herbivorous
All rabbits are Ms

so

All rabbits are herbivorous

And this form will always yield a valid deduction of the conclusion no matter what is substituted for M. For instance it would still be valid if we substituted 'made of wood' for M, thus:

All things made of wood are herbivorous
All rabbits are made of wood

so

All rabbits are herbivorous

But you might well object that while this syllogism may be valid as a deduction, but it will hardly serve as an adequate scientific explanation, since the premises are both false. But, if one is confined to the last line of this syllogism—the conclusion—for one's contact with *reality*, with *truth or falsity*, there will be no way in which that distinction can be made. If we cannot tell which of these theories is the true one then given that they are each successful in prediction, they must be equally acceptable on logicist grounds.

This stage of the argument has recently been revived, without acknowledgment of its renaissance origins, as the problem of the under-determination of theory by data. But Clavius went a step further. Since there is no restriction from within logicism on what can be substituted for the term M, in principle there are infinitely many theories that can be created by putting one thing or another for the middle term. What are our chances, asks Clavius, of hitting on the correct, or even the best theory, considered relative to its capacity to represent the causal mechanisms responsible for phenomena? Clearly they approximate zero. And this is paradoxical. It is worth remarking that this situation is rather the rule than the exception. For instance there are now a great many theories in play to explain the disappearance of the dinosaurs, from overheating to overeating. All make a reasonably good showing from a logical point of view. But we would like to know which one is the nearest to the truth. This notion 'nearest to the truth' is used here only in a colloquial sense. On close philosophical examination it turns out to be very far from satisfactory and will need radical revision before it can properly be incorporated amongst our metascientific concepts.

But this is not all. Deductively organized structures of propositions permit another 'paradox'. We could represent the logic of an experimental prediction in a syllogism in *Darii* as follows:

All rodents are herbivores
This rat is a rodent

so

We can expect it to eat only vegetable matter

However, we find that when presented with meat the rat consumes it with evident relish. It seems obvious that the original hypothesis, that all rodents are herbivorous is surely false. So it would seem if we confine ourselves to simple examples of this sort. But real science is somewhat more complex.

When Michelson and Morley showed that it was impossible to detect the motion of the earth relative to the ether one might have supposed that this spelled out the death knell of the ether hypothesis. Far from it. Lorentz was able to refine that hypothesis using his analysis of the forces on electrically charged matter, to show that the experimental result could be equally well explained by taking an assumption built in to the apparatus to be have been falsified instead, namely that the arms of the cross-shaped interferometer were unaffected by the motion of the whole thing through the ether. If, Lorentz showed, we revised that assumption, and instead supposed that the arm that lay in the direction of motion was forced to contract, by just the right amount, the ether hypothesis could be saved. This simple point has been generalized by Duhem, into the thesis that false predictions do not have a determinate effect on the true values we can rationally assign to the premises from which those predictions sprang. Certainly some amongst the many assumptions and principles, hypotheses and subtheses involved in the formulation and application of a theory are false, but we can never tell from the logic alone which they are.

Finally, there is the classical 'problem of induction', revived from time to time, the problem we usually associate with the writings of David Hume. Again adherence to logicism is the key to understanding the significance of the problem and to appreciating its paradoxical nature. All experimental or observational discoveries have the form of particular or singular facts, expressible as either Aristotelian 'Some A's are B' or as Fregean 'There is an x such that x is A'. Whichever logic we use to express the core of our inductive reasoning the passage from observational or experimental statements to a statement of a general law is logically invalid. We may not validly infer that 'All dinosaurs were cold-blooded' from our current level of knowledge that some were, even though that 'some' comprehends all that we have hitherto investigated. The fallacy of reasoning from 'some' to 'all' becomes even more obvious when the general statement we are aiming at is a law supposedly comprehending all places and all times. If logic is the only source of rationality and the ultimate court of appeal for the justification of reasoning then inductive inferences are irrational.

We have now reached a rather alarming result. It seems that experiment and observation, the very activities which were designed to produce limited but well-attested knowledge and by which all else was to be assessed, are useless. The paradoxes of Clavius and Hume show that experimental results which agree with the theories or hypotheses which entail them can provide no rational grounds for believing these theories. But we do tend to believe them, or if we are wise we allow ourselves to accept them provisionally. The paradox of Duhem shows that the use of disconfirming evidence to eliminate those parts of a scientific theory which we can be sure are false is also problematic, since its effect on a theory of any degree of complexity is indeterminate. But these are the only uses for experiment which logicism can admit. So it seems that we can neither prove nor disprove theories by the use of experiments. And this is surely a very paradoxical result, since it would suggest that experiments are useless.

But there is worse to come. If we return to the actual practices of scientists we find that theories are related to experiments in very different ways from those we have imagined as expressed by the logicist point of view. Theories are not fragile, easily disrupted and for ever in threat of being discarded in the face of contrary evidence. In practice it is theories which are often taken as more robust than experiments and indeed are used to decide whether some experiment has been properly done or an experimental programme well conceived. For instance, Millikan claimed in his published papers that he had done about sixty experiments in his investigation of the charge on the electron by the use of the method of suspended oil drops. All had shown the unit charge or some integral multiple of the unit charge. But Holton, on going through Millikan's notebooks, found that over one hundred and twenty experiments were recorded, about half of which had given unsatisfactory results, from the point of view of the unit charge thesis. Millikan simply discarded these as unsatisfactory. Theory had delivered the judgment. These experiments were defective in either equipment or execution. By taking this attitude Millikan had made it virtually impossible for any experiment to contradict his predetermined idea as to the value of the charge. Since this value was already strongly indicated by the theoretical analysis of Faraday's experiments on electrolysis, to upset it experimentally would have involved a radical rethink of much that was already established physical theory. In a somewhat similar way Mendel seems to have adopted a strategy in dealing with aberrant examples of his pea-breeding experiments that placed theory in a privileged position. It has long been a matter of controversy as to how Mendel got the results he did. It seems that Mendel took it for granted (at the level of *a priori* theory) that characters were ontologically discrete. The apparent natural continua, say between smooth and wrinkled skins and between yellow and green colour, were not scientifically significant. So, according to Root-Bernstein, it would have been quite rational for Mendel to instruct his assistants when counting peas, to distribute those which were not clear cut cases of the discrete characters, randomly amongst those that were. By following this method himself Root-Bernstein has been able to replicate Mendel's figures accurately.

There is also a priority assumption built into logicism. Theory must already exist if experiments and observations are to test it. One could not draw conclusions by deduction from a theory which did not already exist. Thus first theories and then their tests. But again scientific practice does not bear this out. A research programme is written up as a proposal to some funding body and let us say that the application is successful. Apparatus is purchased or manufactured, research assistants are hired and so on. Quite frequently the kind of results which are then obtained run in some way counter to or are not quite relevant to the research programme which was originally proposed. What then happens? In practice the experiments are preserved and a new research programme is invented for which they will be presented as the rational tests or confirming results. First do your experiments and then think out the research programme of which they are the test. This may look at first sight like induction, like drawing a general conclusion from singular premises. But the relation is very much more complicated. There is still the rhetoric of test which entails the possibility of failure. But if the research programme is made up to be that programme which is tested by the experiments it does seem beyond the bounds of practical sense to make a programme which is refuted or shown to be senseless by the experiments one has already done. This is particularly obvious when one remembers that the object of the exercise, considered sociologically, is to make acceptable publications possible.

What has led to this paradoxical position? All along the trouble seems to have come from the logicism which has been an unexamined assumption of much of our way of looking at science. There is no doubt that the scientific community values logically coherent and deductively organized scientific writing. Perhaps we have projected a feature of the rhetoric of the presentation of scientific results to the relevant community as if it were a necessary feature of the inner workings of scientific thought and a paradigm of method. I turn now to expound a naturalistic analysis of theories as they are actually constructed in the day to day conversations of a scientific community. Sometimes it happens that the whole work of building the basis of a successful theory family is the work of one man. For convenience I shall use such an example to introduce the main ideas of the analysis, but it must be remembered that this is nowadays more usually a communal activity, with some division of labour.

With the help of naturalistic analysis we will be able to see what makes a theory plausible, one it would be reasonable to read as if its terms denoted real beings that could be looked for experimentally.

(iii) *A Naturalistic Analysis of Theories*

Unfortunately from the point of view of exposition a naturalistic analysis of a theory expands into a very complex structure. The illusion of simplicity that comes from the logicist programme is bought at the cost of leaving out crucial elements of the underlying cognitive 'entity' of which the written forms of theory are usually rather idealized abstractions, with much left out. I will therefore break down the exposition of the naturalistic analysis into three phases. The first phase will be concerned with the way theoretical concepts are created so that they shall both be intelligible and be capable of referring to objects, properties and processes which have not, when they are introduced actually been observed. The second phase will be concerned with the structure of the relations in which these concepts are juxtaposed to empirical concepts to make the results of experiments relevant to the testing of the theory. In the third phase I will quite briefly introduce the necessary analytical ideas to help us to grasp how in fact an experimental programme is set up, and it will be noticeably different from the idea of a syllogism in *Darii*.

The first phase is nicely illustrated by Darwin's exposition of the theory of natural selection. The question to be addressed is how the concept of natural selection is created and made intelligible. In the *Origin of Species*, Darwin sets out a systematic exposition through two stages. First he demonstrates in great detail that there is an empirically well-established relationship between domestic variation and the appearance of domestic novelties, say new breeds of dog, mediated by the practice of domestic selective breeding or selection. Then he goes on to show that in nature there is also generally much variation between parental populations and their offspring. And there is natural novelty. There are new species and the geological record shows that they have appeared in succession, not at one and only one time. If this is now laid out alongside the results of Darwin's reflections on domestic breeding we get the following scheme:

Domestic variation plus domestic selection yields domestic novelty
Natural variation plus what (?)　　　　　　　yields natural novelty.

The answer stares out at us. If there is an analogy between these processes the missing piece in the jigsaw is Natural Selection. This thought pattern has done two things. It has given us a concept we can understand, and it has given us a theory which refers to a new process which we can perhaps hope actually to observe.

In a very similar way Pasteur exploited an analogy between suppuration in wounds and fermentation. The latter is caused by a micro-organism, the yeasts, so perhaps the latter is also caused by a micro-organism, the bacterium. In this way he reconceptualized Lord Lister's discovery of 'wild' cells in suppurating wounds. Lister had mistakenly thought them to be detatched human cells. But by drawing on the analogy between infected wounds and fermenting juices Pasteur was able to bring his knowledge of the process of wine-making, in the study of which he first made his reputation, to the problem of infection. Similarly the Causius-Maxwell theory of gases in which a gas is thought of as a swarm of randomly moving molecules depends on the underlying analogy between a Newtonian particle obeying the Newtonian dynamics and the molecule obeying analogous laws.

The second phase of our analysis takes us to the role of experiment in assessing theories. The results of experiments present, in compendious form, a description of the behaviour of whatever mechanisms there really are lying behind and responsible for the appearances in some field of scientific interest. We want our imagined mechanism, described in terms of the theoretical concepts expressing the analogy above, described phase one, to be analogous to the behaviour of the real mechanisms which we know about from our experiments. If we call the relation between the concepts of domestic selection and natural selection an instance of a material analogy, we could call the relation between the behaviour of a real gas ($PV=RT$) and the imagined behaviour of the Maxwell analogue, a swarm of molecules ($pv=\frac{1}{3}\ nmc^2$) the behavioural analogy. An important aspect of the dynamics of theory development comes about through the need to maintain both these analogies. As we shall see when either is disturbed by new experiments in the case of the behavioural analogy, or by new developments in theory in the case of the material analogy, the other has to be adjusted to re-establish equilibrium.

A striking example of the interaction between behavioural and material analogies can be found in Amagat's revisions of the gas laws consequent on his experimental programme to test those laws under extreme conditions. He devised apparatus to raise pressures to the order of 400 atmospheres. Under those conditions he found that the simple proportionality expressed in Boyle's law, that pressure is inversely proportional to volume was not borne out. By this experimental programme he had shown that real gases did not behave in ways analogous to the way the imagined Clausius–Maxwell gas behaved. So he went back to the material analogy upon which that theoretical conception of a gas had been based. It involved a molecule which though analogous in behaviour did not have volume. But suppose we changed the material analogy to add volume to the properties we imagine molecules to have. Then the volume available to the free Maxwell motion of those particles would be restricted by volume they themselves occupy, namely 'b'. Then the actual volume available is $V-b$. A new form of Boyle's law is called for, $P\ (V-b)=$constant. This law, derived from reworking the material analogy is found actually to fit the experimental results thus restoring the balance between behavioural and material analogies.

Rom Harré

But there is yet another way in which this analysis of theory in terms of content is instructive. Mendel's research programme depended on an atomistic conception of genetic material and this went along with, of necessity, a way of thinking about the characteristics of organisms, as discrete sets of characters rather than as continuous ranges. Thus the infinite gradations of hue between yellow and green were treated as a simple polar dichotomy between 'green' and 'yellow', just two colours. The experimental programme, look for the distribution of discrete colours and discrete textures of peas, generation by generation, was controlled by an ontological hypothesis, that of the atomic genetic factor, which has descended to us as the gene. Clearly this concept must have been created in the theory, since it could not have been derived from the experimental programme. That programme actually depended upon the ontology of the theory as I have already pointed out. Now, what could the role of the new concept, 'gene' actually be? It cannot be explanatory in the logicist sense on pain of obvious circularity of reasoning. So it is not playing a logical role. But the subsequent history of genetics shows that it played a central ontological role. It served as a guide for the long running programme of research which finally culminated in the work of the molecular biologists who found the chemical basis for the genetic factors. Of course much changed in the concept in the course of this history, but throughout the idea of an atomistic source of genotypical attributes was preserved, the core of the concept. The gene was a new kind of being, though ontologically familiar as a causally potent occupant of a spatial position and enduring for some time.

What then is explaining on this view of scientific theorizing? It is certainly not building up a structure of propositions from which finally a description of what is to explained can be deduced. Explaining is not a logical concept. In the examples that I have developed it is clear that the drive toward completion of the theory is a need to have a clearly formulated conception of a causal mechanism which could produce the phenomena of interest. Explaining is mapping items from a common ontology on to a phenomena.

An example will help to make this clear. When Pasteur was working on the development of an anthrax innoculation he was puzzled by the fact that the disease still spread among the cows on a farm even when infected animals were buried deeply in the earth. His theory of disease was based on the ontological hypothesis of microorganisms, bacteria. Some transporter must then be active to permit the infective agent to travel from the dead cow to the surface of the earth to be taken up by the living herd. Earthworms were an obvious answer. So Pasteur began to collect earthworms in the earth near the dead cows and to look in their guts. There he did indeed find anthrax bacilli. Now this is both a very simple example and very telling philosophically. The crucial step was the postulation of an unobserved process that could become observable. And to try to show that it exists. This is quite different from establishing a Humean and logicist correlation between dead and buried cows and the infection of the living.

This is the position of scientific realism, but of the policy variety. It enjoins us to take the referring expressions in a theory seriously, as if they were indeed denoting real but so far unobserved processes or things, and to use the content of the theory to guide the research process. The source analogue or model of 'organism' controls the general field of research, through the material analogy. We look for a microorganism, which is an enduring entity in a definite spatial location. And the theory also allows us to form hypotheses about the causal powers we should attribute to those beings, thus specifying their natural kind, and giving us criteria by which instances may be specified. Logically the hypothesis 'There are anthrax bacilli in the gut of earthworms' is verified by an instance, in stark contrast to the scepticism that infects our view of general and law like statements even when we do have favourable instantiations of their correlated predicates.

The organization of concepts into theories is evidently controlled by the principle of analogy (and that displacement of concepts we call metaphor). It is not achieved by the interpretation of a logically organized formal core.

Varieties of Defences

In this section I undertake the task of producing a philosophical argument in favour of policy realism. But in doing that I must at the same time make sure that the scope of the argument is sufficiently restricted so that it shall have bite. Scientific theories denote three kinds of beings; realm 1, those which are ordinarily observable; realm 2, those that are actually unobservable but could perhaps be observed; and realm 3, those which we believe to be in principle unobservable. The defence of realism for theories whose terms severally denote beings in the three realms will be different. I will undertake the defence of realism, of the appropriate sort, only for theories denoting beings in realm 2. The argument depends on it being only contingent that such beings cannot be observed, so the policy of making a realist reading is reasonable.

To articulate a fully explicit argument for policy realism a more careful catalogue must be constructed for the kinds of beings the terms in a theory could denote. There are those which are ordinarily and currently observable, such as the gall stones a physician diagnoses and a surgeon looks for and finds or fails to find. Then there are those which at some historical epoch are unobservable but are of the same ontological category (and sometimes even of the same natural kind) as beings currently observable. The smallest moon of Uranus, the AIDS virus, the human genetic layout, are or have been in that status. Finally there is a third realm of beings which are unobservable in principle. By 'in principle' I mean that there are reasons, say in the very ontological category to which they belong, or in the physical or psychological theory with which they are associated, that forces this judgement of unobservability upon us. Three quarks make up a proton, but protons never decay. Field potentials are observable only in their manifestations, never in themselves. A possibility or 'would be' is never an 'is' or realization, and only the latter is observable as such. The boundary between the realm of observable beings and those which are currently unobservable by reason of some lack of technique or lost opportunity etc., those of our second category, is historically variable and therefore contingent. We can never know, in advance, whether some technical development or invention will be made to bring such beings within the bounds of the observable. It is rational then to read the theories which we use to refer to them as if the relevant terms did denote real beings. By doing so we initiate the long process of exploration and technical development which would, did they exist, reveal them. But this is worthwhile only if the theories involved are plausible, that is maintain an ontology of beings which are observable in principle, and work well pragmatically, as devices for predicting and retrodicting testable consequences.

The defence of realism raises different issues in each realm. A realist reading of realm 1 theories is defensible only if there is a good argument for a realist interpretation of perception. A realist reading of the theory that the car will not start because of a loose wire can be taken seriously only if we think that perception in general is a kind of contact with beings that exist independently of ourselves. The argument above is a defence of a kind of realism for theories with which scientists refer to realm 2 beings. But a defence of the reality of the dispositions and powers denoted by terms in use in realm 3 theories involves issues in philosophical logic and metaphysics too complex to undertake here.

Note

[1] K. Donnellan, 'Reference and Definite Descriptions', *Philosophical Review* **75** (1966), 281–304.

Mind and Body

K. V. WILKES

1. Introduction

I expect every reader knows the hackneyed old joke: 'What is matter? Never mind. What is mind? No matter.' Antique as this joke is, it none the less points to an interesting question. For the so-called mind–body dichotomy, which has been raised to almost canonical status in post-Cartesian philosophy, is not in fact at all easy to draw or to defend. This of course means that 'the mind–body problem' is difficult both to describe and to solve—or rather, as I would prefer, to dissolve.

We shall begin by looking at this 'mental/physical' distinction, to see of what stuff it is made. That will be the first half of this lecture. Then, in the second half, I shall try to provide a brief description of the main attempts to understand the relationship between the 'mental' and the 'physical', or 'mind' and 'brain'.

2. 'Mental' and 'Physical'

(a) The Mental

It would be difficult to explain the term 'mental' to an ancient Greek. If we look very fleetingly at Aristotle, for instance, there we find the term *psuche*, which is usually, but very misleadingly, translated as 'soul' (and which is the ancestor of our term '*psych*ological'). Aristotle's *psuche*, though, did not restrict itself to those phenomena covered by our terms 'mind', or 'mental'. For Aristotle,[1] everything that lived had *psuche*—thus maple trees and mosquitoes had it as fully as did mice and men. *Psuche*-functions included seeing, thinking, imagining—but also included other functions of living things: digestion, growth, movement, metabolism.

'The mental', as we have it today, owes its scope to two very different sources. The first is Cartesian: the mind is the sum total of everything of which we are directly and immediately conscious. So my present thought of a Viennese coffee-house is mental, as is the pain in my toe, and my memory of a thunderstorm in Sofia. Mental phenomena are meant to be all those things of which we are immediately, incorrigibly, aware; we have unmediated, direct, and privileged access to them. 'Consciousness never deceives', claimed Hume,[2] in this respect following Descartes—as indeed did Locke and Berkeley before him. So, for instance, a capacity like perception was included *in a sense*, but this was not 'perception of a tree'; rather it was the experience, the feeling, the sensation, of seeing a tree: whatever there is in common between actually seeing a tree and hallucinating one.

This definition of the mental, which made it co-extensive with the conscious mind, was revolutionary. Before Descartes nobody doubted that there was much about human psychology which we did *not* know, of which we were *not* conscious. The Greek demand 'know thyself' would have been fatuous rather than famous if self-knowledge were so easy. Heraclitus said that we could never find out the depths of the soul, no matter how long and hard we tried. Writers, poets and philosophers had all taken it for granted, for centuries, that we were very largely confused, self-deceived, ignorant about ourselves and about what goes on in our minds. Indeed, it is worth remembering that Descartes' primary aim was to combat scepticism, *not* to provide a description of the mind; his account of the *mens* was pulled along by his epistemological strategy. He thought that the only way to defeat the sceptic was to find some unchallengeable foundations of knowledge—some facts which even the most ardent sceptic could not attack. He thought that the only possible candidates to play the role of this unshakeable foundation were statements such as *cogito*—generalized to all first-person present-tense reports on the current contents ('ideas') in the conscious mind. So evidently there must be such current contents; and hence epistemological motivations gave rise to a metaphysical, or ontological, thesis: that 'the mind' just is 'the conscious mind'.

Evidently this will not do, although it is indeed part of the story. The mere everyday fact of self-deception shows that we can be wrong about ourselves: not everything is open to the unblinking gaze of the Inner Eye of conscious introspection. Consider too another everyday phenomenon: you trip at the top of a flight of steps. As you brush yourself down you say 'I thought' (or perhaps: 'I must have thought') 'that there was another step'. But in your conscious mind at the time, let us suppose, were thoughts about the health of your pet canary. It seems true that this thought ('one more step') explains your stumble; but whatever else this thought is, it wasn't in your conscious mind. Then again, whether or not we go along with Freud, we presumably all nowadays admit that factors of which we are not conscious supply much of the warp and weft of our characters, personality, motivation. (Freud, I suggest, didn't 'discover' the unconscious; rather, Descartes *un*discovered it, by equating 'the mind' with the tip of the iceberg that is the *conscious* mind.)

Nevertheless, Descartes left a rich legacy. The importance of the idea that we have some special, privileged, incorrigible access to at least some of our mental states is with us still, and generates the most troublesome part of the mind–body question, as we shall see. In other words, I shall suggest, 'the' mind–body dilemma is most difficult to resolve when it is seen primarily as a question about the relation of *conscious* mental phenomena to physical phenomena. At the moment this is just a promissory note, to be cashed a little later.

Before pursuing the 'Cartesian' notion of mind, we should examine the second source of the present-day scope of the term 'mental'. This goes back further, to the medieval scholastics; but it was most clearly phrased by Brentano (under whom, incidentally, Freud studied for a time). This was called in medieval times 'intentional inexistence'; today it is called 'intensionality', often spelled with an 's' in the middle rather than a 't', to distinguish it from one specific mental state, the state of intending to do something (I shall use the 's' spelling here).

Broadly, an intensional state is a state which has content, which is *about* something. What it is about may not exist (that is, you can have beliefs about Father Christmas; the Greeks believed in Zeus), or may not be true (you can believe that there is a dodo in the bathroom). Alternatively the content of your mental states may exist, or be true. This doesn't matter; it is true *that* you have such thoughts, desires, etc., whether or not what they are *about* exists or is the case, or not. Another way of describing intensionality is the following. Suppose that the man in the brown mackintosh is the Lord Mayor of London. You have beliefs about the man in the mackintosh—you think he's a KGB agent. You don't however think that the Mayor is a Soviet agent (you don't know that the man in the brown mackintosh is the Mayor); in fact you think the Mayor is fanatically anti-Soviet. So there is a property which the man in the brown mackintosh has—being believed by you to be a Soviet agent—which the Mayor lacks, *even though* it is one and the same individual. This is called 'failure of substitutivity', because if I say of you that you believe that the man in the brown mackintosh is a KGB spy, I can't substitute 'the Lord Mayor of London', for the phrase 'the man in the brown mackintosh' when I'm reporting your belief, even though they are one and the same man. By and large failure of sub-stitutivity does not hold for non-mental properties; if the man in the brown mackintosh has the property of having a sore toe, or of being six feet tall, then so does the Mayor. We shall come back to this; it links up with the Leibnizian definition of identity: if *a* just is identical to *b*, then everything that is true of *a* is of course also true of *b*. Mental phenomena seem to violate this principle; 'being believed by Kathy Wilkes to be a KGB spy' is true of the man in the brown mackintosh, not of the Mayor. Brentano saw intensionality as of immense importance; as sundering the universe is the most fundamental possible way, by dividing the mental from the physical.

This too is central to our contemporary characterization of the mental. It is broader than the Cartesian restriction to consciousness, since it easily includes non-conscious thoughts, desires, etc. But it too has its shortcomings; in fact where the 'Cartesian' considerations succeed, intensionality often tends to fail, and vice versa. Intensionality seems not to hold for some paradigm mental phenomena: 'I have a pain' does not fit readily the criteria for intensionality, whereas it is easily accommodated by the equation of the mental with the conscious. Conversely, intensionality seems to include too much. Consider: some neuropsychologists describe the amygdala of the rat's brain as a 'comparator', which compares received rewards or punishments with expected ones. 'Expecting' is a thoroughly intensional notion; but do we really want to ascribe mental states to bits of a rat's brain? Again: we find intensional terms freely employed to describe operations in a computer; but it is at least an open question whether we want to commit ourselves to the idea that computers have a mental life.

The brute fact is that there is no single and agreed characterization of what it is to be *mental*, as distinct from non-mental, or physical. The two main candidates we have been discussing are of very different stripes; one is epistemologically motivated and relies heavily upon a notion, 'consciousness', that did not come into English (or French, or German) in its present range of senses until the second half of the seventeenth century. The other is a logical criterion, resting on the differences between the truth-conditions for statements concerning the mind, and those for statements concerning the physical. We can use the two together, and get a hybrid sort of notion that covers *most* of what we want the term 'mental' to cover, and which doesn't include too much that we would rather exclude. Possibly, however, the source of the problem is that there isn't a sharp line here at all; that 'the' dichotomy isn't either clear, nor even important. I shall develop this line further in the second half of this lecture; for the moment just reflect that when we describe other people we use large numbers of terms that are not clearly either obviously mental, nor obviously physical: 'has a toothache', 'is sleepy', 'is tired', 'is nervy', 'is suave', 'is an extrovert'; or alternatively reflect on the number of 'mental' terms that are routinely used by neuropsychologists, or computer scientists, to describe bits of the brain, or to describe programs.

(b) The Physical

The difficulty of delimning 'the mental' is familiar; far too many assume that there's no difficulty with 'the physical'. Or rather, philosophers take a hand-waving attitude, according to which 'the physical' is 'whatever physical scientists talk about'; when it comes to issues of mind and brain, 'the physical' is whatever *neurophysiologists* talk about: neurons, synapses. But such hand-waving is often a way of bidding farewell to what is crucially important.

There are of course nerve cells in the brain; billions of them. BUT: each has an immensely complex internal economy, and needs to be dissected into its microconstituents. Evidently there is a chemical level of description of each neuron, and after that too an atomic level; and then, as we now know, atoms have hideously complex internal economies of their own. So far forth we simply do not know how much of the explanation for the workings of the mind will require us to examine the *sub*-cellular workings of the brain. Equally and conversely, why go as 'micro' as the neuron? This may be unnecessary; it seems that much of the explanation for some features of our mental life derives from the operations of cell-*columns*, or *collections* of cell-columns, or the *pattern-properties* or *spiking frequencies* of neural networks. Or, again: neuroscientists talk about functions performed by 'macro' cerebral chunks: the amygdala, the hippocampus, the temporal lobe, the right hemisphere.

It is an obvious fact, but one too often ignored by philosophers, that there are dozens of levels of description for 'the physical'. (Philosophers often oversimplify areas they know little about; there is a nice comment here by Austin:[3] '. . . oversimplification, which one might be tempted to call the occupational disease of philosophers if it were not their occupation'.) If we restrict ourselves just to the brain, we can take at one end of the spectrum 'the brain', and at the other end, quarks and neutrinos. The choice of anything in between, such as 'the neuron', or 'the left hemisphere', is arbitrary and needs defence—which, of course, it can often receive. We must break loose of the idea that 'the physical' is something stuff-like. 'The brain' may be stuff-like; but 'pattern-properties of neural excitation' is a highly *abstract* notion, and there is nothing 'stuff-like' about quarks. We must also break free from the idea that there is one, privileged, level of description of the brain to which 'the mental' must somehow be related. It is I think entirely true that the best description of 'the physical' is: 'whatever is picked out by the terminology that physical scientists use in their theories'. But then we must also recognize that there is a hierarchical host of levels about which neuroscientists talk; and that they talk not only about stuff-like things, but also about physical *functions*. These functions include not only the 'firings' of synapses, but also the 'expectancies' of the rat's amygdala, or the 'face-recognition' capacity of subsystems within the right hemisphere.

(c) The Distinction

So: what price 'the' mental–physical dichotomy? I suggest the following. 'The mental' (equivalently for our purposes, 'the psychological') is

73

best defined as: 'whatever is picked out in the terminology of the psychological sciences'. 'The physical'—as far as brain science is concerned—will be: 'whatever is picked out by the terminology of neuroscience'. This means that there is *no* line between the two, just as there is no God-given 'line' between a bump in my lawn and the Alps. There is, usually, a difference; neurophysiologists won't often talk about neuroses, and psychoanalysts usually have little to say about neutrinos. Equally I can skip over a bump in my lawn, but would leave Alpine climbing to others. But since there is no absolute line, demarcation point—just as there is no absolute line between a hill and a mountain—we must accept that there will be a whole host of terms that are indeterminately both, or neither, 'mental' and 'physical'. Indeed, there is a branch of science that is called 'neuropsychology' (or, equivalently, 'psychophysiology'). This discipline has its own conceptual apparatus which, inevitably, straddles the so-called divide between the neural-physiological and the psychological. Here is an example, taken directly from the literature: 'the septal-hippocampal system *sends a signal* via the fornix to *the decision centre* in the medial hypothalamus'.

The lesson to be drawn, a lesson which makes a vast difference, I think, to any worthwhile examination of the mind–body problem, is that we do not have two sharply distinct sorts of thing to relate. We have instead a muddled, complex hierarchy of mind–brain interrelations to discuss.

3. Mind–Brain Relationships

(a) Two Main Sources of Complexity

If this is right, then, we do not have 'the' mind–body problem; we should not expect to pick on *one* type of relationship that obtains between mental kinds of things and physical kinds of things. Both mental and physical are wildly heterogeneous. Few things are less similar than an Oedipal complex and the sensation of a pinprick; or subliminal perception and a state of irritability. Oak trees and quarks are both 'physical phenomena'; as are lumps of gold and pattern-properties of atomic lattices. This heterogeneity—found in both 'mental' and 'physical'—makes our problem messier, but has the virtue of greater plausibility.

Another very important source of messiness is the question whether we want to relate types of mental things to types of physical things, or tokens to tokens, or something in between. To understand this important distinction, compare 'all men are sons' with 'the man holding the gun is my brother'. All men, Adam being the sole exception, are identical with someone's son; the type, man, is systematically related to the class of sons. So this is a *type–type* relation, in this case the relation of identity. But not all my brothers hold guns, and not all men holding guns are brothers of mine; 'the man holding the gun is my brother' is a *token–token* claim of relationship, also in this case the relation of identity. Thus when we are considering mental–physical relationships, we have to decide whether, and when, we hope for the stronger type–type kind of relationship, or for the weaker token–token form. Probably it is true to say that almost all instances of physical pain involve (*inter alia*) firing of C-fibres in the brain stem. So there might be a type–type relationship between pains and C-fibre firing (although it would not be a relationship of *identity*, since pain involves far more than just C-fibre firing). But 'my thought at 12.01 that I was running out of coffee' may have few if any *systematic* correlations with what goes on in your head when you have such a thought; in other words, there may be no type of brain-state that goes along with coffee-thoughts rather than tea-thoughts or toothpaste-thoughts. That thought at 12.01 might then be identical to some complex brain process, but in a token–token way.

Given that we have these complexities to take on board, let us look through some of the candidate theories that are in the game of elucidating the mental–physical relationship.

(b) Some Competing Theories

The simplest view of the mind–brain relation is one of identity: pain just is such-and-such a state of the brain, my thought that I need to buy more coffee is another. But this needs careful exploration.

(i) *Identity*. If *a* is identical to *b* then—since identity is symmetric—*b* is identical to *a*. A trivial point, perhaps; but it means that if all mental events are physical, some physical events are mental: the relation of identity has no favourites. Certainly some writers who call themselves 'identity theorists' want the physical to be somehow more fundamental, more important, than the mental. We shall soon return to this. A second complication of any identity theory is that Leibniz's law, mentioned above, must be observed: all properties (bating intensional properties and some others) true of *a* must be true of anything—*b*—to which it is identical. Thus if my mental image is horse-shaped, or my pain is stabbing, they cannot be identical to any brain state, since brain states lack such properties. But this difficulty can be circumvented by a bit of fast footwork, sleight of hand: we can decide to identify, *not* mental images, or pains, but the states of *having* images and pains, and *being in* certain brain states. Evidently, 'having an image of a horse'— or, equivalently, 'visualizing a horse'—is not the sort of thing to be called 'horse-shaped', and '*having* a pain' is not 'stabbing'. A third complication is whether we hope for *type* identities, or *token* ones, or some mixed type–token identities.

K. V. Wilkes

How might one prove or disprove any identity thesis? Empirical work will be inconclusive, for a very simple reason: all the evidence for identity is, equally, evidence for dualistic parallelism. That is, if a scientist establishes that whenever anyone experiences a pain there is such-and-such a sequence of cerebral processes, the dualist can easily argue that this shows only that whenever there is a pain, there is *also* this sequence of cerebral processes; he need not be forced into conceding that they are *identical*. 'Whenever A, then B' is a far cry from 'A *is* B'. Whenever there is a heart (in any organism) then there is also a kidney, and vice versa; but hearts are not kidneys.

Partly for this reason, the most discussed and notorious argument for identity does not rest on empirical evidence but argues *a priori*; this is an argument of Donald Davidson's.[4] It relies on three premises: first, that mental and physical interact causally. Second, that wherever there is causality, there is a law: all true singular causal statements instantiate *some* general law. Third, that there are no laws linking phenomena described in mental terms with anything, mental or physical; all laws must relate events under physical descriptions. Now; there is no time here to assess the three premises; the third, certainly, needs a great deal of defence and examination. But if the premises are accepted, then the conclusion follows, in this way. Suppose a physical event—an ambulance siren—causes a mental event—your hearing the noise. Since one causes the other, there must be *a* law (every true singular causal statement instantiates a law). But there are no laws relating mental phenomena (you hearing the noise) to anything. All laws have to be physical–physical. Therefore the mental event of hearing the noise must be token-identical to a physical event. (Only token-identical, note; if there are no laws relating mental to physical, there cannot be type-correlations between them.) Since this is an important point, I'll reinforce it by considering an analogous case. Suppose you say 'the event reported on page 3 of the *The Times* caused the event reported on page 4 of the *Morning Star*'. Suppose further that the first event was an earthquake in a populated area, the second destruction of property and loss of life. Evidently there are no laws linking 'events described on page 3 of the *The Times*' with 'events described on page 4 of the *Morning Star*'—Murdoch hasn't taken over the *Morning Star* yet. However, one event just is an earthquake, another just is destruction of property; and given an adequate statement of the standing conditions, we are at least getting close to a law that relates earthquakes of certain strengths to the destruction of buildings of certain kinds in the earthquake zone.

Unfortunately the issue cannot be quite so swiftly resolved, since not everyone by any means accepts all Davidson's premises. Moreover, his thesis needn't even be considered as a thesis about *identity*. It gives one a monistic conclusion, certainly—there aren't two sorts of thing or state, only one.

(ii) *Monism without identity (A): eliminative materialism*. We might however prefer to think of mental phenomena not as *identical* to physical phenomena, but rather as *constituted by, made up of, nothing but,* them, in the sort of way that tables are made up of, constituted by, nothing but, molecules. Note here that the relation 'X-es are made up of Y-s' is not symmetric: molecules aren't made up of tables. So it isn't strict identity. The relation between mental and physical is rather a relationship which is expressed by saying (e.g.) 'X-es are nothing but Y-s'—e.g. 'pains are nothing but C-fibre firings'. This is not symmetric: if we say 'X-es are nothing but (constituted by) Y-s', we do not need to accept in return that 'Y-s are nothing but (constituted by) X-es'.

There is a moderate and an extreme version of this general position. Moderate proponents consider that the 'macro' phenomena (tables, or pains) which are shown to be 'made up of', or are 'nothing but', 'micro' phenomena (clouds of molecules, or brain processes) are thereby endorsed and validated: there really are such things as tables/pains, and this microanalysis shows exactly what they are. Extreme proponents of this sort of view however argue that the 'nothing but' relation licenses the further claim 'so, there are really no X-es', in the same sort of way that the claim 'witches are nothing but neurotic women' might be held to license the claim 'so, there are really no witches'. The picture we are offered, sometimes, is then that in some splendid and enlightened future we won't find children crying 'Mummy, Mummy, my leg hurts', but rather 'Mummy, Mummy, I'm in brain state B351c'.

To the extremists I am disposed to respond 'well, maybe; let's wait and see'. More seriously, one can surely agree that there might be *some* mental phenomena which we could agree one day to be 'nothing but' states or processes in the brain, and which moreover are such that we might in time come to drop the 'mental' description of them, and use instead a physical one. For that to come about, though, we shall need to have discovered *type–type* relations between the 'old' mental phenomena and the 'new' physiological description, otherwise we couldn't eliminate smoothly the old terminology: it would be 'nothing but' a different brain state every time it occurred. For the vast majority of what we talk about, and need to talk about, extreme eliminative materialism is just wildly implausible, though. 'Pain', and 'table', are simple, short, easy words. The series of events in and throughout the brain that are implicated in pain experiences, and the description of the molecular cloud which makes up the table, by contrast, are incredibly complex and would take several minutes to describe. The point would be clearer if we took a different example: it is just ludicrous to imagine that we might ever find 'a' cerebral process that correlated smoothly and systematically with your and my and everyone else's thought that gaslamps are more romantic than electric lamps.

Parenthesis: there's nothing odd about psychology in this respect. There is nothing fishy or funny about the *brute* fact that many mental phenomena have at best only token–token realizations in our neurophysiology. This is true throughout the physical world as well. For it is just as clear that there are no systematic correlations between fences, ashtrays, and ornaments, on the one hand, and their microstructures on the other. The sciences—psychology and physiology included—search primarily for natural kinds—classes of things which *do* get governed by systematic law; like gold, water, tigers, but not ashtrays, fences, police uniforms. So *systematic* psycho–physical relationships will hold only between whatever these mental and physical classes prove to be; and it is more likely that such categories will include 'face recognition' than that they'll include 'beliefs that gaslamps are more romantic than electric ones'.

(iii) *Monism without identity (B): functionalism.* So far I have touched briefly on a number of theses that are *monistic*: that claim that mental phenomena are not other than physical phenomena. The identity theory plays no favourites; the 'composed of' and 'nothing but' theories give preference and priority to the physical. Let us turn now to a different approach to (part of) the question of the mind–brain relationship. This is the set of views called functionalism; but we can work up to it by first considering classical behaviourism, since functionalism is most clearly seen as 'reiterated behaviourism'.

Behaviourists decided to ban talk of the mental (some of them denied that mental phenomena existed; other considered that reference to them was unnecessary). The organism was a big black box, and the behaviour (output) was a function of the state of the system, and the stimulus (input). All behaviour could in principle be explained as a function of these two variables. See here Figure 1.

Well, this was too simple-minded to work, although it could go a long way. Ultimately, though, it proved unable to explain the behaviour of mice, let alone men. Functionalism however takes up and runs with the essential idea. It does not rest content with the behaviourists' single big box; it opens up this box, and inserts a *nest* of boxes. Each of these smaller boxes has its own 'behaviour'; its output is a function of its current state, and of its input (which might be from the external world, or from another box; and boxes/functions later in the series can loop, or feed, back on to earlier boxes/functions). See here Figure 2.

So each box has its input and output: the input may be from the external world (e.g. box f_1 in the diagram), which receives data from outside and passes on an output to other functions; maybe other boxes send signals to the 'output box' (f_z in the diagram) which, say, then

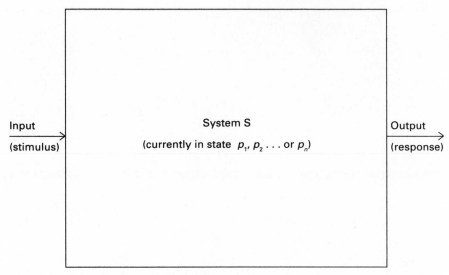

Figure 1

activates muscles to generate or suppress physical movement (walking, talking). Those in the middle receive input from, and send output to, other functions (f_2–f_x and f_y in the diagram).

So far this is very abstract, and could as easily describe a tractor factory, or a banking system, as an intelligent organism. But we can clothe the formal model by noting that these 'boxes', these functions,

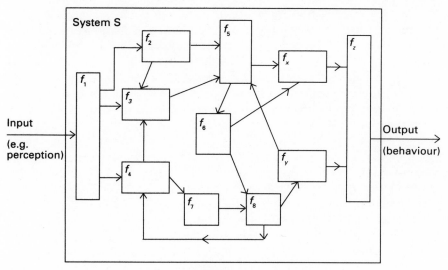

Figure 2

K. V. Wilkes

can be equated with psychological phenomena. They would be *theories* for explaining behaviour. That is, one box might be labelled 'desire', another 'belief', another 'memory', another 'perception'. Or, to take an actual example from neuropsychology, the labels might be 'classifier', 'expectancy generator', 'comparator', 'amplifier'. These labels pick on capacities of the mind, and the schema tries to show how they interact to explain behaviour. For example: if you see a wasp on your hand, you might want to jerk your hand to throw it off, because of a belief that wasps can sting and a desire to avoid the pain. But if you also knew that you were on a tightrope, then *that* information, together with stored information or memory about the effects of sudden movement on precarious balancing, might result in the suppression of the movement.

The method can of course be reiterated. Suppose one box, one function, is called 'memory'. Well, perhaps we can open up that box, and insert a smaller nest of contributory boxes: short-term memory, long-term memory, habit memory, propositional memory, iconic memory, and so forth. We then create a nest of subfunctions (these are labelled '*s–f*' in the diagram). See here Figure 3.

Then: consider only short-term memory, and suppose that it is the central box in figure 3, which I have called 'sub-function sf_m'. How is *that* function fulfilled? We may need sub-sub-functions like 'information-retrieval mechanisms' (labelled '*s–s–f*' in the diagram). Again,

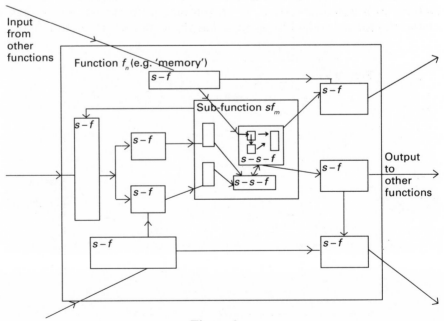

Figure 3

another subordinate nest of 'boxes'. The primary point is that in principle one could go on for a long time, breaking down complex psychological functions into smaller, more 'stupid', functions, until—in principle!—we reached such relatively simple functions as 'edge detection', for which we could perhaps seek a neurophysiological realization.

Such a view sidelines 'the' identity debate. Indeed, it makes talk of 'identity' a category mistake: one can't equate functions with the things that perform those functions, any more than one can identify bottle-opening with a corkscrew. Opening bottles is what corkscrews do, not what corkscrews are. Similarly 'edge detection' is what cell-columns do, not what they are. But nor is it a dualist position. One and the same thing can be described *via* its function or *via* its structure; a group of cells, that is, might legitimately be called an 'edge detector', just as a corkscrew can be called a 'bottle-opener'. Or, look at it this way. 'The' function/structure distinction can be—and very often is—compared to 'the' difference between computer software and computer hardware; but *that* distinction isn't absolute but is relative to the level at which you look at your PC. Someone writing the machine code is writing a program, software; one level higher you get the assembly language, which is another program—but for the writer of the assembly language, the machine code counts as the hardware with which he's working. Right at the top of the scale, the programmer working in ADA, PASCAL, or BASIC, treats everthing 'beneath' as hardware.

It is tricky to assess functionalism, because there are so many stripes of it. You'll by now be able to guess that there'll be a big difference depending on whether one wants a *scientific* version or a *common-sense* version: that is, depending on whether the boxes, or functions, selected are more like water and gold—with systematic relationships (type–type) to the physiological mechanisms that ultimately explain them—or whether they are more like fences and ashtrays, where there are at best token–token relationships. Put another way, the Russian neuroscientist Sokolov[5] explains habituation in the rat by postulating functions he labels as 'expectancy generators', 'amplifiers', 'comparators'—these are not typically 'mental' terms, as we think of them. But philosophers, who are generally concerned to examine common sense psychology, may use the friendlier everyday terminology of 'beliefs', 'memories', 'desires'.

(iv) *Problems for functionalism*. Functionalism may be said to beg the mind–body problem in advance; it assumes that the brain is (somehow) capable of instantiating the 'software' of mental states. But I hope that by now you won't be surprised to discover that functionalism—whatever form you take of it—isn't the panacea to all our problems. Very many people believe that in some guise it can handle most of the

K. V. Wilkes

'Brentano' mental, the intensional terms—our thoughts, beliefs, desires, memories. These are psychological competences for which cerebral structures, at some level of description, are ultimately responsible. But it leaves much unexplained. In particular, it seems to fail with the 'Cartesian' mental: our pains, visual experiences, and the like. To put the problem most clearly, consider a computer which had all the 'boxes' that we suppose we have in your heads to explain visual perception. So, like us, it can tell when something is red, when blue, and so forth. But there still seems to be a question: does it have *the experience of redness*? It can discriminate; but is there, to adopt the famous question of Tom Nagel,[6] anything 'that it is like to be' seeing red? To put the general question another way, and very crudely: we could with a bit of robotics design a robot that had analogues to C-fibres which could be 'stimulated', with an 'information store' that led it to avoid situations which tended to damage it physically; a robot that hopped and squealed when kicked, that had little sacs to allow water to roll down from its 'eyes' to its humanoidal cheeks; but no 'mere' behaviour adds up to pain. Nagel thinks that there is 'something that it is like to be' a human, or a bat, but nothing that it is like to be any computer, any more than there is anything that it is like to be a hamburger.

Perhaps we need a little bit of both—a little bit of the 'classical' identity debate, and a bit of functionalism. This would accord well with the earlier comments that the mental and the physical are alike *heterogeneous*, so why should we expect there to be just one strategy for aligning the two? We might for example speculate that the processes of vision need a functionalist account of the various subordinate functions that go to explain our perceptual abilities; this would successfully explain our abilities to discriminate colours and shapes. But the subjective or experiential side of things might require us to identify *visual experience* with something like 'the spiking frequency of a neural network'. Maybe we cannot at present understand how anything like *the sensation of seeing red* is the right sort of thing to be identified with a 'spiking frequency'. But then, how do non-physicists understand the identification of matter with energy? This is something non-physicists tend to accept as a fact—because *Scientific American*, or Sunday colour supplements, tell them so—even though in its own way it is just as perplexing to the layman.

4. Conclusion

Most of the problem of 'the' mind–body relationship needs to be dissolved rather than solved. As we learn more about how the brain is organized to underpin our mental competences, we'll be less and less inclined to puzzle over 'the' mental–physical relationship. For instance, something like 'edge detection' is 'mental', in a way; but neurophysiology has already uncovered a great deal about how men—and mice, and mosquitoes—detect edges, and few I think find a deep philosophical problem with this low-level, non-conscious, psychological subfunction with respect to its relationship to the physical. Put another way, computers can be programmed to detect edges. The more 'sexy', grander, psychological states, such as feelings of Weltanschauung, of euphoria, of transcendental joy, are much farther from any neuroscientific explanation, and hence seem more puzzling. The conscious, subjective, experiential—cherished—properties of our mental life will always seem more problematic, because we find it so hard just to understand the idea that they might in principle be analysed out, dissected, into the push–pull operations of neurons and synapses. However: the fact remains that even though virtually everything that is significant is left out by a statement such as 'Leonardo's *Last Supper* is no more than a collection of paint-molecules on canvas', this is, none the less, in a sense true.

Notes

[1] *Aristotle's De Anima,* Books II, III. ed. and tr. D. Hamyln (Oxford: Clarendon Press, 1968).

[2] D. Hume, *An Enquiry Concerning Human Understanding,* L. Selby-Bigge (ed.) (Oxford: Clarendon Press, 1963), s. vii, part 1, para, 52, p. 66.

[3] J. L. Austin, *How to Do Things with Words* (Oxford: Clarendon Press, 1962), 38.

[4] D. Davidson, 'Mental Events', in Davidson, *Essays on Actions and Events* (Oxford: Clarendon Press, 1980), 207–225. First published 1970.

[5] For Sokolov's theory see J. A. Gray, *Elements of a Two-Process Theory of Learning* (London: Academic Press, 1975), 22.

[6] T. Nagel, *Mortal Questions* (Cambridge University Press, 1979), Ch. 12, "What is it Like to be a Bat?"

Free Will

I: GODFREY VESEY

Responsibility and 'Free Will'

As a rule we treat people as responsible for what they do. We admonish them if they behave badly, praise them if they do well. We punish people. And we reward them.

There are exceptions, of course. For example, we do not punish someone for doing something he has been compelled to do, perhaps by having a gun in his back. And we even recognize such a thing as psychological compulsion, as in the case of kleptomania.

A word we sometimes use in discussing responsibility is the word 'will'. We ask, for example, 'Did John resign *of his own free will?*', 'Did Mary give up the child *against her will?*'

Besides our everyday use of the word 'will', in expressions like 'of his own free will' and 'against her will', there is a philosopher's use of the word. In this respect the word 'will' is a bit like the word 'idea'. There is the ordinary use of the word 'idea', in everyday expressions like 'Have you any idea of the time?' and 'I've no idea what she sees in him'. And there is the philosopher's use, the use of the word by people like Thomas Hobbes[1] (1588–1679) and John Locke[2] (1632–1704) in their theorizing about how language works. Roughly, the theory is that linguistic communication involves the speaker or writer putting her ideas into words and the hearer or reader translating the words back into ideas of his own. Words are needed because mind cannot act on mind directly. To people who are thinking philosophically about language for the first time this may seem so obviously true as hardly to be a theory at all. Even some people whose business it is to think about language philosophically find it irresistible. All the same, it *is* a theory, and a questionable one at that. For instance, how can different people know they mean the same by some word, if the meaning of a word is an idea, and a person's ideas are, as Locke says, 'all within his own breast, invisible and hidden from others, nor can of themselves be made to appear'?[3] The 'ideas' of Locke's scepticism-prone 'way of ideas' are not the innocuous non-theory-laden 'ideas' of everyday expressions like 'Have you any idea of the time?'

Philosophers use the word 'idea' in a special sense because they want to explain linguistic communication. What about the word 'will'? Why do philosophers use the word 'will' in a special sense? What is the point of it? And what do they mean by 'the will', and by the will being 'free'?

To see the point of what philosophers say about 'free will' one has to imagine being asked what I can only describe as an extraordinary question. It is this. What justifies us in engaging in the practice of treating people as responsible for what they do? It is an extraordinary question in that it is about the practice in general. Ordinarily we ask such questions as 'Under the circumstances—threats to his life, and so on—can Peter really be held responsible for what he did?', on the assumption that some people, some of the time, *can* properly be held responsible. We unthinkingly assume that we are, in general, justified in engaging in the practice of treating people as responsible. But are we? That is the question. The idea is that if human beings had not 'free will' then it would not even make sense to ask the sort of questions we ordinarily ask.

So much for the point of saying that the will is free. It has to do with the notion that we need a general justification for our practice of treating people as responsible. Now, what do we *mean* by 'the will'? What is 'the will' in the philosopher's special sense? And what is meant by the will being 'free'?

If I had to pick out one philosopher who has given the word 'will' a special sense I would pick out René Descartes (1596–1650). Descartes was the first philosopher to talk of willing as an activity, something a person *does*. According to Descartes willing is not just *being* willing; it is not just having a favourable attitude to something happening, as it seems to have been for the Greeks;[4] it is performing a special sort of mental act, an act of 'volition'.

Descartes combined his notion of willing as an activity with the notions that, essentially, human beings are no more than thinking things, 'minds' or 'souls', and that a soul is somehow 'joined' to the body via a little gland in the head. Accordingly, he wrote, in his *Passions of the Soul* (1649), Article 41: 'The activity of the soul consists entirely in the fact that simply by willing something it brings it about that the little gland to which it is closely joined moves in the manner required to produce the effect corresponding to this volition'.[5] It is this 'activity of the soul' that Descartes held to be performed 'freely'.

By the will being free, then, Descartes means that the soul acts freely. But what does that mean? Freely as opposed to what?

In an earlier work, *The Principles of Philosophy* (1644), Part 1, Principle 37, Descartes wrote, not of the *soul* acting freely but of *man* acting freely. And in that work he opposed 'freely' to 'out of necessity'. The passage is as follows:

> And it is a supreme perfection in man that he acts voluntarily, that is,
> freely; this makes him in a special way the author of his actions and

deserving of praise for what he does. We do not praise automatons for accurately producing all the movements they were designed to perform, because the production of these movements occurs necessarily. It is the designer who is praised for constructing such carefully-made devices; for in constructing them he acted not out of necessity but freely.[6]

To understand this we need to know what is meant by 'necessity'. It is a word that was used by philosophers long before Descartes, such as Plato (428–348 BC) and Aristotle (384–322 BC); and by philosophers who succeeded Descartes, such as David Hume (1711–76), David Hartley (1705–57), John Stuart Mill (1806–73) and T. H. Huxley (1825–95).

Let us begin with Plato and Aristotle.

Plato and Aristotle

In the dialogue *Timaeus* (46d–e)[7] Plato says we should acknowledge two kinds of causes. He refers to them in a shorthand sort of way as 'mind and necessity'. On the one hand there are causes 'which are endowed with mind and are the workers of things fair and good'. He means gods and human beings. On the other, there are things like fire and water, earth and air. He says that most people think that things like fire and water, earth and air, are 'the prime causes of all things, because they freeze and heat, and contract and dilate, and the like'. But, Plato says, they are not. Fire and water, earth and air, cannot be prime causes 'for they are incapable of reason or intellect'. We ought to attend to the kinds of causes which are endowed with mind first of all, and only secondly to 'those things which, being moved by others, are compelled to move others'.

To understand this we need an example. Plato provides one, though in a different dialogue (*Phaedo* 98c–99b).[8] Socrates has been condemned to die, by drinking hemlock. He can either sit down, to await the arrival of the poison-bearer, or he can run away. He sits down. The question is: What causes his sitting? One explanation is in terms of Socrates and his thoughts. He thinks it more right and honourable to submit to the penalty ordered by his country than to take to his heels and run away. The other kind of explanation is in terms of sinews relaxing and contracting, limbs bending, and so on. Socrates puts the second kind of explanation as follows:

> The reason why I am lying here now is that my body is composed of bones and sinews, and since the bones move freely in their joints the sinews by relaxing and contracting enable me somehow to bend my limbs, and that is the cause of my sitting here in a bent position.

Which kind of explanation should be given priority? Socrates is in no doubt: the first. He says:

> If it were said that without bones and sinews I should not be able to do what I think is right, it would be true. But to say that it is because of them that I do what I am doing, and not through choice of what is best, would be a very lax and inaccurate form of expression. Fancy being unable to distinguish between the cause of a thing and the condition without which it would not be a cause!

Plato's distinction between two kinds of causes has a counterpart in present day philosophy. Since the 1960s a number of philosophers have distinguished between 'agent-causation' and 'event-causation'.[9] Expressed in this modern terminology, Plato's view is that the agent-causation explanation of Socrates' sitting has priority. Admittedly Socrates' legs bend (so that he assumes a sitting position) because certain sinews relax. But they would not relax unless Socrates, an agent, had chosen to sit rather than run.

This makes sense, but notice a word Plato uses in what he makes Socrates say. The word is 'somehow'. Socrates says: 'the sinews by relaxing and contracting enable me somehow to bend my limbs'. To me, this suggests uncertainty about something; specifically, about what Plato's answer would be to the question, 'Does Socrates bend his limbs *by* relaxing and contracting his sinews?' That is, is the relaxing and contracting of sinews something Socrates, *qua* agent, *does*, or is it only something that *happens* in his body, just as whatever happens in his nerves, which causes the sinews to relax and contract, is something that happens in his body and not something he does?

To the best of my knowledge, Plato never answered this question. But it was taken up by his most famous pupil, Aristotle.

At the beginning of Book 8, Chapter 5, of his *Physics* II, Aristotle[10] considers the case of a man moving a stone with a stick held in his hand. Whereas the man moves the stone by doing something else (namely, hitting it with the stick), and moves the stick by doing something else (namely, moving the hand in which he is holding it), he does *not*, Aristotle implies, move his hand by doing something else. He moves it *immediately*. In other words, his sinews or muscles are not instruments he uses to bring about a movement of his hand.

Expressed in terms of agent-causation and event-causation, Aristotle's position is that what the agent causes, immediately, is the movement of his hand, not something that comes earlier in the event-causation regress, such as a muscle-contraction, or a nerve-impulse, or a brain-event. The man's agency is expressed directly in his hand-movement. The movement of his hand is, in 1960s terminology, his 'basic action'.[11] That is, there is no other action the man performs that causes his hand to move, as moving his hand causes the stick held in it to move.

I want to draw your attention to three features of Aristotle's answer to the questions 'What does the man do immediately? What is his basic action?' I shall call them the dependence feature, the fallibility feature, and the compatibility feature.

First, the dependence feature. Plato made Socrates say, 'If it were said that without bones and sinews I should not be able to do what I think is right, it would be true'. Aristotle, I am sure, would agree with Plato. He would say that the man in his example could not do what he does immediately, namely move his hand, unless his muscles were capable of relaxation and contraction, unless they could be caused to relax and contract as a result of something else happening, and so on. In other words, the possibility of agent-causation is dependent on things going right in the realm of event-causation. If the man's muscles were atrophied, and so could not function properly, then he would not be able to move his hand.

Secondly, the fallibility feature. A person can think he has moved his hand when he has not done so. His body can let him down without his knowing it. An interesting variation on this is provided by the American psychologist, William James (1842–1910), in his *Principles of Psychology*.[12] A patient had anaesthesia of the moving parts. If he raised his hand, he could not feel it rising. If someone held it, he could not feel it being held. He was willing to do whatever he was told to do. The experimenter closed the patient's eyes, held the anaesthetized arm still, and told the patient to raise his hand to his head. When the patient opened his eyes, James says, he was astonished to find that the movement had not taken place. Evidently the patient thought he had done as he was told; he thought he had raised his hand. He thought this until he opened his eyes. He thought he had performed a basic action which he had not performed.

The fallibility feature is, of course, a consequence of the dependence feature.

Thirdly, the compatibility feature. What I mean by this is that Aristotle's answer 'He moves his hand', to the questions 'What does the man do immediately? What is his basic action?', is compatible with our giving the answer 'Relaxation and contraction of muscles', to the other kind of question, 'What bodily events cause his hand to move as it does?' When Plato said that we ought to attend to the kinds of causes which are endowed with mind first of all, and only secondly to 'those things which, being moved by others, are compelled to move others', he did not mean to rule out our attending to the latter. His concern was to correct our priorities, not to rule out one kind of question as improper.

89

Descartes

Now let us turn to Descartes and his special sense of the word 'will'. Descartes uses the word 'will', in his special sense, in his own answer to the question what a person does immediately. According to him, a person's basic action is not a bodily action at all; it is a *mental* action. The agent *wills* his hand to move, and this mental action somehow brings about a movement of a little gland in the head. It brings about just the movement that is needed to produce the movements in the nerves and muscles that will make the hand move in the way willed.

The significant thing about this answer is that it differs from Aristotle's in respect of every one of the three features we have been considering. Whereas the features of Aristotle's answer are dependence, fallibility, and compatibility, the features of Descartes' are *in*dependence, *in*fallibility, and *in*compatibility.

For the independence and infallibility features of Descartes' answer the key passage in his works is that containing the definitions of 'mind' and 'thought', at the beginning of the *Arguments proving the existence of God and the distinction between the soul and the body arranged in geometrical fashion.*[13] Descartes defines 'mind' as 'the substance in which thought resides'. But what is 'thought'? Descartes writes:

> *Thought.* I use this term to include everything that is within us in such a way that we are immediately [i e non-inferentially] aware of it. Thus all the operations of the will, the intellect, the imagination and the senses are thoughts. I say 'immediately' so as to exclude the consequences of thoughts; a voluntary movement, for example, originates in a thought but is not itself a thought.

It follows from this that an 'operation of the will', which is what Descartes holds to be what a person does immediately (i.e. non-instrumentally, or without having to do something else to bring it about), can be performed regardless of whether or not the person's body is functioning properly. And since his awareness of his act of will is immediate (i.e. is non-inferential, does not involve any questionable assumptions, such as that if he wills something to happen it will happen), there is nothing for him to be wrong about. So Descartes' answer to the question what a person does immediately (what his basic action is), unlike Aristotle's answer, has the two features of independence and infallibility.

This can be illustrated by reference to the case of William James' patient with anaesthesia of the moving parts. Descartes would say that the patient *did* do something. He was not merely willing to raise his hand; he actually willed it to rise. So he did perform a basic action, the mental act of willing, and he was not wrong about what he did. He was wrong only about the consequences. To his astonishment the movement he willed did not take place.

Incidentally, William James followed Descartes in this. He concluded a discussion of 'the more *intimate* nature of the volitional process' as follows:

> In a word, volition is a psychic or moral fact pure and simple, . . . The supervention of motion is a supernumerary phenomenon depending on executive ganglia whose function lies outside the mind.[14]

Now for the incompatibility feature. I believe that Descartes, when he says that the soul determines a movement of 'the little gland to which it is closely joined', is implicitly ruling out an explanation of that movement in physical terms.

The relevant passages are in Descartes' *Description of the Human Body*, Part 1, and in his *Passions of the soul*, Part 1, Articles 34, 41 and 44.[15] In these passages Descartes repeatedly opposes the production of bodily movement by the soul to its production by 'other causes'. The implication is that if a movement is produced by the soul then that movement cannot be explained physically. He allows, of course, that the bodily organ that is to be moved must be appropriately disposed. We cannot, by willing, produce a movement of 'the little gland' if the little gland is not disposed to be moved, rigid. But when the gland *is* moved by the soul it is the *soul alone* that is responsible for the movement.

It is not difficult to see the significance of this. If someone were to hold, as a matter of principle, that all physical events have physical causes, then he could not consistently allow that some movements do not have physical causes. He could not allow for the possibility of movements of glands in heads being produced by mental causes. So if the possibility of such movements is required for man to be 'in a special way the author of his actions' he could not allow that man is the author of his actions. And so he could not allow that man can properly be held responsible for his actions.

In short, belief in Cartesian 'free will' requires disbelief in universal physical causation.

It may seem strange that Descartes himself seems not to have been worried by the incompatibility of 'free will' and universal physical causation. I think the explanation must be that when he opposed 'freely' to 'out of necessity', in Principle 37 of *The Principles of Philosophy*, Part I, he was thinking exclusively of the necessity that may be thought to be involved in God creating us, and pre-ordaining all we do. In Principle 40 he wrote that, when we came to know God, 'we perceive in him a power so immeasurable that we regard it as impious to suppose that we could ever do anything which was not already preordained by him'.[16] And Principle 41 has the title 'How to reconcile the freedom of our will with divine preordination'.[17] Now, althought he uses the expression 'the freedom of our will' in that title, it could equally well have been 'How to reconcile our responsibility for what we do with divine preordination'. For the attempted reconciliation has nothing to do with 'the will' in his special sense.

It would certainly be interesting to discuss the problem of how to reconcile our responsibility with divine preordination, but since this lecture is explicitly on 'Free Will' I shall have to leave it for another occasion. Instead, let us turn to some of Descartes' successors. First, Hume, Hartley and Mill.

Hume, Hartley and Mill

Some of Descartes' successors were less concerned about the possible incompatibility of responsibility and divine pre-ordination than Descartes was. It might be thought that they would turn their attention to the other seeming incompatibility, that of free will and universal physical causation; and that their major project would be that of showing them not to be incompatible after all. But to think this would be to leave out of account Descartes' dualism, his reification of the mind, making 'the mind' into a thing in its own right, and the inner life into a series of states of this thing.

If it is a thing in its own right then may there not be a self-contained science of its workings, as necessitarian and mechanistic as the science of matter? And in this science may not acts of will be shown not to be 'free' after all but to be determined by the occurrence of other mental states?

The position of Hume, Hartley and Mill takes quite a lot of explaining. They reacted against Plato and Aristotle in one respect, and against Decartes in another, and neither of the respects are ones about which I have said anything up to now.

I said that Plato wrote of 'mind and necessity' as two kinds of causes, and that this corresponds to the 1960s talk of 'agent-causation' and 'event-causation'. Necessity rules in event-causation, but not in agent-causation. (Doing something because you think it is better to do it is not doing it out of necessity; you are free *not* to do what you think is better.) But did Plato think the converse holds? That is, would he have said that it is nonsense to talk of things in the physical world happening as they do because it is better that they should? Is it nonsense to talk of mind, in some rarefied sense, being at work in the physical, non-human, world?

The answer is that Plato did *not* think it nonsense. In fact the passage in which he writes of Socrates sitting down to await the arrival of the poison-bearer because he thinks it better to do so than to run away (*Phaedo*, 98c–99b) follows directly on from one (97c–98b) in which he expresses his pleasure on reading a book said to be by Anaxagoras (499–422 BC), 'asserting that it is mind that produces order and is the cause of everything' (my italics), Socrates lost no time in procuring the book but, when he did so, was disappointed, for, he said, 'the fellow made no use of mind and assigned to it no causality for the order of the world, but adduced causes like air and aether and water and many other absurdities'.

Aristotle was equally disappointed. Anaxagoras, he said, 'uses reason as a *deus ex machina* for the making of the world, and when he is at a loss to tell from what cause something necessarily is, then he drags reason in, but in all other cases ascribes events to anything rather than to reason' (Aristotle, *Metaphysics*, Bk 1, Ch. 4, 985a20).

Plato reacted to his disappointment with Anaxagoras by producing a theory of causation which he had worked out himself (*Phaedo*, 100b), his theory of 'Forms'. Aristotle reacted differently. He distinguished between what he called 'the final cause' and 'the motor cause' (sometimes called 'the efficient cause'), and declared 'the good end and the final cause' to be first, 'for this is the Reason, and the Reason forms the starting-point, alike in the works of art and in works of nature' (*Parts of Animals*, Bk 1, Ch. 1, 639b12–22). He realized that giving priority to the final cause might be challenged. 'Why should not nature work, not for the sake of something, nor because it is better so, but just as the sky rains, not in order to make the corn grow, but of necessity?' (*Physics*, Bk II, Ch. 8, 198b17). But he was not deterred by such challenges. Obviously, human beings do what they do for the sake of something. For example, school children work hard in order to pass examinations and get on in life. (They are, as we say, motivated by ambition.) And, it is arguable, plants, also, do things for the sake of something. For example, their leaves turn to face the sun in order to facilitate the process of photosynthesis. But Aristotle went further. He maintained that there is a place for final causes even in non-life sciences, such as astronomy. He wrote:

> . . . we are inclined to think of the stars as mere bodies or units, occurring in a certain order but completely lifeless; whereas we ought to think of them as partaking of life and initiative. Once we do this, the events will no longer seem surprising . . . with these considerations in mind, we must suppose the action of the planets to be analogous to that of animals and plants (*On the Heavens*, Bk II, Ch. 12, 292c14–b27).

In saying this, Aristotle might appear to have gone too far, but his influence was so great that it was not until the first half of the seventeenth century AD that the reaction set in. Scientists and philosophers like Galilei Galileo (1564–1642) and Pierre Gassendi (1592–1655) ridiculed the Aristotelian conception of science; and the search for 'final causes' gave way to one for 'motor causes'. Scientists looked for mechanisms instead of ends.

There were risks in this, for the Church was on the side of Aristotle. Galileo was prosecuted for heresy and spent the last eight years of his life under house arrest. Descartes was understandably cautious about how he expressed himself. In private correspondence with Marin Mersenne (1588–1648), he wrote, on 28 January 1641, that he hoped readers would gradually get used to his principles, and recognize their truth, 'before they notice that they destroy the principles of Aristotle.'[18] I can think of only one passage in his published work in which he opposed the Aristotelian view that 'the Reason forms the starting point' in science. This was in the Fourth Meditation: 'I consider the customary search for final causes to be totally useless in physics'.

Notice, however, that Descartes only said, 'in physics'. He did not say that final causes have no place in explaining why people act as they do. He did not deny that they act as they do in order to attain certain ends, that they want to become famous, or rich, or whatever. He did not deny that we can explain human behaviour by reference to motives, such as ambition and avarice.

This fairly long account of the views of Aristotle and Descartes on final causes makes it possible to give a fairly brief account of the views of Hume, Hartley and Mill on Cartesian 'free will'. All three of them wanted there to be a science of the workings of mind that was as similar as possible to the new mechanistic science of matter. To this end they construed motives not as final causes but as motor causes. They wrote of motives 'producing' actions, and even said that the same motives always produce the same actions.[20, 21] There is, they said, a mechanism, the so-called 'association of ideas', which accounts for the workings of mind in much the same way as Newton's gravitational attraction accounts for some of the workings of matter. It is, in Hume's words, 'a kind of ATTRACTION, which in the mental world will be found to have as extraordinary effects as in the natural, and to show itself in as many and as various forms'.[22]

Hartley spelt out the consequence for Cartesian free will of construing motives as motor causes, and accepting the doctrine of association:

> The consequence I mean is that of the mechanism or necessity of human actions, in opposition to what is generally termed free-will . . . By the mechanism of human actions I mean that each action results . . . as other effects do from their mechanical causes . . . If

by free-will be meant a power of beginning motion . . . man has no
such power.[23]

Mill called this 'the doctrine of Necessity', and declared his support for
it, and his rejection of 'the metaphysical theory of free-will'.[24] But he
was reluctant to go all the way with Hartley. The doctrine of Necessity
seemed 'humiliating to the pride, and even degrading to the moral
nature, of man'. Man must have *some* 'power', even if not a power of
beginning motion.

Correctly conceived, Mill said, the doctrine of Necessity is 'simply
this: that given the motives which are present to an individual's mind,
and given likewise the character and disposition of the individual, the
manner in which he will act might be unerringly inferred'.[25] The
reference to 'character' provided him with the means of rescuing man
from humiliation and degradation. A man has power to a certain extent,
but it is power, not over his limbs, but over his character: 'His character
is formed by his circumstances, but his own desire to mould it in a
particular way is one of those circumstances, and by no means one of
the least influential'.[26]

Let me try to sum all this up in a few sentences, using the concept of
agent causation to do so. Aristotle held that agent causation applies to
such things as movements of hands and legs. That is, a person can move
his hands and legs without having to do something else to make them
move. Descartes held that it applied to a special sort of mental act, an
act of 'volition'. A person can move his hands and legs only by doing
something else, willing them to move. Hume and Hartley went a stage
further. They construed the reason a person has for willing something,
his motive in willing it, as a motor cause of the volition. Finally, Mill,
realizing that this was leading to a total rejection of agent causation, and
hence of our practice of holding people responsible for what they do,
maintained that the concept of agent causation *does* have application to
human beings, but only at the *recherché* level of character formation. A
man is powerless to do anything except to desire to mould his character
in a particular way.

Tucker

Hume and Hartley did not have it all their own way. That most lucid
and readable of eighteenth-century philosophers, Abraham Tucker
(1705–74), in *The Light of Nature Pursued*, which he began in 1756,
within ten years of the publication of Hume's *Enquiry Concerning
Human Understanding* and Hartley's *Observations on Man*, distinguished between final causes and the sort of causes billiard balls are,
and wrote:

> To prevent mistakes, when I speak of the efficacy of motives and of
> their moving the mind to exert herself, I desire it may be understood

that these are figurative expressions; and I do not mean thereby to deny the efficacy of the mind, or to assert any motion, force or impulse implanted to her from the motives as there is to one billiard ball from another upon their striking; but only to observe that motives give occasion to the mind to exert her endeavours in attaining whatever they invite her to, which she does by her own inherent activity, not by any power derived from them. And all mankind understand the matter so, except perhaps some few persons of uncommon sense and superfine understandings . . .

Nobody will deny that we sometimes act upon motives, . . . but we run into frequent mistakes . . ., for want of first settling accurately with ourselves what they be. A motive I conceive is the prospect of some end actually in view of the mind at the time of action . . .[27]

In short, motives are final causes, not motor causes. If there is a science of mind in which motives figure as causes, it is not on a par with the new mechanistic science of matter.

Huxley

The plan had been to show, within a mechanistic science of mind, that acts of will are not 'free', but are as much necessitated as anything else. Cartesian willing would not thereby be shown to be compatible with universal physical causation, but at least it would be legitimized by being brought within a necessitarian science of sorts. And perhaps, someone, some day, would find a way of bringing the sciences of mind and matter into relation (like electricity and magnetism!), so that we need no longer insist on the closed shop of universal physical causation.

With the recognition that motives do not operate like billiard balls, and hence that the science of mind, if such there be, is not on a par with the science of matter, it was realized that a new plan was needed. What courses were open?

One possible course would have been to revert to Aristotle's answer to the question what a person does immediately: he moves his hand. He does not contract his muscles, or send an impulse down a nerve, or move a gland in his head, or perform an act of will to make the gland move; he simply moves his hand. As we saw, a feature of this answer is that it is compatible with our giving the answer 'Relaxation and contraction of muscles' to the other kind of question, 'What bodily events cause his hand to move as it does?' There is nothing in Aristotle's answer to conflict with the principle of universal physical causation. But Aristotle was out of favour, and Descartes was in favour, at least as regards his dualism. It was not the existence of acts of will that was suspect, only the notion that they interfere with the physical world.

Descartes held that mind and body interact causally. What was needed, to protect universal physical causation, was a variation on Cartesian interactionist dualism, dualism without the action of mind on body.

What was needed was provided, in 1874, some thirty years after the publication of Mill's *System of Logic*, by the English biologist and philosopher, T. H. Huxley (1825–95):

> The consciousness of brutes would appear to be related to the mechanism of their body simply as a collateral product of its working, and to be as completely without any power of modifying that working as the steam-whistle which accompanies the work of a locomotive engine is without influence upon its machinery. Their volition, if they have any, is an emotion indicative of physical changes, not a cause of such changes . . .
>
> It is quite true that, to the best of my judgement, the argumentation which applies to brutes holds equally well of men; and, therefore, that all states of consciousness in us, as in them, are immediately caused by molecular changes of the brain-substance. It seems to me that in men, as in brutes, there is no proof that any state of consciousness is the cause of change in the motion of the matter of the organism. If these positions are well based, it follows that our mental conditions are simply the symbols in consciousness of the changes which take place automatically in the organism; and that, to take an extreme illustration, the feeling we call volition is not the cause of a voluntary act, but the symbol of that state of the brain which is the immediate cause of that act. We are conscious automata, endowed with free will in the only intelligible sense of that much-abused term—inasmuch as in many respects we are able to do as we like—but none the less parts of the great series of causes and effects which, in unbroken continuity, composes that which is, and has been, and shall be—the sum of existence.

Would Descartes have been content with free will in what Huxley called 'the only intelligible sense of that much-abused term'? Hardly. He opposed 'freely' to 'out of necessity', and to illustrate movements occurring necessarily he referred the reader to automatons. What Descartes called 'a supreme perfection in men' is, precisely, that he is *not* an automaton.

Review

It is our normal practice to treat people as responsible for what they do. ordinarily we do not question this practice. We unthinkingly assume that it is all right. But if it is questioned then one way of justifying it may be in terms of what Mill calls 'the metaphysical theory of free-will'. This is Descartes' theory that a person can, by a mental act of willing that is not itself caused (in the 'motor cause' sense of 'cause') by anything else, originate a movement of a little gland in the head, a movement that eventuates in a movement of the limbs. We have noticed that although this was Descartes' own theory, he himself makes no use of it to explain our acting freely. He opposed 'freely' to 'out of necessity', but the necessity he had in mind was that with which automatons accurately produce all the movements they are designed to perform. The question that evidently worried him, as 'Are *we* God's automatons?' What may be called 'divine determinism' worried him so much that he ignored physical determinism in what he said about our acting freely. All the same we can consider his theory of 'free will' as providing an answer to the question 'Given universal physical causation, how can we be justi- fied in treating people as responsible for what they do?' The answer is: 'Mental acts of willing originate certain physical movements, so univer- sal physical causation is not true, so the question does not arise'. In other words, Descartes in effect deals with the problem of human responsibility being incompatible with universal physical causation by denying universal physical causation.

Hume, Hartley and Mill have a different project altogether. They want to defend the notion of a necessitarian science of mind against Cartesian 'free will'; that is, against the notion that there are some mental phenomena, acts of will, that do not have motor causes. They do so by construing motives as motor causes—and so qualify for being described, ironically, by Abraham Tucker, as 'some few persons of uncommon sense and superfine understandings'.

Finally, Huxley has the project of defending universal physical causation, which he does by declaring 'the feeling we call volition' to be, not 'the cause of a voluntary act', but merely 'the symbol of that state of the brain which is the immediate cause of that act'—a theory philos- ophers call 'epiphenomenalism'.

Incidentally, psychological determinism based on the doctrine of association is a thing of the past, as is the combination of physical determinism and epiphenomenalism, but both sorts of determinism have representatives in the twentieth century. The psychological deter- minist looks to Sigmund Freud (1856–1940), perhaps, or to B. F. Skinner (1904–). The erstwhile epiphenomenalist now declares the workings of the mind to be 'contingently identical' with those of the brain.

Conclusion

I said that philosopers talk of 'free will' with a view to justifying our engaging in the practice of treating people as responsible for what they do. But why do they feel the need for a justification? Is it because they want, also, to engage in the practice of looking for (motor) causes of everything that happens, and feel that the two practices are somehow incompatible? If so, then it is very paradoxical that they should turn to Descartes, and his theory of willing. Descartes' answer to the question 'What does a person do immediately?', namely 'he performs an act of will', has what I called 'the incompatibility feature', whereas Aristotle's answer has not. Why are they not content to say, with Aristotle, that the two practices are compatible, and hence that there is no need for justification?

That is not a purely rhetorical question. I would like to know the answer.

Notes

[1] T. Hobbes, *Leviathan* (London: Dent, 1914).

[2] J. Locke, *An Essay Concerning Human Understanding*, P. H. Nidditch (ed.) (Oxford: Clarendon Press, 1975).

[3] Locke, op. cit. III, ii, i.

[4] M. Pohlenz, *Die Stoa* (Göttinghen: Vandenhoeck and Ruprecht, 1959); A. A. Long, *Problems in Stoicism* (London: Athlone, 1971).

[5] R. Descartes, *The Philosophical Writings of Descartes*, tr. J. Cottingham, R. Stoothoff and D. Murdoch (Cambridge University Press, 1985), 343.

[6] Descartes, op. cit. 205.

[7] Plato, *The Collected Dialogues of Plato*, E. Hamilton and H. Cairns (eds) (New York: Pantheon, 1961).

[8] Ibid.

[9] R. M. Chisholm, 'Human Freedom and the Self', in G. Watson (ed.) *Free Will* (Oxford University Press, 1982); D. Davidson, 'Agency', in D. Davidson, *Essays on Actions and Events* (Oxford: Clarendon Press, 1980); A. Kolnai, 'Agency and Freedom', in G. Vesey (ed.), *The Human Agent, Royal Institute of Philosophy Lectures,* Vol. 1, 1966/7 (London: Macmillan), 20–46; R. Taylor, *Action and Purpose* (Englewood Cliffs, NJ: Prentice-Hall, 1966); I, Thalberg, 'Do We Cause Our Own Actions?, *Analysis* **27** (1967), 196–201; J. Yolton, 'Agent Causality', *American Philosophical Quarterly* **3** (1966), 14–26.

[10] Aristotle, *The Basic Works of Aristotle*, edited and with an introduction by R. McKeon (New York: Random House, 1941).

[11] A. Danto, 'What We Can Do', *Journal of Philosophy* **60** (1963), 435–445; 'Basic Actions', *American Philosophical Quarterly* **2** (1965), 141–148; M. Brand, 'Danto on Basic Actions', *Nous* (1968); F. Stoutland, 'Basic Actions and Causality', *Journal of Philosophy* **65** (1968), 467–475.

[12] W. James, *The Principles of Psychology* (London: Macmillan, 1891).

[13] Descartes, op. cit. II, 113–114.

[14] James, op. cit. II, 560.

[15] Descartes, op. cit. I, 315, 341, 343–345.

[16] Descartes, op. cit. I, 206.

[17] Ibid.

[18] A. Kenny (tr. and ed.), *Descartes: Philosophical Letters* (Oxford: Clarendon Press, 1970), 94.

[19] Descartes, op. cit. II, 39.

[20] D. Hume, 'An Enquiry Concerning Human Understanding', in *Hume's Enquiries*, L. A. Selby-Bigge (ed.), with revisions by P. H. Nidditch (Oxford: Clarendon Press, 1975), 82.

[21] D. Hartley, *Observations on Man, His Frame, His Duty and His Expectations* (Hildesheim: Ohms, 1967).

[22] D. Hume, *A Treatise of Human Nature*, 2nd edn, L. A. Selby-Bigge (ed.), revised by P. H. Nidditch (Oxford: Clarendon Press, 1978), I, i, 4.

[23] D. Hartley, op. cit.

[24] J. S. Mill, *A System of Logic: Ratiocinative and Inductive*, Robson (ed.), in *Collected Works of John Stuart Mill* (London: Routledge and Kegan Paul, 1974), VI, ii, 1.

[25] Ibid. VI, ii, 2.

[26] Ibid. VI, ii, 3.

[27] A. Tucker, *The Light of Nature Pursued* (London: Thomas Tegg, 1837), I, 39–40.

[28] T. H. Huxley, 'On the Hypothesis that Animals are Automata, and its History', in T. H. Huxley, *Collected Essays,* Vol. I, *Methods and Results* (London: Macmillan, 1912), 240, 243–244.

II: A. PHILLIPS GRIFFITHS

Is Free Will Incompatible with Something or Other?

Professor Vesey poses the following question:

> ... philosophers talk of 'free will' with a view to justifying our engaging in the practice of treating people as responsible for what they do. But why do we feel the need for a justification? It is because they want, also, to engage in the practice of looking for (motor) causes of everything that happens, and feel that the two practices are somehow incompatible? If so, then it is very paradoxical that they should turn to Descartes, and his theory of willing. Descartes' answer to the question 'What does a person do immediately?', namely 'He performs an act of will', has what I call 'the incompatibility feature', whereas Aristotle's answer has not. Why are they not content to say, with Aristotle, that the two practices are compatible, and hence there is no need for a justification?[1]

In my view, in those cases in which we would treat someone as responsible, as being subject to moral praise and blame, then something must have been done which was willed by the agent. That I regard as an invariable necessary condition. I do not regard it as a sufficient one: what has done must not only have been willed, but freely willed, by the agent.

I would therefore want to reformulate Vesey's question as follows:

> We are justified in treating people as responsible only when they freely will to do what they do. Philosophers may want to 'engage in the practice of looking for (motor) causes of everything that happens', presumably because they believe that they are there; and some of us also believe that everything that happens in the Universe is the outcome of God's creative Will. Why should we think that these beliefs are incompatible with freely willing to do things, or *a fortiori*, willing to do things, and that we are therefore never justified in holding people responsible?

But in putting the question this way I may seem already to have accepted the 'incompatibility feature', which Vesey attributes to Descartes' theory of willing.

Vesey quotes the following passage of Descartes:

> By the term *thought*, I comprehend all that is in us, so that we are

immediately conscious of it. Thus, all the operations of the will, intellect, imagination, and senses, are thoughts. But I have used the word *immediately* expressly to exclude whatever follows or depends upon our thoughts: for example, voluntary motion has, in truth, thought for its source (principle), but yet it is not itself thought.[2]

Vesey comments:

It follows from this that an 'operation of the will', which is what Descartes holds to be what a person does immediately [i.e. non-instrumentally, without having to do something to bring it about], can be performed regardless of whether or not the person's body is functioning properly.

If Vesey is right this already implies the 'incompatibility feature': that the will is independent of any 'motor causes' of what may happen, and in particular of motor causes constituted by the functioning of the body.

But I don't think this follows from Descartes' quoted passage: Descartes claims only that the content of our thoughts, of which we are immediately aware, is independent of anything which might or might not follow from or depend on them; not that our thinking these thoughts is independent of all motor causes. This must be so because among thoughts he includes *imaginatio*, the senses. There is no doubt that he thought that the content of *imaginatio* was not independent of the functioning of the body; that, for example, one could not be aware of what something looked like if one kept one's eyes closed.

The 'incompatibility thesis', does not, as might be thought, follow from Descartes' two-substance, mind–body metaphysics; at least, he doesn't think it does. He holds that these two substances can affect one other: for example the will affects bodily motions, and perceptible physical events affect the mind in *imaginatio*.

Anyone who accepts what Descartes says in the quoted passage, as I do, can still hold that there are thoughts which are wholly dependent on outside factors. And I would indeed hold that: I cannot but be aware of the colour of this paper as white, and that is just because it is white, and not 'itself thought'. There is so far no reason to say that something similar may not be true of my will: that it is dependent on something or other distinct from my thought.

However, Descartes was committed to the 'incompatibility feature', not because of his doctrine of the soul, but because of a specific doctrine concerning the will. This doctrine depends on Descartes' view that the will, as a God-given faculty of the mind, must be perfect: completely independent and autonomous, without limitations, and hence subject to no prior conditions or aetiology.[3]

My reformulation of Vesey's question does not presuppose this specific doctrine of the will. It does not require that I follow Pelagius in denying any possible condition or aetiology of willing, or deny the doctrine of grace; only that I consider explanations involving conditions which might be thought to rule out any explanation in terms of willing, and explanations of conditions which might be thought to rule out free willing.

My reformulation does, however, presuppose that there is sense and application to the term 'willing'.

Let us take the case Vesey uses in this context, William James' patient with anaesthesia of the moving parts.

> A patient had anaesthesia of the moving parts. If he raised his hand, he could not feel it rising. If someone held it, he could not feel it being held. He was willing to do whatever he was told to do. The experimenter closed the patient's eyes, held the anaesthetized arm still, and told the patient to raise his hand to his head. When the patient opened his eyes . . . he was astonished to find that the movement had not taken place. Evidently the patient thought he had done as he was told; he thought he had raised his hand.[4]

The patient was aware of some state of affairs, or event, or perhaps something he had done, which led him to think he must have raised his arm, only to find he had not raised his arm. What could this be? That he had *willed* to raise it?

How else might this be described? Not merely as his having had a favourable attitude towards his raising his arm; for then his consequent belief that he had raised it would have been mere wishful thinking. Not merely as his having intended to raise his arm; because one might intend to do something before the time comes to do it, and then at the last instant not do it. Not as his having chosen to, because that suggests he was pondering alternatives, or at least had in mind the possibility of doing something else. Attention to the *nuances* of these ordinary expressions tends to rule out their use as ways of describing what the patient was aware of; attention J. L. Austin would recommend, when philosophers might try to describe what the patient was aware of as an act of will, to show it couldn't be that; and then to suggest it couldn't be *anything*, for our ordinary talk about 'being willing' or 'making a will' or 'having a strong will' doesn't pick it out either. Which leaves philosophers to talk about only a nothing as an act of will, as Ryle pointed out in the *Concept of Mind*;[5] as indeed he once pointed out very sternly to me, telling me to talk instead about trying. But I don't think we can say that the patient was aware of trying to raise his arm; though it may appeal more than any of the other answers; because it is true that he tried to raise his arm. It is true, because he didn't ignore the experimenter's request, yet he failed to raise his arm. But for the patient, when he tried to raise his arm, there was no thought of possible failure (or why was he so astonished at his failure?). And in the awareness of trying (and here it is *our* awareness of *his* trying), there must be a belief in the possibility or certainty of failure. One can try to do what one is convinced is impossible; for example, in response to robust encouragement, to be pleasantly astonished at the outcome. But where there is conviction that one cannot fail, one might say 'I don't have to try'. I can be aware of testing myself in seeing how long I can hold my breath, but not in fact in seeing whether I can refrain from holding my breath.

The patient must surely have been aware of *something*. Willing is not a nothing, and more can be said about what it is—one is not condemned to saying just 'well, after all, we all know what an act of will is'. And to do this one does not have to search for other everyday locutions, with Austin standing over us again; we need not turn to talk for example of 'setting oneself to', which carries with it associations of 'on your mark', steeling oneself, and so on.

The trouble is, that we seem to need to talk about an act of willing only in extraordinary cases like that of James's patient. People raise their arms, to scratch their heads, or in expostulation, or more pressingly when they want to leave the room, and everything is clear about that: why attribute anything to them other than the simple, and I mean simple—not structured or consisting of discriminable or, still less, sequent parts—*simple* raising of their arm? So I shall try to get at the notion of willing in quite another way, considering only everyday cases and having nothing to depend on but common sense.

Take the case of one Levebrachia, who: draws attention to herself; exposes her dirty fingernails; touches the ceiling; raises her arm; interrupts the lecture; and tries to get permission to leave the room. She doesn't do these things one after another, but all in one, so to speak. Given certain reasons for puzzlement (which I shall supply) we might ask various questions. Why (since she likes to be thought a more fastidious person than she is) did she expose her dirty fingernails? Why (the ceiling has just been decorated, and the paint is still wet) did she touch the ceiling? Why (her arthritis being so bad, it must have been a discomfort) did she raise her arm? Why (at just the point at which the lecturer was saying something interesting after a half hour of platitudes) did she interrupt the lecturer? Why (she being so anxious not to miss the lecture, and having traipsed some miles through the snow to get to it) did she try to get permission to leave the room?

One set of answers might be that she drew attention to herself because she needed to leave the room: she exposed her dirty fingernails because she couldn't avoid it in raising her arm; she touched the ceiling because it was much lower than she had thought; she raised her arm because she thought it would attract the lecturer's attention; she interrupted the lecture in order to get permission to leave the room; she tried to get permission to leave the room because of the demands of a categorical imperative (you can supply whatever content you fancy Kant might allow to that).

None of these explanations would be correct unless Levebrachia had certain beliefs. She must have believed that by drawing attention to herself she would be enabled to leave the room. She needn't have thought she was exposing her dirty fingernails, but if she did then she must have accepted that it was necessary to do so if she were to raise her arm. She believed the ceiling was higher than it was. She believed that if she raised her arm she would attract the lecturer's attention. She believed she would be permitted to leave the room only if she interrupted the lecture. She believed she could satisfy the demands of a categorical imperative only if she left the room.

These answers tell us a lot about what she wanted. She wanted to leave the room. She didn't want to expose her dirty fingernails, but possibly was willing to because she wanted to raise her arm. There is no reason to think she wanted to touch the ceiling. She wanted to attract the lecturer's attention. She wanted to satisfy the demands of a categorical imperative.

There may have been many other things she wanted: to be introduced to the charming and handsome chairman, to light a cigarette, to be the cynosure of all eyes, to blow her nose though she had no handkerchief; and likewise many other things she believed: that the lecture room was wood-panelled, that the chairman was charming and handsome, that she had no handkerchief, that her name was Levebrachia. But none of these beliefs or wants had anything to do with her raising her arm.

But among the beliefs which did, there is a certain order.

Though she may have believed that in raising her arm she was suffering discomfort, she did not raise her arm because in so doing she would be suffering discomfort. But her believing that in raising her arm she would be attracting the lecturer's attention is essential to explaining what she did, indeed of understanding what she did. She raised her arm because she believed that in raising her arm she would be attracting the lecturer's attention and thereby getting permission to leave the room and so enabling herself to satisfy the demands of a categorical imperative.

That would still be true if her belief were untrue; as far as our understanding or explanation of Levebrachia's action is concerned, it doesn't matter if it turns out that the lecturer was not only daft but blind, so long as she didn't know it.

Let me now make a general suggestion which will seem like jumping to a conclusion. Of all the class of things Levebrachia or any one else does of which it is true that they do it of their own free will, a condition of the following form must apply to them:

Levebrachia believed that in x'ing she was y'ing.

Notice I do not say that where this condition holds, Levebrachia acted of her own free will, nor that if this truth had not held, Levebrachia would not have done it.

The belief can be represented as a hypothetical one, thus:

If I am x'ing then I am y'ing.

This is the agent's reason for x'ing.

I shall refer to what is before the 'then' as the protasis, and what is after it as the 'apodosis'. The logical subtleties here are very great; but I hope that this is clear without going into these complications (as I have done elsewhere).

For such a true explanation, in a further explanation what is the protasis can become in turn an apodosis. Thus Levebrachia believes that

If I raise my arm, then I shall be attracting the lecturer's attention.

But this explains her raising her arm only because she also believes

If I attract the lecturer's attention, I shall get permission to leave the room.

Clearly, such a chain of apodoses becoming in turn protases clearly cannot be infinite. Eventually we come to a stop: to what we might call the agent's basic reason for acting.

Take here Hume's famous finite regress, which is something of the same sort in other terms:

Ask a man *why he uses exercise*; he will answer, *because he desires to keep his health*. If you then enquire, *why he desires health*, he will readily reply, *because sickness is painful*. If you push your enquiries farther, and desire a reason *why he hates pain*, it is impossible he can ever give any. This is an ultimate end, and is never referred to any object.[6]

I do this, because it avoids pain. Why do I avoid pain? Well, here is another hypothetical proposition, with another apodosis.

If I am avoiding pain, then I am avoiding what is painful.

Clearly, this isn't a new apodosis; the new hypothetical says no more than that if I am avoiding pain, then I am avoiding pain.

But that doesn't mean that at this point *all* explanation comes to a stop. Asked why I avoid pain, I could say that pain is generally connected with what damages the organism, and in common with the rest of the human species I avoid it because any species whose members did not would not survive. But notice that what we have here is a quite different kind of explanation from the ones we have been considering. It is not my *believing* this evolutionary hypothesis which leads me to avoid pain, and the explanation does not imply that. It is the evolutionary *fact*, if it is one, which explains; not my *belief*: which is just as well, because if it were necessary to convince people of dodgy, if sophisticated, evolutionary theories in order to give them reasons for avoiding pain, the human species would never have survived the Stone Age. What then, is the belief, the final or basic reason, for my avoiding pain? It is my belief that pain is painful, which amounts to no more than the belief that pain is pain.

It may seem shocking for me to say that a mere tautology can be someone's reason for acting, and his basic reason at that. But I want to say more: to claim that someone's basic reason can *only* be a tautology.

Some cleverdick in the Prince's retinue goads Fluellen:

CD   *Why did you make Pistol eat the leek?*
F   *Because he gleeked at my country.*
CD   *Why challenge those who who mock your country?*
F   *Because it galls at my honour.*
CD   *Why bother about your 'honour'?*
F   *Honour's honour; and there's an end on't.*

The dialogue isn't up to Shakespeare's, but now we know where we stand with Fluellen. Sociologists may very well go on to explain where he stands, by talking about the development and social function of the concept of honour (cogently and illuminatingly); and Fluellen's basic reasons can be criticized. But, with Fluellen's final answer, the particular kind of interrogation to which he is subjected must come to an end. And his final answer is a tautology.

How can a reason be a tautology? Nothing follows from a tautology. The answer is that it is a *practical* reason. All reasons the agent has for acting (though not all the reasons *why* he acts) are beliefs; not all his beliefs are his reasons for acting. A belief, one among others, even if a tautology among other tautologies, turns out to be someone's reason for acting. To hold a belief in that way is to hold it in a way differently from the way one holds other beliefs. The belief held in that way is what gives content to the willing: is indeed the willing.

Sometimes, the chain of reasons begins and ends with a tautology. Someone is humming a tune. Why are you humming? Oh, I'm just humming, dee-de-de-dee. I'm humming just because humming is humming, not because it's annoying someone or showing my musical genius or aiding my digestion.

To will to do something is to have a belief which has this hypothetical form and is the explanation of what one does. It is what, in fact, Kant[7] called a particular maxim of action: one example is of someone who makes a lying promise to get money: her maxim is 'in making a lying promise I shall be getting money'. Anyone may believe that of herself, but only in her case is it a maxim.

That beliefs are held in this way, and have this role, is something everybody knows. People show this every day, constantly, in what they accept as the explanations of someone's actions in the sense of *her* reasons for doing something (not the same as *the* reason, or a (*good*) reason, or what she *thinks* is a good reason); and in the fact that they know what their reasons for doing things are: what beliefs explain their actions: what they are *up* to. How do they know which among their many beliefs constitute their reasons, explain their actions? That question is no more nor less difficult than the question how they know which things, among the many things they can imagine, they believe to be the case. Suffice it to say that people do know what they will and that they will, as they know what they believe and that they believe.

Let us return to William James's patient. In ordinary cases of failure, not only is the agent usually aware of his failure, but he does do *something*. And he can explain what he actually did in terms of the hypothetical belief, the apodosis of which was not satisfied. Thus, for example, if someone flicked the switch, but nothing else happened, he can explain what he did by saying 'I thought that if I flicked the switch, the light would come on'. His belief, that if he flicked the switch, the light would come on, is one of very many such hypothetical beliefs (which would include, for example, his belief that if he clapped his hands, he would make a noise); but it can be singled out, as one held somehow differently by him, as one explaining *something* that he did. But James's patient didn't do *anything* (a neuron in his brain may have fired, but that isn't anything he *did*, nor have any beliefs about); so that way of putting the matter isn't available to us. But can't we single it out by saying that his hypothetical belief—perhaps that, if he raised his arm, he would be doing as he was asked—would, in any normal circumstances be the belief, as distinct from all his other beliefs, which would alone have explained his raising his arm; and that, this being so, he knows this in holding the belief in this way, except that in fact he does not know that he did not—astonishingly, until one is told the unusual circumstances—raise his arm. So he was holding a belief in just the same way that people do when they ordinarily raise their arms, or for that matter when they write novels, or stand for Parliament, or scratch their heads, in the normal way of doing things, that is, willing to do things.

But if this is right, what is it that makes a hypothetical belief a maxim for one person yet not for another? On many occasions, that I believe that if I am smoking a cigarette I am ingesting tobacco fumes explains my smoking a cigarette (if I lit one and it turned out to be made of wood shavings, I should throw it away). But Professor Vesey believes, just as firmly as I do of myself, that if he is smoking a cigarette he is ingesting tobacco fumes, but that never explains his smoking a cigarette, because he never smokes; indeed that very belief of his possibly explains why he refrains from smoking. Why does one and the same belief explain my actions where it never explains his?

Clearly no theory of action can depend on reference to the relation between belief and action alone. Some other factor is needed to complete the story and make sense of it all. And one seems ready to hand. I've already said that knowing what Levebrachia did and what beliefs explained her actions we could say a lot about what she wanted. People act differently, where they have the same beliefs, because they have different wants, it is said. Professor Vesey doesn't *desire* to ingest tobacco fumes, I almost always do. Action is explained by belief plus desire. This is the conventional wisdom about the matter, developed and convoluted and refined by many very clever philosophers and respectably old; held not only by Holbach and Bentham, but by Kant, though unlike Bentham, Kant didn't make a virtue of it. But I think it is nonsense; nonsense on stilts.

Nonsense, that is, if wanting or desiring is something which is supposed to go on in the soul or psyche. There may be some little conical grey jiggersnicket in the brain which explains what needs explaining here, but I don't think there is, and I *know* that nobody *knows* there is, and even if there were I can't see that it would be come across by research in the Royal Institute of Philosophy, and it would be simply naughty to call it a desire, which is after all the sort of thing that infests the soul rather than the brain. Fortunately I can know a lot of what goes on in my soul or psyche without applying for a research grant, and even more about what doesn't go on. And I'm afraid I have to disappoint the action theorists and report that very often when I light a cigarette I have no desire whatever, though I do if I am deprived of one long enough. Indeed, desire is just the apposite word for what I feel when I am long deprived of nicotine. And just the *in*apposite word to connect with almost all I do.

Last night, I went to bed, and before I went to sleep, I satisfied my desires. I said my prayers.
?!

I marked thirteen boring undergraduate essays this morning, having thirteen successive desires to mark a boring undergraduate essay. I got tired and fed up with it after that and left the rest to tomorrow; obviously, I had lost my desire to mark essays.
?!

It is simply wrong to suggest that there are desires connected with all the multifarious everyday things we all the time do, like tying one's shoelaces or turning over the next page or washing one's hands or shutting the door. Well, it might be said, not strong desires, but little, undetectable, teensy-weensy desires, which must be there to explain why we do these things; but isn't that just to insist on the conventional action-theory by importing a *virtus dormitiva*?

Again, it might be said, perhaps desire is too narrow a word; what about pro-attitude? I smoke cigarettes because I have a pro-attitude to ingesting tobacco fumes. What's the evidence for that? How are pro-attitudes detected? Easily enough: I will only smoke a cigarette if I believe it contains tobacco; and when I smoke, it is because I believe the cigarette contains tobacco. But if that is the only evidence for the existence of a pro-attitude, what has been added to talk in terms of belief? Pro-attitudes are just another *virtus dormitiva*, only this time not masquerading as something we are acquainted with, like desires. It also has the disadvantage of being too broad, being infected with an earlier now generally defunct incarnation the term once had, as a way of talking emptily of what it is to believe something to be good. I hope I do not compound the folly of ingesting tobacco smoke by being at the same time under the misapprehension that it is good.

But what, then, about treating the explanatory factor as *wants*, or *wanting to*? After all, we were able to infer Levebrachia's wants *immediately* from her beliefs and actions. Yes, and that's the trouble. We often *aren't* able to infer people's beliefs from their actions (a rock on which many a philosophical behaviourist has foundered) and hence finding out about beliefs independently enables us to give edifying, illuminating explanations of what people do. We can immediately infer someone's wants from their actions and from their basic reasons for acting, because it is necessarily true that if someone does something willingly or of his own free will then there must be some description of the action in terms of which he wants to do it, simply because there is nothing to so acting beyond having a basic reason for doing it.

It is true that wanting has an existence independent of acting, because people can want to do things without ever doing them. This is not a difficulty if I am right in my view, which I haven't time to argue now, that the notion of wanting without doing can only be explicated in terms of our understanding of doing. It is also true that people can know what they want without having to see or avert to what they do or discover or avert to what they believe. But this is no difficulty, because we can know what we are doing without seeing or averting to what we are doing and know what we believe without discovering or averting to what we believe.

Well then: where can we turn, instead, for a theory of action? I haven't the slightest idea, It's not so much that I don't know where to look as that I don't know how to look, or what it would be to find one.[8]

Not that from here on everything is inexplicable. We have lots of plausible and many more barely plausible particular explanations: someone won't eat pork because she was brought up in an orthodox Muslim household, though she has long ceased to be a Muslim. We and she may accept that as the reason she won't eat pork, but *that she was brought up in a Muslim household* wouldn't be *her* reason for not eating pork. She is mean with her money because she's from Carmarthen. She over-indulges herself because she was spoilt as a child. She is vicious about homosexuality because she has unconscious homosexual tendencies. She talks in that sententious way because she's a judge. All sorts of explanations, some good, some bad, and no doubt you could mention many of a better kind, enable us to explain and predict what people will do without knowing about their beliefs or their basic reasons, or to explain why their basic reasons are what they are. But this can't be called a theory. At best it is what Spinoza called knowledge from vague experience.

Some explanations of what people do, however, are not explanations of, or consequent on, or supplementary to, explanations in terms of what beliefs constitute their basic reasons for doing things; they are incompatible with explanations in terms of beliefs. In these cases, the agent did not only not act of his own free will, he did not act of his own will at all. No one will be bothered by the existence of such explanations because no one is seriously going to believe that explanations which clearly rule out any explanation in terms of the agent's beliefs are plausible in every case. It could have been that when Levebrachia raised her arm, it was because someone had tied a string to her wrist and was pulling on the string from above a hole in the ceiling; in which case the fact that she believed that by raising her arm she would get permission to leave the room could have had nothing whatever to do with her arm going up. But who on earth would take seriously a claim that our beliefs have nothing to do with our actions, because everything we do may be the result of our being attached to strings being pulled through holes in ceilings—that we are all puppets? Or even more generally that if people's beliefs were different, or indeed, if people, like trees or computers, didn't have any beliefs, their actions would be just the same? One of the things that makes me think that facts about atomic events make a difference to what happens is that knowing these things enables technologists to achieve great things, like blowing up whole cities. In the same way I am impressed by my own capacity to make things happen on the assumption that when people acquire certain beliefs they will act differently than they otherwise would. Sometimes I succeed in getting people to clean my windows by leading them to believe that I will pay them if they do.

A. Phillips Griffiths

By making this point about a totally unserious objection to free will, have I answered Vesey's question? If so, his is not a serious question. The incompatibilist worry can't be that there are always some motor explanations which imply that people would have acted the same way, whatever their beliefs might have been. I have already said that this was not the source of Descartes' incompatibilism. A thesis like it, about non-human animals, does seem to have been the source of a similar thesis about beasts, which he thought of as machines. He seems to have thought that beasts, not having language, do not have any beliefs at all;[9] but Descartes's thesis about beasts does not imply that if everything that happens has motor causes, then people do not have beliefs and hence that these do not explain their actions. The incompatibility which might need to be taken seriously is not between all that happens being explicable, if not explained, in terms of motor causes—or that what happens is universally explicable by God's pre-ordination—and explanations of people's actions as being dependent on their beliefs. It must be that what would be ruled out is not that we act out of our beliefs: not of our willing to act; but that we do not act out of our own free will, so that we cannot be held responsible.

Real cases do introduce this kind of worry. Let me adumbrate one, which merited a documentary programme on television. A young woman, call her Furia, was awaiting sentence for manslaughter, having brutally assaulted and killed a girl she was quarrelling with while they were working as barmaids. It was expected that the sentence would be a severe one especially because she had a long series of convictions followed by imprisonment for assault and damage to property. The record spoke of a bad character, but her father knew her at other times as a pleasant and equable person. He was puzzled, and eventually noticed, because he had kept a record, that these offences had a certain periodicity, being related to phases of the moon. This in itself should be enough to raise a question of Furia's responsibility. At one time, it would have suggested the explanation that she was under the influence of the moon, and hence a lunatic. We don't believe in that sort of thing any more, but another kind of dependency on the moon has been discovered: pre-menstrual hormonal imbalance. She was given a series of examinations by a distinguished consultant on whose consequent advice the anticipated sentence was suspended, and a course of hormone treatment which seemed to have been successful when she was interviewed on television some months later.

We have only recently had any knowledge of pre-menstrual tension. In the eighteenth century Furia would have been hanged or transported. That she was subject to the curse of Eden, it would have been thought, made her no different from any other women, though probably not enough connection would have been made with that even to

112

have to dismiss it as irrelevant. How can we be sure that no such sort of explanation holds whenever a punishable act, or for that matter rewardable act, indeed any act whatever, is done? Not necessarily, of course, an explanation in terms of hormones, or nutrition, or astral influence, or damaged brain cells, or porphyria, or massive doses of alcohol or lysergic acid, because in the vast majority of cases such explanations can be ruled out. I am sure Professor Vesey isn't chairing this meeting because he is suffering from porphyria (however else he may be suffering). But then, of in terms of what? Well, in terms of some at present unknown sort of motor causal explanation.

What is it, in this account of Furia's case, which convinces us that she was not responsible for what she did?

It is not that Furia's beliefs are ruled out as irrelevant; she didn't suddenly cut loose as it were unconsciously: she was engaged in a quarrel, aware that the object of her attack was a person who annoyed her (she didn't attack the beer barrel, or her left foot). She wielded the knife in a way that showed she was fully aware of what she was doing (and, for the benefit of McNaughten, it is plausible to think she knew it was wrong).

One might represent Furia's father as simply desperate. He was naturally most anxious to get his daughter off, and would grasp at any straw, though not like Clarence Darrow who in pleading in court for two vicious men who conspired to murder a young boy just for the thrill of it argued that they should not be held responsible, because there may be an unknown motor causal explanation in every case of lawbreaking; an argument which one might expect of a shyster lawyer without the ghost of a defence case, and one which did not in the slightest impress the court. No, Furia's father already had reason to look for some explanation: there was something very odd and fishy about the case. He knew his daughter; she usually didn't act like that; was usually equable and reasonable, no more quick and ready to respond violently to little real or imagined provocations than anyone else; possibly even less so. She could, of course, resent provocations just as much as anyone else, but like everyone else her awareness of what constitutes good behaviour, as well as her prudent awareness of consequences and her natural understanding of other people's feelings would lead her to behave reasonably. Normally, the knowledge, or belief, that such behaviour would lose her her job, would lead to prosecution and imprisonment, and, whether or not, would cause injury and even death to an acquaintance who had done very little to offend, would have made it, for Furia, out of the question. But, oddly, extraordinarily, not so, once a month. Why would she suddenly behave like the fearsome delinquent she generally was not?

Never wind why; the observation is enough. She is not herself on these occasions, can't help herself, goes round the bend despite herself. But that's not much use in court; if it were then every villain would get off through the mendacious testimony of her doting relatives. We reserve such appeals for sceptical attention in pleas of mitigation.

The discovery about menstrual tension is not needed to convince Furia's father that she was not responsible; he already believes that. It enables him to convince others she was not by explaining why she was not. What I suggest is this. We can regard someone as acting of their own free will only when they have a basic reason for acting. But that is not enough. Furia assaulted her victim because she believed that in so doing she would be hurting someone who had annoyed her. What is lacking is that she would not have acted differently whatever else she might have believed; her believing something is a necessary part of accounting for what she did, but her *other* beliefs play no part.

Where that is not lacking; where what is done arises from a belief, but where the agent's behaviour is responsive to what other beliefs the agent may have, no recourse to explanations in terms of possible known physical causes such as hormonal imbalance, still less unknown physical causes, is in place. I now compare two fictional but quite credible examples which I hope will bring this out.

Vesey says 'we do not hold someone responsible for doing something he has been forced to do by irresistible physical compulsion. And we recognize varieties of mental compulsion, such as kleptomania, an irresistible tendency to theft in persons who are well-to-do.' I take it to be true of the keptomaniac as much as of any other thief that she knows what she is doing: that she is taking someone else's property without the owner's consent with a view to depriving the owner of it; not the absent-minded picking up of things lying about that one is later surprised to find in one's pocket! Imagine two persons, ordinary housewives and equally not particularly legitimately well-to-do, Volentia and Purloinia.

Volentia has a bulky and specially designed fur coat, lined with enormous pockets, which she stuffs with valuable, portable, and saleable goods during weekly visits to Harrod's, making sure beforehand that she can get rid of the goods quickly and profitably to a receiver she knows in Shepherd's Market; and when she finds she won't be able to fence the stuff, she doesn't pinch it. She knows perfectly well that what she is doing is illegal, but this bothers her no more than it does to falsify her tax returns and open other people's letters; and her friends have learned that it is unwise to lend her money. She knows her shopping enterprises are risky, but she goes to great lengths to minimize the risk, and is careful not to be seen in the same department too often and to call off the project if she has the slightest suspicion that someone might be watching. Such behaviour is indeed quite common. There are in fact many shoplifters.

Purloinia, a more unusual case, makes no special arrangements to steal things, but does so when shopping or idly wandering about department stores. She makes no use of what she steals, and certainly is not concerned to sell it. She is desperately anxious to avoid scandal and cherishes her reputation, to the extent that when she is finally caught at it and charged, she commits suicide (I have an actual case in mind). She is extremely honest in other things, and could not bring herself to open other people's letters and goes to great lengths to repay her debts.

Volentia is surely a criminal shoplifter, and would be treated severely in a court. We would take Purloinia to be a typical kleptomaniac. Not because she has been infected by the kleptomanic virus; kleptomania, unlike pre-menstrual hormonal imbalance, signifies nothing but a pattern of behaviour: it has no aetiological significance. If we wish to speak of an irresistible compulsion, that is only another way of picking out the behaviour, not the diagnosis of an independently known factor. So what is the difference between the two thieves? Volentia is someone whose actions are not determined in relation to just one belief, but subject to the whole complex relation of all her beliefs; and in many ways, if her beliefs were different she would act differently. She could also have done otherwise, had her beliefs been different. But Purloinia is going to go on stealing, no matter what *else* she thinks.

Now if that is roughly how we distinguish between people who act of their own free will, and those who do not, then what of the threat posed by the possibility of universal motor causes? It is a threat if universal motor causes are such that they rule out that people could do otherwise than they do, if their possible beliefs were different. Is there any reason to think they might?

Perhaps the causes of human actions are the same as the causes of the actions of automata? If automata are just things that work on their own, like internal combustion engines (nobody has to keep pushing the pistons up and down) then human beings are automata (nobody has to keep opening and closing my mouth for me to talk); and there are therefore clearly automata whose movement is governed by factors quite different from those which explain the workings of an internal combustion engine. But perhaps, what is meant by automata is automatic machines, such as pianolas. Human beings are like automatic machines in *some* ways; so are dogs, pulsars, whirlpools and the solar system. But surely, not *just* like machines, not being machines. They are not contrivances. We don't know altogether how they work, and that means we don't only not know how to contrive them, we don't even know whether they are contrivable. Nobody can make a fly, let alone something just like me. I was generated, not made.

This kind of response, it may be thought, is not sufficiently serious. When someone calls a railway engine an iron horse, it is not enough to point out that this must be merely metaphorical talk because no one would say that a horse is a protein and carbohydrate railway engine; the metaphor is used only to point to a similarity of function between a living thing and a machine. Talk of automata, or machines, or engines, or self-replicating mechanical systems, or whatever, as comparisons with human beings, is intended to bring out that mere complexity of function does not necessarily require a different kind of aetiology. Not in the case of machines, so why not in the case of human beings? In short, couldn't everything that happens be explained by the laws of physics, in such a way that reference to beliefs are ruled out?

Well, the laws of physics don't explain anything. *Physicists* do, in terms of theories of physics. Well, couldn't a physicist, being clever enough, explain Mrs Thatcher's decision to remain Prime Minister? Perhaps, if he were *so* clever that we couldn't even *imagine* him, and if what is called physics became something entirely different. But there is no place for notions like prime minister in any kind of physics known to any actual or imaginably clever physicists. I can't say that there won't be a great theory which explains everything, and which rules out not only free will but prime ministers and human beings and trees and the solar system; we have after all been surprised, if not so much, before (discovering, for example, that rainbows aren't really there, up in the sky, like clouds or stars). But I don't know what that admission shows, beyond a certain modesty. If I'm worried about where the next meal is coming from it's only because I don't know where Professor Vesey is going to take me to dinner, not because some scientist may possibly show that eating has to be explained away as an illusory phenomenon like a rainbow.

Perhaps I can make the point by adverting to the other worry, about God's omniscient will, by which every detail of everything is of His pre-ordination. God said 'Let there be light' and there was light. I haven't the slightest idea how He did it. I wish I did, because it could help a lot with my electricity bills. Not knowing that, I can't learn from it anything which might be true of light, whether for example it consists of waves, or particles, or both, or neither, or both and neither, or none of these. All I know is that whatever light might be it is as God wills it. Nothing is but that God wills it. I believe man has free will, and I must also therefore believe that God said 'Let man have free will' and man had free will, without knowing how He did it, except that He made no other arrangements which would exclude it. My not really understanding God's strange, atemporal pre-ordinative power allows me to infer nothing, without the aid of revelation, about what might be or not be, because it is necessarily compatible with *whatever* there is.

If there is some true but unknown theory which uses causal laws (causal laws somehow like those supposed to be known in macro-physics, though how like them and how much like them and how different from them we obviously can't know without knowing the theory) to explain absolutely everything—prime ministers, jokes, the sublime, the ridiculous, joy, bereavement, free will and all the other things there seem obviously to be—then, if there are prime ministers, jokes, free will and so on these causal laws will have to be compatible with prime ministers, jokes and free will. But not knowing what theory or even what kind of theory this great theory might be, I can't tell whether it is compatible with there being prime ministers, jokes and free will, or not.

Vesey has asked why philosophers are not content to say that the two practices of treating people as responsible for what they do, on the one hand, and looking for (motor) causes of everything that happens, on the other, are compatible. What I have tried to suggest is that certain idle and contentless fantasies can lead philosophers into thinking that *something or other*—something I know not what—is incompatible with treating people as responsible for what they do. This does not make me content to say that the two practices are compatible, however, because I am not clear what the second one is.

But what, then, of the second practice, in which, Vesey says, philosophers want to engage, of looking for (motor) causes of everything that happens?

Kant did say that it is one in which reason demands we should engage.[10] But he not only denied any possible application to the concept of its completion (reserving that, and that only as a transcendental idea, to non-motor, 'spontaneous' causality—the 'causality of freedom'); his argument for it applies only to the objective temporal succession of events, in the Second Analogy.[11] This should be limited to matter, if we conjoin to it the argument of the First Analogy,[12] and it would do very well as a metaphysical backup for Newtonian physics; however Newtonian physics deals only with point-masses, though Kant uses such examples as heated stoves[13] and ships going down rivers.[14] Hume denied real causal necessity to relations between such things;[15] but, oddly, claims it is demonstrated inductively for psychological events (ideas and impressions).[16] One may, despite Hume, see that Newton's principle of attraction gives us some application for a theoretical notion of causality, even action at a distance, over a very important range of happenings. But neither Kant nor Hume—despite its being the Hume's ambition to be the Newton of psychology—gives any applicable theory, other than a crass and incoherent egoistic psychological hedonism which is the ancestor of contemporary 'theory of action' in

A. Phillips Griffiths

the case of the former, and crude causal associationism in the case of the latter for dealing with mental events.

Professor Vesey—and I advert to this again with no syndeiretical intent—has offered to give me dinner after this meeting. If one of these philosophers tries to engage in the practice of looking for the (motor) causes of this kind invitation, I should be very surprised. That is not only because the offer is hardly so extraordinary a happening as to merit investigation, nor only because it suggests an unworthy suspicion of the sources of Professor Vesey's characteristic good will. I should be most surprised, because somebody was proposing to set out on an investigation which he hadn't the slightest idea not only of how to complete, but of how to begin.

The practice which Professor Vesey says philosophers may want to engage in is just another something I know not what.

Notes

1 P. 82.

2 P. 86.

3 See Descartes' *Philosophical Writings,* tr. N. Kemp-Smith (London: Macmillan, 1952), *Meditation IV,* 232ff. Thus, for Descartes, Reason is perfect, and cannot mislead us; but the will, being perfect, can will anything, including the acceptance of beliefs against all reason, or beyond what reason allows. It is because of this that while the faculties of reason and will are both perfect, we can have erroneous beliefs. This particular doctrine of Descartes' is not one which appeals to many, including many of the most inveterate Cartesian mind–body dualists. I would not reject it entirely; I think a distinction can be made between believing and freely believing which is parallel to that between willing and freely willing. But it is only the latter distinction with which I can be concerned here.

4 P. 85.

5 G. Ryle, *The Concept of Mind* (London: Hutchinson, 1949), Ch. III.

6 D. Hume, *An Enquiry Concerning Human Understanding and Concerning the Principles of Morals,* L. A. Selby-Bigge (ed.) (Oxford: Clarendon Press, 1975), App. 1, 293.

7 I. Kant, *Groundwork of the Metaphysics of Morals*, tr. H. J. Paton as *The Moral Law* (London: Hutchinson, 1948).

8 This does not mean I cannot give any explanations of our actions. Biographical narrative is no more devoid of explanation than is history. Neither constitutes theory.

9 *Descartes Selections,* M. Eaton (ed.) (New York: Scribners, 1927); *Automatism of Brutes: Letter to the Marquis of Newcastle*, 335ff.

10 I. Kant, *Critique of Pure Reason*, tr. N. Kemp-Smith (London: Macmillan, 1929), 449ff.

11 Ibid., 218–233.

12 Ibid., 212–217.

[13] Ibid., 227.

[14] Ibid., 221.

[15] D. Hume, op. cit., Sect. VII, Part II, 73.

[16] D. Hume, *A Treatise of Human Nature,* L. A. Selby-Bigg (ed.) (Oxford: Clarendon Press, 1978), 4–5.

[17] Ibid., xvi.

Faith and the Existence of God

I: R. G. SWINBURNE

Arguments for the Existence of God[1]

Arguments move from premises to conclusions. The premises state things taken temporally for granted; if the argument works, the premises provide grounds for affirming the conclusion. A valid deductive argument is one in which the premises necessitate, that is, entail, the conclusion. (It would involve a self-contradiction to assert the premises but deny the conclusion.) What I shall call a 'correct' inductive argument is one in which the premises in some degree probabilify the conclusion, but do not necessitate it. More precisely, in what I shall call a correct P-inductive argument the premises make the conclusion probable (i.e. more probable than not); in what I shall call a correct C-inductive argument, the premises add to the probability of the conclusion (i.e. confirm it, make it more probable than it was; but do not necessarily make it overall probable). Arguments only show their conclusions to be true if they start from true premises; arguments of the above types which work (i.e. are valid or correct) and do start from such premises I will call sound arguments. Arguments are only of use to show to an individual that the conclusion is true if he already knows the premises to be true. Most of what I shall have to say today concerns arguments with respect to which there is no doubt that the premises are true.

Philosophical arguments for the existence of God may be *a priori* or *a posteriori*. *A priori* arguments have as their premises purported logical or conceptual truths; *a posteriori* arguments begin from purported observable facts of experience. A logical or conceptual truth is one which could not but be true whatever the world is like, or even if there is no world at all; 'All squares have four sides', '$2+3=5$', and 'If there is a God, he is omnipresent' are logical truths. *A priori* arguments to the existence of God begin from some such purported logical truths, including some truth about what God would have to be like, if he existed; and they they go on to claim that it follows that he must exist. Such *a priori* arguments include the traditional ontological argument put forward by Anselm and Descartes; but there have been plenty of other arguments put forward which conform to this general pattern. They normally purport to be deductive arguments. My own view of such arguments is that either they are invalid or (more usually) their premises are highly dubious. However, occasional eminent philosophers have thought otherwise.[2]

Much more interesting to my mind are *a posteriori* arguments, which begin either from very evident general phenomena of experience or from some fairly special phenomenon alleged to have occurred, and then claim that God's action explains the occurrence of the phenomenon and so he must exist. Among such arguments are the cosmological argument (which argues from the existence of the Universe), versions of the teleological argument or 'argument from design' (which argues from the universe being orderly in various respects), the argument from consciousness (which argues from the existence of conscious animals and men), all of which argue from very evident general observable phenomena. Then there are arguments from miracles and religious experience, which argue from special phenomena within the world. All these arguments may be construed either as inductive or as deductive. But the arguments have much more plausibility if we regard them as inductive, and I shall so construe them. Arguments of this type, unlike *a priori* arguments, do, I believe, attempt to codify in a rigorous form the vague reasons which many ordinary believers have for believing in God. They all seem to me to have a common pattern.

Some phenomenon E is considered. It is claimed that E is puzzling, strange, not to be expected in the ordinary course of things; but that E is to be expected if there is a God; for God has the power to bring about E and (with some probability) he might well choose to do so. Hence the occurrence of E is reason for supposing that there is a God. If the arguments are correct C-inductive arguments, then they will 'add up'. Each phenomenon by itself will not make its conclusion on balance probable, but several of the phenomena put together may do so, and thus, in my terminology, provide a correct P-inductive argument. This pattern of argument is one much used in science, history, and all other fields of human inquiry. A detective, for example, finds various clues—John's fingerprints on a burgled safe, John having a lot of money hidden in his house, John being seen near the scene of the burglary at the time when it was committed. He then suggests that these various clues, although they just *might* have other explanations, are not in general to be expected unless John had robbed the safe. Each clue is some evidence that he did rob the safe, confirms the hypothesis that John robbed the safe; and the evidence is cumulative—when put together it makes the hypothesis probable.

Let us call arguments of this kind arguments to a good explanation. Scientists use this pattern of argument to argue to the existence of unobservable entities as causes of the phenomena which they observe. For example, at the beginning of the nineteenth century, scientists observed many varied phenomena of chemical interaction, such as that substances combine in fixed ratios by weight to form new substances (e.g. hydrogen and oxygen always form water in a ratio by weight of 1:8). They then claimed that these phenomena would be expected if there existed a hundred or so different kinds of atom, particles far too small to be seen, which combined and recombined in certain simple ways. In their turn physicists postulated electrons, protons and neutrons and other particles in order to account for the behaviour of the atoms, as well as for larger-scale observable phenomena; and now they postulate quarks in order to explain the behaviour of protons, neutrons and most other particles.

Arguments of this kind give significant probability to their hypothesis in so far as they satisfy three criteria.[3] First, the phenomena which they cite as evidence must not be very likely to occur in the normal course of things. We saw in the burglary example how the various clues, such as John's fingerprints on the safe, were not much to be expected in the normal course of things. Secondly, the phenomena must be more to be expected, to be much more likely to occur if the hypothesis is true. If John did rob the safe it is *quite* likely that his fingerprints would be found on it. Thirdly, the hypothesis must be simple, That is, it must postulate the existence and operation of *few* entities, *few* kinds of entities, with few *easily* describable properties behaving in mathematically *simple* kinds of way. We could always postulate many new entities with complicated properties to explain anything which we found. But our hypothesis will only be supported by the evidence if it postulates few entities, which lead us to expect the diverse phenomena which form the evidence. Thus in the detective story example we could suggest that Brown planted John's fingerprints on the safe, Smith dressed up to look like John at the scene of the crime, and without any collusion with the others Robinson hid the money in John's house. This new hypothesis would lead us to expect the phenomena which we find just as well as does the hypothesis that John robbed the safe. But the latter hypothesis is supported by the evidence whereas the former is not. And this is because the hypothesis that John robbed the safe postulates *one* object—John—doing *one* deed—robbing the safe—which leads us to expect the several phenomena which we find. Scientists always postulate as few new entities (e.g. subatomic particles) as are needed to lead us to expect to find the phenomena which we observe; and they postulate that those entities do not behave erratically (behave one way one day and a different way the next day) but that they behave in accordance with as simple and smooth a mathematical law as is compatible with what is observed. There is an old Latin saying, *simplex sigillum veri*, 'The simple is the sign of the true'. To be rendered probable by evidence, hypotheses must be simple.

R. G. Swinburne

We have available to us for explaining phenomena two different kinds of explanation which we use in ordinary life. One is scientific explanation, whereby we explain a phenomenon E in terms of some prior state of affairs F (the cause) and some regularity L in the behaviour of objects involved in F and E. We explain why a stone took two seconds to fall from a tower to the ground (E) by its having been liberated from rest at the top of the tower 64 feet from the ground (F) and the regularity derivable from Galileo's law of fall that all bodies fall towards the surface of the Earth with an acceleration of 32 ft/sec^2 (L). E follows from F and L. Science can also explain the operation of a regularity or law in some narrow area, in terms of the operation of a wider law in the particular conditions of that narrow area. Thus it can explain why Galileo's law of fall holds for small objects near the surface of the Earth. Galileo's law follows from Newton's laws, given that the Earth is a body of a certain mass far from other massive bodies and the objects on its surface are close to it and small in mass in comparison.

The other way which we use all the time and see as a proper way of explaining phenomena is what I call personal explanation. We often explain some phenomenon E as brought about by a person P in order to achieve some purpose or goal G. The present motion of my hand is explained as brought about by me for the purpose of writing a philosophical paper. The cup being on the table is explained by me having put it there for the purpose of drinking out of it. In these cases I bring about a state of my body which then itself causes by processes susceptible of scientific explanation some state of affairs outside my body. But it is I (P) who bring about the bodily state (E) conducive to producing that further state (G) rather than some other. And the kind of explanation involved here is a different way of explaining things from the scientific. Scientific explanation involves laws of nature and previous states of affairs. Personal explanation involves persons and purposes. In each case the grounds for believing the explanation to be correct are, as stated earlier, the fact that to explain the cited phenomenon and many other similar phenomena we need few entities (e.g. one person rather than many), few kinds of entities with few, easily describable properties, behaving in mathematically simple kinds of way (e.g. a person having certain capacities and purposes which do not change erratically) which give rise to many bodily phenomena. In seeking the best explanation of phenomena we may seek explanations of either kind, and if we cannot find a scientific one which satisfies the criteria, we should look for a personal one.

We should seek explanations of all things; but we have seen that we only have reason for supposing that we have found one if the purported explanation is simple, and leads us to expect what we find when that is otherwise not to be expected. This history of science shows that we

124

judge that the complex, miscellaneous, coincidental and diverse needs explaining, and that it is to be explained in terms of something simpler. The motions of the planets (subject to Kepler's laws), the mechanical interactions of bodies on Earth, the behaviour of pendula, the motions of tides, the behaviour of comets, etc., formed a pretty miscellaneous set of phenomena. Newton's laws of motion constituted a simple theory which led us to expect these phenomena, and so was judged a true explanation of them. The existence of thousands of different chemical substances combining in different ratios to make other substances was complex. The hypothesis that there were only a hundred or so chemical elements of which the thousands of substances were made was a simple hypothesis which led us to expect the complex phenomena. When we reach the simplest possible starting-point for explanation which leads us to expect the phenomena which we find, there alone we should stop and believe that we have found the ultimate brute fact on which all other things depend.

The cosmological argument argues from the existence of a complex physical Universe (or something as general as that) to God who keeps it in being. The first three 'ways' of St Thomas Aquinas are forms of such an argument,[4] but the best classical statement of it to my mind is to be found in the version given by Leibniz.[5] He, however, represented it as a deductively valid argument, and that, I suggest, it cannot be; for there is no apparent inconsistency involved in supposing there to be a Universe and yet no God. Rather, it is an inductive argument to the best explanation of the existence of the Universe.

Here is my own version of the argument, based on Leibniz, but put in the form of an inductive argument rather than a deductive one. The premise is the existence of our Universe for so long as it has existed (whether a finite time or, if it has no beginning, an infinite time). The Universe is a complex thing. There are lots and lots of separate chunks of it. The chunks have each a different finite and not very natural volume, shape, mass, etc.—consider the vast diversity of galaxies, stars and planets, and pebbles on the seashore. Matter is inert and has no powers which it can choose to exert; it does what it has to do. There is a limited amount of it in any region, and it has a limited amount of energy and velocity. There is a complexity, particularity, and finitude about the Universe which looks for explanation in terms of something simpler. The existence of the Universe is something evidently inexplicable by science. For, as we saw, a scientific explanation as such explains the occurrence of one state of affairs in terms of a previous state of affairs and some law of nature which makes states like the former bring about states like the latter. It may explain the planets being in their present positions by a previous state of the system (the Sun and planets being where they were last year) and the operation of Kepler's laws which state that states like the latter are followed a year later by states like the former. And so it may explain the existence of the Universe this year in terms of the existence of the Universe last year and the laws of cosmology. But either there was a first state of the Universe, or there has always been a Universe. In the former case, what science cannot explain is why there was the first state; and in the latter case it still cannot explain why there was ever any matter (or, more correctly, matter-energy) for the laws of nature to get a grip on, as it were. By its very nature science cannot explain why there are any states of affairs at all.

But a God can provide an explanation. The hypothesis of theism is that the Universe exists because there is a God who keeps it in being and that laws of nature operate because there is a God who brings it about that they do. He brings it about that the laws of nature operate by sustaining in every object in the Universe its liability to behave in accord with those laws. He keeps the Universe in being by making the laws such as to conserve the matter of the Universe, i.e. by making it the case at each moment that what there was before continues to exist. The hypothesis is a hypothesis that a person brings about these things for some purpose. He acts directly on the Universe, as we act directly on our brains, guiding them to move our limbs (but the Universe is not his body—for he could at any moment destroy it, and act on another universe, or do without a universe). As we have seen, personal explanation and scientific explanation are the two ways we have of explaining the occurrence of phenomena. Since there cannot be a scientific explanation of the existence of the Universe, either there is a personal explanation or there is no explanation at all. The hypothesis that there is a God is the hypothesis of the existence of the simplest kind of person which there could be. A person is a being with *power* to bring about effects, *knowledge* of how to do so, and *freedom* to make choices of which effects to bring about. God is by definition an omnipotent (that is, infinitely powerful), omniscient (that is, all-knowing), and perfectly free person; he is person of infinite power, knowledge and freedom; a person to whose power, knowledge and freedom there are no limits except those of logic. The hypothesis that there exists a being with infinite degrees of the qualities essential to a being of that kind is the postulation of a very simple being. The hypothesis that there is one such God is a much simpler hypothesis than the hypothesis that there is a god who has such and such limited power, or the hypothesis that there are several gods with limited powers. It is simpler in just the same way that the hypothesis that some particle has zero mass or infinite velocity is simpler than the hypothesis that it has 0.32147 of some unit of mass or a velocity of 221,000 km/sec. A finite limitation cries out for an explanation of why there is just that particular limit, in a way the limitlessness does not.

That there should exist anything at all, let alone a universe as complex and as orderly as ours, is exceedingly strange. But if there is a God, it is not vastly unlikely that he should create such a universe. A universe such a ours is a thing of beauty, and a theatre in which men and other creatures can grow and work out their destiny, a point which I shall develop further below. So the argument from the Universe to God is an argument from a complex phenomenon to a simple entity which leads us to expect (though does not guarantee) the existence of the former far more than it would be expected otherwise. Therefore, I suggest, the argument is a correct C-inductive argument.

The teleological argument or 'argument from design' has various forms. One form is the argument from temporal order, from the fact that almost all natural phenomena conform to simple natural laws. It argues not from the existence of a universe, but from its orderliness. St Thomas Aquinas gave such an argument as his 'fifth way' to prove the existence of God. He may or may not have intended it as a deductively valid argument. I shall expound his argument in a more modern and clearly inductive way.

The phenomenon which forms the premise of the argument is the operation of the most general laws of nature, that is, the orderliness of nature in conforming to very general laws. What exactly these laws are, science may not yet have discovered—perhaps they are the field equations of Einstein's General Theory of Relativity, or perhaps there are some yet more fundamental laws. Now, as we have seen, science can explain the operation of some narrow regularity or law in terms of a wider or more general law. But what science by its very nature cannot explain is why there are the most general laws of nature that there are; for, *ex hypothesi*, no wider law can explain their operation.

The conformity of objects throughout endless time and space to simple laws cries out for explanation. For let us consider what this amounts to. Laws are not things, independent of material objects. To say that all objects conform to laws is simply to say that they all behave in exactly the same way. To say, for example, that the planets obey Kepler's laws is just to say that each planet at each moment of time has the property of moving in the ways that Kepler's laws state. There is, therefore, this vast coincidence in the behavioural properties of objects at all times and in all places. If all the coins of some region have the same markings, or all the papers in a room are written in the same handwriting, we seek an explanation in terms of a common source of these coincidences. We should seek a similar explanation for that vast coincidence which we describe as the conformity of objects to laws of nature—e.g. the fact that all electrons are produced, attract and repel

127

other particles, and combine with them in exactly the same way at each point of endless time and space.

That there is a Universe and that there are laws of nature are phenomena so general and pervasive that we tend to ignore them. But there might so easily not have been a Universe at all, ever. Or the Universe might so easily have been a chaotic mess. That there is an *orderly* Universe is something very striking, yet beyond the capacity of science ever to explain. Science's inability to explain these things is not a temporary phenomenon, caused by the backwardenss of twentieth-century science. Rather, because of what a *scientific* explanation is, these things will ever be beyond its capacity to explain. For scientific explanations by their very nature terminate with some ultimate natural law and ultimate physical arrangement of physical things, and the questions which I am raising are why there are natural laws and physical things at all.

There is available again the same simple explanation of the temporal orderliness of the Universe, that God makes protons and electrons move in an orderly way, just as we might make our bodies move in the regular patterns of a dance. He has *ex hypothesi*, the power to do this. But why should he choose to do so? The orderliness of the Universe makes it a beautiful Universe, but, even more importantly, it makes it a Universe which men can learn to control and change. For only if there are simple laws of nature can men predict what will follow from what—and unless they can do that, they can never change anything. Only if men know that by sowing certain seeds, weeding and watering them, they will get corn, can they develop an agriculture. And men can only acquire that knowledge if there are easily graspable regularities of behaviour in nature. It is good that there be men, embodied mini-creators who share in God's activity of forming and developing the Universe through their free choice. But if there are to be such, there must be laws of nature. There is, therefore, some reasonable expectation that God will bring them about; but otherwise that the Universe should exhibit such very striking order is hardly to be expected.

The form of 'argument from design' which has been most common in the history of thought and was very widely prevalent in the eighteenth and early nineteenth centuries was the argument from spatial order. The intricate organization of animals and plants enabling them to catch the food for which their digestive apparatus was suited and to escape from predators suggested that they were like very complicated machines and hence that they must have been put together by a master machine-maker, who built into them at the same time the power to reproduce. The frequent use of this argument in religious apologetic came to an abrupt halt in 1859, when Darwin produced his explanation of why there were complexly organized animals and plants, in terms of the laws of evolution operating on much simpler organisms. There seemed no need to bring God into the picture.

That reaction was, however, premature. For the demand for explanation can be taken back a further stage. Why are there laws of evolution which have the consequence that over many millennia simple organisms gradually give rise to complex organisms? No doubt because these laws follow from the basic laws of physics. But then why do the basic laws of physics have such a form as to give rise to laws of evolution? And why were there the primitive organisms in the first place? A plausible story can be told of how the primeval 'soup' of matter-energy at the time of the 'Big Bang' (a moment some 15,000 million years ago at which, scientists now tell us, the Universe, or at least the present stage of the Universe, began) gave rise over many millennia, in accordance with physical laws, to those primitive organisms. But then why was there matter suitable for such evolutionary development in the first place? With respect to the laws and with respect to the primeval matter, we have again the same choice, of saying that these things cannot be further explained, or of postulating a further explanation. Note that the issue here is not why there are laws at all (the premise of the argument from temporal order) or why there is matter at all (the premise of the cosmological argument), but why the laws and the matter-energy have this peculiar character, that they are ready wound-up to produce plants, animals and men. Since it is the most general laws of nature which have this special character, there can be no scientific explanation of why they are as they are. And although there might be a scientific explanation of why the matter at the time of the Big Bang had the special character it did, in terms of its character at some earlier time, clearly if there was a first state of the Universe, it must have been of a certain kind; or if the Universe has lasted forever, its matter must have had certain general features if at any time there was to be a state of the Universe suited to produce plants, animals and men. Scientific explanation comes to a stop. The question remains whether we should accept these particular features of the laws and matter of the Universe as ultimate brute facts or whether we should move beyond them to a personal explanation in terms of the agency of God.

What the choice turns on is how likely it is that the laws and initial conditions should by chance have just this character. Recent scientific work has drawn attention to the fact that the Universe is fine-tuned.[6] The matter-energy at the time of the Big Bang had to have a certain density and a certain velocity of recession; increase or decrease in these respects by one part in a million would have had the effect that the Universe was not life-evolving. For example, if the Big Bang had caused the quanta of matter-energy to recede from each other a little more quickly, no galaxies, stars or planets, and no environment suitable for life would have been formed. If the recession had been marginally slower, the Universe would have collapsed in on itself before life could be formed. Similarly, the constants in laws of nature needed to lie within very narrow limits if life was to be formed. It is, therefore, most unlikely that laws and initial conditions should have by chance a life-producing character. God is able to give matter and laws this character. If we can show that he would have reason to do so, then that gives support to the hypothesis that he has done so. There is available again the reason which (additional to the reason of its beauty) was a reason why God would choose to bring about an orderly Universe at all—the worthwhileness of the sentient embodied beings which the evolutionary process would bring about, and above all of humans who can themselves makes informed choices as to what sort of a world there should be.

The arguments which I have considered so far are all arguments from phenomena which are too 'big' for science to explain; they start from the fact and general character of the Universe as described by science. Either these things have no explanation or it is not of a scientific kind. Other arguments start from phenomena which allegedly are too 'odd' for science to explain. It has first to be shown that it is most unlikely that science can explain these phenomena. One example of such an argument is the argument from consciousness. Locke gave a version of this argument.[7] Here is my own tidied-up version.

Men have thoughts and feelings, beliefs and desires, and they make choices. These are events totally different from publicly observable physical events. Physical objects are, physicists tell us, interacting colourless centres of forces; but they act on our senses, which set up electrical circuits in our brains, and these brain events cause us to have sensations (of pain or colour, sound or smell), thoughts, desires and beliefs. Mental events such as these are no doubt largely caused by brain events (and vice versa), but mental events are distinct from brain events—sensations are quite different from electrochemical disturbances. They are, in fact, so different—private, coloured or noisy or felt—from public events such as brain events, that it is very unlikely indeed that science will ever explain how brain events give rise to mental events (why this brain event causes a red sensation, and that one a blue sensation). Yet brain events do cause mental events; no doubt there are regular correlations between this type of brain event and that type of mental event, and yet no scientific theory can say why there are the particular correlations there are, or indeed any correlations at all (why did not evolution just throw up unfeeling robots?). Yet these correlations which science cannot explain cry out for explanation, and explanation of another kind is available. God brings it about that brain events of certain kinds give rise to mental events of certain kinds in order that animals and men may learn about the physical world, see it as imbued with colour and smell making it beautiful, and learn to control it. Much of the value of the evolutionary process would be lost if the embodied creatures to which it gave rise were not conscious. Brain events caused by different sights, sounds and smells give rise to different characteristic sensations and beliefs in order that men may have knowledge of a beautiful physical world and thus have power over it. Darwinism can only explain why some animals are eliminated in the struggle for survival, not why there are conscious animals at all.

Then there are arguments from particular events within history, purported violations of laws of nature (miracles). If it can be shown that some such event E occurred and that science is quite unable to explain its occurrence, then that is grounds for supposing that it has a quite different kind of explanation from the scientific; and the simplest one readily available is divine agency—so long as we can suggest a good reason why God might have chosen to intervene in history to bring about E. E might be an event good in itself, an answer to prayer, or an event which helped the religious progress of men. Of course, historical evidence that some event E occurred may be misleading; or it may be that, while E is inexplicable by current science, the science of the future will be able to explain it. But we are always in this kind of situation with regard to any argument about anything—we may be mistaken. But the reasonable man bases his conclusions on the evidence currently available while acknowledging that tomorrow's evidence may show something quite different. If today's evidence shows that probably a violation of a natural law occurred, we ought so to believe and to seek the best explanation we can of it.

Then there is the argument from the existence of moral obligations, made famous by Kant.[8] I do not myself think that this argument is of any use for showing the existence of God. It does not seem to me deductively valid; moral obligations could exist and yet there be no God. Nor does it seem to me to have any inductive force. For an argument has inductive force only if the phenomenon described in the premise is such that it is more to be expected if the conclusion is true than it would be otherwise. And it seems to me that, if there are, as I believe, moral obligations, many of them will exist whether or not there is a God—one ought to keep one's promises whether or not there is a God. Hence the existence of obligation is no evidence for God's existence.

And then finally there is the argument from religious experience, in the sense of experience which seems to the subject to be an experience of God. Since this is an argument which I believe to have some force, let me put it again in my own words. To so many men it has seemed at different moments of their lives that they were aware of God and his guidance. It is a basic principle of knowledge, which I have called the principle of credulity, that we ought to believe that things are as they seem to be, unless and until we have evidence that we are mistaken. If it seems to me that I am seeing a table or hearing my friend's voice, I ought to believe this until evidence appears that I have been deceived. If you say the contrary—never trust appearances until it is proved that they are reliable, you will never have any beliefs at all. For what would show that appearances were reliable, except more appearances? And if you can't trust appearances as such, you can't trust these new ones either. Just as you must trust your five ordinary senses, so it is equally rational to trust your religious sense. An opponent may say, you trust your ordinary senses (e.g. your sense of sight) because it agrees with the senses of other men—what you claim to see they claim to see; but your religious sense does not agree with the senses of other men (they don't always have religious experiences at all, or of the same kind as you do). However, it is important to realize that the rational man applies the principle of credulity before he knows what other men experience. You rightly trust your senses even if there is no other observer to check them. And if there is another observer who reports that he seems to see what you seem to see, you have thereafter to remember that he did so report, and that means relying on your own memory (i.e. how things seem to have been) without present corroboration. Anyway, religious experiences often do coincide with those of many others in their general awareness of a power beyond ourselves guilding our lives. If some men do not have our experiences, even when our experiences coincide with those of others, that suggests that the former are blind to religious realities—just as a man's inability to see colours does not show that the many of us who claim to see them are mistaken, only that he is colour-blind. It is basic to human knowledge of the world that we believe things are as they seem to be in the absence of positive evidence to the contrary. Someone who seems to have an experience of God should believe that he does, unless evidence can be produced that he is mistaken. And it is another basic principle of knowledge that those who do not have an experience of a certain type ought to believe any others when they say that they do—again, in the absence of evidence of deceit or delusion. Hence there became available to those of us who do not ourselves have religious experiences the reports of others who do, and to which therefore we can apply the principle of credulity. In the absence of counter-evidence, we ought to believe that things are as they seem to others to be; and we do, of course, normally so assume. We trust the reports of others on what they see unless we have reason to suppose that they are lying, or deceiving themselves, or simply misobserving. We ought to do the same with their reports of religious experience.

These are complicated matters. Both where I have defended an argument for the existence of God and where I have attacked it, there are one hundred and one counter-arguments which can be given. I believe that I have available one hundred and one replies to them. But that is a promise; one lecture does not give me time to fulfil it. Inevitably, in order to give unity to my lecture, I have given an overall view of the field, and to some extent defended one overall position. I have claimed that many of the arguments which I have discussed have some inductive force (i.e. are correct C-inductive arguments). Inductive arguments are, as we saw, cumulative. They add to or subtract from the force of each other. I have considered only arguments for the existence of God. They need to be weighed against any arguments against the existence of God, of which the most famous is the argument from evil. Whether all the arguments taken together make the conclusion, that there is a God, more probably than not (i.e. form a correct P-inductive argument) is a very important question. I have expressed elsewhere my own view on this matter; it would be inappropriate to press it too hard in this context.

Notes

[1] This paper is based on the much fuller and more rigorous account which I gave of *a posteriori* arguments for the existence of God in my book, *The Existence of God* (Oxford: Clarendon Press, 1979). (Some of the wording of this present paper is taken from a small pamphlet which I wrote for a different purpose, *Evidence for God*, published by Mowbrays for the Christian Evidence Society, 1986. I am grateful to the society for permission to re-use this material.) For detailed criticism of my approach, see J. L. Mackie, *The Miracle of Theism* (Oxford: Clarendon Press, 1982).

[2] See A. Plantinga (ed.), *The Ontological Argument* (London: Macmillan, 1968), and many other collections of writings on the philosophy of religion for the versions of the ontological argument given by Anselm and Descartes, and a modern version given by Norman Malcolm.

[3] More formally, they are correct C-inductive arguments if the phenomena cited as evidence are more likely to occur if the hypothesis is true than otherwise; and the more each of the criteria is satisfied, the more probable on the evidence is the hypothesis.

[4] See A. Kenny, *The Five Ways* (London: Routledge and Kegan Paul, 1969), for exposition and criticism of Aquinas' 'ways'.

[5] G. W. Leibniz, *On the Ultimate Origination of Things*.

[6] See, for example, the simple description of this fine-tuning in John Leslie, 'Anthropic Principle, World Ensemble, Design', *American Philosophical Quarterly* **19** (1982), 141–151.

[7] John Locke, *An Essay Concerning Human Understanding*, 4.10.10.

[8] See (e.g.) I. Kant, *Critique of Practical Reason*, 1.2.2.5.

II: D. C. BARRETT

Faith and Rationality

In the previous lecture Professor Swinburne discussed arguments for the existence of God. I do not propose to put forward arguments for the non-existence of God, precisely. Rather I want to discuss the view that the whole enterprise of putting forward arguments for the existence of God is misguided. Moreover, I hold that it distorts the nature of religious belief. This in turn raises the question of the rationality of religious belief. A belief that cannot be based on argument, however broadly understood, does not seem to be a rational belief. Is religious belief, therefore, irrational, contrary to reason? We shall see. This, at least, is my programme.

Before embarking on it two points have to be made clear: what I mean by religious belief, and what makes a belief 'religious'. I shall deal with these questions more closely later in the paper. For the moment we can say that, on the one hand, religious belief has got to be distinguished from scientific, commonsense and other such beliefs that have no claim to be considered religious; on the other hand, it has to be distinguished from superstition and beliefs that claim to be religious for various reasons, including tax relief. Clearly the great religious beliefs—Judaic, Christian, Hindu, Islamic—as well as those of pagans, animists and even so-called primitives are religious beliefs or, at least, *regarded* as such. Provisionally, I have these in mind. It is not my intention to adjudicate between them. I have not mentioned Buddhism, especially Zen Buddhism. It is arguable that it is a form of mysticism and asceticism, rather than a religion. This is as may be; it does not concern me in this paper. What I am concerned with is the *concept* of religious beliefs. What does it mean to say that a belief is religious simply because one thinks it is?

* * *

But to return to arguments for the existence of God. As I have said I do not think that they have anything to do with religious belief.

At least four principal arguments can be advanced in favour of the proposition that whether or not there is a God or gods, his existence cannot be proved. These I label: (1) presumptive, (2) cosmological, (3) semantic, and (4) ontological. Whether there are ancillary arguments I do not know, nor have I been able to devise any.

(1) The *Presumptive* argument for the non-existence of God. This has been proposed by Professor Flew. It is a good argument which can be summarized as follows. Since we have no direct evidence of the existence of a Deity, the onus of proof that there is one lies with those who believe that there is. However, whatever proof they could produce, the world would still look the same. That is an uncreated, godless world would not differ in any particular from a created world depending on a Deity.

(2) What I call the *Cosmological* argument for the non-existence of God is better known as the 'problem of evil'. (It might also be called the *Moral* argument.) This argument takes its colour from the argument it is attempting to refute. Thus, if it is Paley's argument from design, it says simply that the world has been so badly designed that there are no grounds for believing in a divine Designer. At a somewhat more sophisticated level it can be argued that in a world full of natural disasters, there cannot be an intelligence governing it: it is out of control. But the strongest argument is moral. How can an all perfect intelligence, which is wise, just and merciful, allow not only physical disasters, pain and agony to take place—wars, famine, poverty, etc.— but also moral evil—torture, murder, extortion and exploitation—to happen?

This is not the place to discuss the problem of evil. I merely wish to note and outline it. But I cannot refrain from two observations. The first is that it does not *prove* the *non-existence* of God. At most it proves that he is not very nice. The second is that it still has to make sense of what Aquinas noted as the order and seeming purpose in the world. Undoubtedly the problem of evil is a problem for theists of whatever persuasion. But it is not a knock-down argument for the non-existence of a Deity. It can be coped with in various ways, scandalous, persuasive or neutral according to one's extra-philosophical views.

(3) The *Semantic* argument has a certain charm. It is that: not only is there nothing that could answer to what could claim to be a Deity, but there could be nothing. The notion of a Deity is vacuous. It is like asking do smoos exist without having a coherent concept of a smoo, or indeed, any concept whatsoever. This, indeed, is the difference between smoos and God, that, whereas we have no idea what a smoo might be—it could be a furry mammal, a splodge in print, a suave way of brushing off a difficult question, a type of cleric, a rare Alaskan cactus, the detritus of a Tuareg cooking vessel, a ravine, a piece of computer software—we do have at least a quasi-concept of God as, for example the being on whom we and everything else depends, the omnipotent, omniscient, all just, all wise, all merciful. Kant was probably the first to hold this concept was inapplicable, though he held, rightly or wrongly, that it was a necessary assumption for comprehend-

ing the world, as a reality, not as a conglomerate of things. But he did not think that the concept was meaningless. That task was left to his successors, the Logical Positivists and linguistic philosophers of various hues. It is, in their various opinions, either unverifiable in principle (and hence meaningless) or incoherent, i.e. internally contradictory.

This is a highly convenient way of disposing of God. If the notion of God is meaningless for whatever reason, then one does not have to argue for his non-existence, since the question of the existence or non-existence of something, the notion of which is meaningless, is itself meaningless, or at best purely verbal. One can construct the sentence: does God exist?, just as one can construct the sentence: are there square circles? And one can answer these pseudo-questions in the negative and support the negation by proving that both are impossible because they are either incoherent or inapplicable notions.

This line of attack on proofs for the existence of God poses problems for the rationality of religious beliefs that are not based on arguments for the existence of God. I shall deal with these in due course.

(4) The *Ontological* argument for the non-existence of God is most ingenious. It was proposed by Professor Findlay, who later repudiated it, but for reasons other than those which I shall offer. In effect it turns Anselm's and later ontological arguments for the existence of God on their heads. As Findlay says: 'it was an ill day when St Anselm proposed his proof for the existence of God . . .'

Findlay agrees with Anselm and the others that, if there is a God, he must be a cut above every other kind of being. He must be in a class of his own, a class totally distinct from all other classes. (Strictly speaking, in no class at all. But that is a refinement into which we need not go at present.) The notion of a being greater than which none other can be conceived fits the bill nicely. But the notion of a necessary being, that is, a being that cannot not exist, fits even better, since it clearly distinguished between those beings that can not-exist (ourselves and all we know) from this one being that cannot not-exist.

Thus, argues Findlay, if there is a God, he must be such a being: i.e. greater than any that can be conceived, i.e. necessary, i.e. whose non-existence is impossible. If there cannot be such a being, then there cannot be a God. But, Findlay continues, there cannot be such a being. Why not? because, as Kant had pointed out long before, existence is not a predicate. There is nothing whose non-existence is not conceivable. One has to establish first *what* the being is before deciding whether it can exist or not; and much more, whether its non-existence is possible or not. If this is so, Findlay argues, the non-existence even of a being that cannot not exist is conceivable. Therefore the non-existence of God—the being that cannot not exist—is conceivable, and hence possible. So God is no different from creatures, in that, like any contingent being, it is possible to conceive of the necessary being not existing. But this cannot be God, the being greater than which none other can be conceived, the truly necessary being. He is contingent like the rest of us. Hence there cannot be a God, or not one worth his salt, one whose non-existence is absolutely unthinkable.

One could take issue with this line of argument by challenging the shibboleth that existence is not a predicate. But a simpler way to deal with it is to right the boat, to turn the ontological argument back onto even keel. Put briefly, Findlay's argument is as dependent on the ontological argument to prove the impossibility of, and hence, non-existence of God, as Anselm's and the other arguments are to prove the existence of God. If one sinks, they all sink: they all go together. So Findlay's argument founders with the rest, which is a pity, since there are few proofs for the non-existence of God. It would be nice to have the matter settled philosophically once and for all. But that is not to be, as I hope to argue in the next section

* * *

No one has, to my knowledge and satisfaction, so far proved either that a God exists or does not exist. (By 'proving' here I mean giving sufficiently cogent argument so that dissent would be irrational.) That is the conclusion of the previous section.

In this section I want to argue that even if the existence of God and certain other religious beliefs could be proved philosophically that would have nothing to do with religious belief as such.

Religious belief is not based on logical argument. How could you prove that Jesus of Nazareth was (a) God incarnate, (b) the Saviour of the world through his death on a cross, (c) now living, and (d) will come again to judge the living and the dead? (I give instances from Christian belief simply because I feel on safer ground, but instances could be given from other religions.) There are no premises on which to base anything remotely resembling a logical argument for such beliefs.

Allowing the historicity of the Gospel narrative—that Jesus was born (not necessarily in Bethlehem), died on a cross, was claimed to have been seen after his death and foretold a Judgment Day—it does not follow that he was God incarnate, saved the world, rose from the dead or will come in judgment. Christian belief may be *based* on the Gospel narrative, but that narrative is *not evidence for* Christian belief in any logical sense, even the broadest and loosest. What is believed—the Incarnation, Redemption, Resurrection and Last Coming—goes far, far beyond anything that can be based on the historical evidence. Even if we accept the historicity of the angel's message to Mary, what Jesus said about his death, the testimony of the apostles, and so forth, this *in itself* is not evidence for the belief. A child being born and a man dying is evidence for nothing but itself. An empty tomb is not evidence that its former occupant is still living. And even if we could prove by some scientific principles that the world would some day come to an end, that would not be evidence for a Day of Judgment.

Hume and other sceptics saw in this a reason for *doubting* the beliefs of Christians. Positivists saw in it a positive reason for *disbelieving*. In so doing they exposed the true nature of religious belief or faith. Faith gives a significance to events and people and even inanimate and non-human objects which they do not have in themselves. The animist who sees a rushing stream as a manifestation of a spirit gleefully leaping from rock to rock or a pagan who sees in a thunderstorm the wrath or warning of a deity, or in a plague a punishment for some serious communal offence, is not regarding these phenomena as a hydrologist, a meteorologist or a bacteriologist would. The explanations of the phenomena by the latter would be totally different. This is not to say that the religious believer ignores the phenomena, whether witnessed or recorded. It is simply that the phenomena—natural or historical events—*taken in themselves* have no religious significance. It is faith which endows them with it.

For this reason faith and science are not in conflict. Science cannot refute faith nor faith science. The religious believer who believes that a plague was a punishment of God or the gods is not proved wrong by the bacteriologist who diagnoses its cause as a particular kind of bacterium. Nor is the bacteriologist proved wrong by the religious believer who attributes the cause of the plague to the gods. They are talking two different but compatible languages. But, more importantly, their methods are totally different. The bacteriologist needs hard evidence to support his diagnosis—symptoms, laboratory tests, previous cases, etc. He must be able to show that a particular bacillus was the cause of the plague, otherwise the cure may be ineffectual. The religious believer does not have to provide anything like such a rigorous proof. But at least he has to give reasons, if not very good ones. He has to point to some wrong-doing or suspected wrong-doing that caused the gods to punish the community as they had done before to the same or other communities.

This raises the question of the rationality of religious belief, which is my third topic.

* * *

If religious belief is not a matter of evidence or strict proof in the logical sense, however broadly understood, can it in any sense be called rational? If not, is one morally justified in indulging in such beliefs, at least when one knows that they have no scientific—astronomical, biological, archaeological, physical, etc.—or historical basis?

In answer to the first question I would say: no, religious belief is not rational; it is beyond reason; it is in the unknown, if not the unknowable. That is its nature. That is what makes it *religious* as against scientific, historical or commonsense belief in the first place, though not all non-rational beliefs are religious.

Is it then irrational? Tertullian in a fit of madness wrote: *Certum est quia impossible est* ('It is certain because it is impossible') (*De Carne Christi*, 5). This is not only untrue, but if it were, every daft belief would have to be dubbed 'religious'. Even Tertullian made distinctions among impossibilities. Some were acceptable, some not. There are reasons for accepting some beliefs and not others. To that extent faith is rational. But what are these reasons?

Reasons in faith are difficult to establish. One must bring in the distinction between a reason for believing and someone's reason for believing. The former may be reasonable, if not rational in the sense of logically provable; the latter may be irrational—'The vicar told me and I like the colour of his hair'. But in general the reasons supporting faith are contained in the word 'faith' (*fides*) itself. 'Faith' in its root means 'trust'. If someone promises to look after my cat and plants while I am away, I believe him, particularly if (a) I have no reason to doubt his word, and (b) he has never let me down before. If someone tells me that Spinks is a good mechanic and that person knows something about mechanics, I will believe him. If someone whom I trust in other respects tells me he is an adviser to the government on financial matters, and I do not think he is just bragging, I will believe him. Are these irrational beliefs? Surely not. It is not irrational to believed something on the testimony of someone whom one has learnt by experience to trust, even though what he says cannot be rationally justified.

This, it might be said, is good enough in everyday or scientific or other acadmic affairs. It can be rationalized thus. A is both knowledgeable and trustworthy; A tells me that X; therefore either X is true or, at least, I have reasonable grounds for believing that X. But what is the criterion of trustworthiness in religious matters? In ordinary and even extraordinary cases of expert advice we have at least some criteria of trustworthiness. Does the thing work as he said it would? Do other experts agree with him? Does it make sense, i.e. is it non-contradictory? Does he tell lies, romanticize, deceive to tease, etc.? Are any of these criteria applicable to religious belief? I would not say that none of these criteria, particularly the last, apply; but there are other criteria.

Obviously there cannot be criteria based on pragmatic or experiential evidence such as one gets in everyday life. What a prophet or an evangelist tells us is beyond any ordinary criteria or credibility. If someone said he had seen flying saucers on many occasions, one might treat his testimony with some respect, since such objects might just be possible and his testimony was otherwise good. If someone said that he regularly saw leprechauns or fairies at the bottom of his garden, however reliable he might be in other respects, we would not take his word for it. So why should we take the word of a prophet or evangelist who is telling us things that not only cannot be verified, but neither can his testimony?

The criterion Wittgenstein offers is the way of life that is contained in the prophecy or revelation. To this might be added the way of life of the prophet himself (or herself). I think this latter is essential if one is to take the prophecy seriously. If the way of life is appealing on moral grounds, that is, if the way of life that is implied by an incomprehensible utterance seems not only acceptable but superior to any other way of life, then one may accept the incomprehensible part from which it subtends or to which it is inextricably united. An illustration of this is St Peter's remark after the discourse on the Eucharist (which was too much for most of the disciples of Jesus) when asked: 'Will you also go away?' He replied: 'Lord, to whom shall we go? Thou hast the words of eternal life' (John vi. 68–69).

One might ask how one can judge and assess a way of life if one is not a moral expert oneself, and, hence, how can one adjudicate between one faith and another—Hindu, Buddhist, Jewish, Christian, Muslim, etc. Is it just a matter of what suits you that you are prepared to accept the incomprehensible doctrine that goes with it? Or is it that you genuinely assess its moral content and come to the conclusion that the way of life it prescribes is preferable to any other? If the latter, how is this conclusion reached, if one is not oneself a prophet? This is not a great problem. One does not have to be a good mathematician or solver of crossword puzzles to see that a mathematical problem or a crossword puzzle has been successfully solved. Nor does one have to be a moral genius to see that, say, slavery is wrong, once the arguments against it are properly presented to you. Nor, again, does it require great expertise to see that there is something wrong with allowing others to go hungry or homeless or badly clothed or neglected in hospital and prison. What might not be so obvious is that such negligence was in some mysterious way directed not only at the person concerned but also at Jesus Christ himself. And yet, having accepted the moral principle, the doctrinal mystery may help to enforce it. The great St Peter Clavier who tended the sick and dying slaves arriving at Cartegena once called after a black helper who could no longer bear the stench and revolting condition of the slaves: 'Martha, come back. These people have been redeemed by the blood of Christ.'

I am not here suggesting a moral or pragmatic argument for religious belief, whether it be Atonement, Redemption, the Mystical Body of

Christ, or whatever. I am merely suggesting that the moral consequences or at least the moral content of a religious belief may lead one
into that belief. No more than that. Even if the religious belief—the
Fatherhood of God, Redemption, a Last Judgement, Life Everlast-
ing—may help to sustain a way of life, this in itself is not sufficient to
justify the religious belief.

Religious belief is ultimately, as Kierkegaard so dramatically presented it, a leap in the dark: the leap of faith. For Kierkegaard there are
three stages on life's way: the aesthetic, where one follows one's whims
and is committed to nothing; the ethical where one makes rational
choices and commits oneself; and faith, which is beyond reason and
without rational justification, based solely on faith in the word of Jesus
Christ. Of course, it need not be Jesus Christ, it could be the word of
God to Moses or the Prophets, of Allah to Mohammed, or any other
religious source. But the important point is that it is beyond reason. It is
an act of trust.

If this is so then it is clear that *arguments* for God's existence, or
anything to do with faith, cannot be reasons for believing. At best they
are elucidatory. This is especially true of St Anselm, who showed that
God had to be a necessary being. (I am not so sure of Aquinas. I think
that he thought he was proving something.) They may also serve to
show that faith is compatible with reason. This works well enough with
the doctrine of immortality. While it cannot be proved philosophically,
Aquinas did a good rearguard action in showing that immortality is not
unreasonable, given the nature of the human mind. But the theory of
transubstantiation, as propounded by Aquinas and defended (or interpreted) by Leibniz, does more harm than good to an understanding of
the mystery of the Eucharist.

It is equally clear where religious belief differs from superstition.
Superstition, as I see it, is false scientific belief masquerading as
religious belief. It resembles religious belief in so far as it has no rational
foundation. It differs from religious belief in that, though purporting to
invoke supernatural agencies by means of spells, curses, incantations
and other rituals, it believes in the efficacy of natural powers. In turn it
differs from bad or pseudo-science in that the latter does not invoke the
supernatural.

* * *

If, as I have argued, religious belief is essentially non-rational, is one
morally justified in believing it? Is one not being irrational in believing
in something that is not only not susceptible of rational proof but defies
and repudiates it? And, moreover, if one is prepared to base one's whole
way of life on these non-rational beliefs—celibacy, indissolubility
of marriage, fasting and abstinence, regular observance at church,

asceticism, and so forth—is there any moral justification for all this? Some people would say this life of renunciation and rigid religious observance was immoral. That seems to go too far, though one can see why someone should think so. Such behaviour is certainly not normal human (i.e. humanist or pagan) behaviour. Nor is it moral in the sense of rational, since it is based on non-rational beliefs. What, then, is the justification for such behaviour and such beliefs?

To answer this one has to distinguish between the rationality of the beliefs and the rationality or reasonableness of believing them. We hold innumerable beliefs—scientific, geographical, social, i.e. about family history, local gossip, etc.—that one cannot rationally justify because one cannot justify them personally. Yet no one would say that it was irrational to hold such beliefs. Now religious beliefs are, admittedly, not quite in that category. There are what might be called vulgarly 'whoppers', i.e. monstrous lies such as fishermen and Irishmen are wont to tell. One is expected to see through them and one usually does. One does this because they exceed the bounds of possibility or, at least probability. Religious beliefs, however, are super-whoppers. Notions such as 'possible', 'probable', 'likely' are inapplicable to them. It would be reasonable to say that it is *likely* that Uncle George did steal the family jewellery but not that it is *likely* that Jesus rose from the dead, or even that it is possible, much less probable. The claim is too monstrous a whopper to merit these adjectives. And yet in the context of the gospels as they are narrated by two one-time ignorant fishermen, a tax collector and a not-so-ignorant doctor, not to mention a scholar who came late on the scene, however much their testimony has been tampered with, it is not unreasonable to believe the Gospel story, monstrous though it may seem. This is not to say that it compels acceptance by a rational person. Nor is anyone who rejects it less moral for doing so.

But one must emphasize the monstrousness of religious belief and its non-rationality in order to bring out its true nature. On the other hand one must emphasize the fact that it is not irrational, much less that its virtue lies in its irrationality. Tertullian went much too far.

Value Judgments

I: MARCUS G. SINGER

Value Judgments and Normative Claims

A person's values are what that person regards as or thinks important; a society's values are what that society regards as important. A society's values are expressed in laws and legislatively enacted policies, in its mores, social habits, and positive morality. Any body's values—an individual person's or a society's—are subject to change, and in our time especially. An individual manifests his or her values in expressions of approval or disapproval, of admiration or disdain, by seeking or avoidance behaviour, and by his or her characteristic activities. What one values one seeks for or tries to maintain. Sometimes attaining it leads to unexpected enlightenment—that isn't what one wanted after all. But a person's values are discovered most significantly in a reflective way by becoming aware of what one is willing to give up to attain or maintain one's values. This is the price one is willing to pay for it, and values are occasionally, and in the money and stock markets always, expressed in terms of price. This can be significant or it can be misleading; it depends on how it is interpreted. Not everything has a monetary equivalent, despite the attempts of the law to provide recovery for damages in monetary terms, and despite the cynical maxim, 'Everyone has his price'.

In addition to value behaviour, one expresses one's values in value judgments. Sometimes these are called evaluations, and an evaluation is either a mental process, a result of that process that remains unexpressed, or a statement expressing it. The latter, an oral or written statement expressing a valuation, is what, for convenience of access, is most often referred to in philosophical discourse as a value judgment.

But our topic is not restricted to value judgments as just described, it is meant to incude under one general heading moral judgments as well, and sometimes in philosophical discourse one finds the expression 'ethical statements' being used as an omnibus word, covering all and sundry. There are distinctions that this usage obscures, and I shall get to them presently. The omnibus term I propose to use is 'normative claims', and I shall use this to cover both value judgments in the more restricted sense mentioned and also moral judgments. A normative claim is a claim to the effect that some standard ought to prevail, a claim

145

about what ought to be done or would be good if it (did exist or) were (done). In sociological usage, a normative claim is one about norms, and in this sense a norm is a standard in the sense of average or usual or normal that *does* exist among a certain group; in this sense a normative claim is a statistical measure. This is not the philosophical use of 'normative'. A normative claim is one about what standard *ought* to be followed, as distinct from what is normal, standard, or average.

The distinction just presented presupposes a distinction between statements of fact and judgments of value, sometimes called the 'fact/value' distinction, sometimes the 'is/ought' distinction, and to explain this I must say something about other kinds of statements. The account I am about to give is fairly standard if not canonical; we shall later see reason to question some of its claims.

A statement of fact is a statement about what is, was, or will be; about what did occur, is now occurring, will occur, or would occur under certain conditions which may or may not be realized; the category also covers generalizations about past, present, or future events or existences. 'I am now in London' is such a statement; so is 'Last week I was in Wisconsin preparing this lecture'; and so is 'Next week I shall be in Oxford and in two weeks I shall be home' (though this last part involves some measure of hope as well as anticipation). The examples just provided happen to be true, but statements of fact, so-called, can be false, do not necessarily state facts. To call them statements of fact is merely to say that they make factual claims, and not to evaluate them as true. This indicates, notice, that a statement of fact may not be a fact, and also that statements of fact can themselves be evaluated. But statements of fact are also not 'necessary' statements, though some of them can state physical or natural necessities. Though it is true that I am now in London, it could be false. 'I am now in Moscow', though a statement of fact, is (I hope) false. If I were in Moscow it would be true, but I am not and it is not.

Another standard category of statements, then, is called in accordance with tradition necessary statements or statements of logic. These are what Hume called 'relations of ideas' in distinction from 'matters of fact'. A relation of ideas can be determined to be true or false by reasoning about it, or merely from the meanings of the terms used in its statement. Statements of fact cannot; their truth-value has to be ascertained empirically, by experience, observation, experiment. Some relations of ideas are trivial, such as 'A lecturer who talks too long is one who talks too long', or 'A person who stammers has a stammer'. Others are not, require elaborate and complex reasoning to establish, such as in mathematical proofs. Given the axioms of Euclidean geometry, the Pythagorean theorem, 'the square of the hypotenuse of a right triangle is equal to the sum of the squares of the other two sides', holds necessarily. So does the proposition that '5,876×4,321=25,390,196' (a result obtained by calculation—I must admit that I used my pocket calculator, and I am not sure that pressing buttons on a calculator is an operation identical with calculating itself; but I took a calculated risk). Another proposition having this *a priori* character is—listen carefully now!—'If there are more trees in the world than there are leaves on any one tree, and there are no trees with no leaves at all, then there are at least two trees with the same number of leaves'. Some people on first hearing are not sure whether this proposition is true or false, but the proof is easy once you get the right idea. If you don't get the right idea right away, it can be frustrating, even deceiving. I shall put the solution in a note, so as not to deprive connoisseurs of the pleasure of figuring it out for themselves; and I add an admonition to readers: don't look down yet![1]

Now one prime question about value judgments and normative claims is this: are they capable of being established by empirical means, as are statements of fact; or are they discoverable by the operations of our reason, as are relations of ideas; or are they incapable of being established at all? If normative claims were deducible from premises containing statements of fact alone, we should have a ready answer to this question. The standard view of the matter is that no 'ought'-statements—normative claims—can be deduced from 'is'-statements—statements of fact—alone. Similarly the standard view is that no value judgments can be deduced from statements of fact alone, that a value judgment must be among the premises of the deduction. This view, though not uncontroversial, is widely held; and the controvery about it is called 'the is/ought controversy'. Professor Hare calls this principle—namely, 'No "ought" from an "is"'—Hume's law; others call it Hare's rule. Still others call it false; these are usually those who call it Hare's rule.

The is/ought problem is the problem of determining how factual and normative claims are related, how facts are related to values, and this is in effect the question of how value judgments and normative claims are to be established. If value judgments could be deduced from statements of fact alone, to establish a judgment of value we should need only to establish the statements of fact from which it is deducible. If this route is not open, as Hare's rule claims, then what route is? How, in other words, are normative claims to be established, justified, proved? Although some can be regarded as tautologous, such as 'Murder is wrong' (since murder is by definition simply wrongful killing), this does not take us very far, and actually takes us nowhere with respect to the interesting and controversial cases. Indeed, it could be argued, and perhaps should be, that 'murder is wrong' is for this reason not a normative claim at all. Other instances, e.g. 'Business is business', have the *form* of tautologies, but simply beg the question. This only looks like a tautology, is used under this tautological cover to advance the normatively dubious claim that the rules that apply in the conduct of ordinary life are inapplicable to the affairs of business, so that whatever one does in the conduct of business is justified because it is in the conduct of business. (Of course no one believes this is who is in the role of recipient as distinct from agent.) A similar example with no tautological disguise is 'All's fair in love and war'; this is not established by the fact that it is often stated and apparently widely accepted—at least by the winners.

Some philosophers have claimed that normative claims are self-evident or deducible from self-evident truths, or are in general establishable by *a priori* means. Kantian ethics is a very elaborate form of this view. The alternative view is that normative claims are to be established by establishing some connection to matters of fact, albeit complicated matters of fact. Utilitarianism, in any of its multifarious varieties, maintains this. Rationalism in ethics is the view that certain ethical propositions or principles can be established or proved *a priori*. Empiricism in ethics denies this, maintains that ethical propositions are establishable as facts or by their connections with facts. And both alternatives are denied by moral sceptics, who deny that normative or value claims can be proved at all; some even deny that there are any. But there are many and manifold varieties of moral or value scepticism. It is not any unitary view, must be defined by disjunction, and this is a topic, or set of topics, in itself.[2]

Non-sceptical normative theories take different forms, depending on how they answer this basic question of moral philosophy. One standard distinction is that between teleological and deontological theories. I think it more adequate (though still troublesome) to distinguish between deontological theories on the one hand, and teleological and consequentialist theories on the other, and will presently say something about this conventional distinction.

However, first I must go back to draw a distinction between value judgments and moral judgments; this often overlooked distinction is often vital.

I

A value judgment is an opinion, assessment, estimate, or claim about the value, worth, quality, merit, or desirability of something—a thing, a state of affairs, or an activity. Such judgments are either comparative or non-comparative. In a comparative value judgment one makes a comparison of the relative merits or value of two or more things, for a certain purpose, in a certain context, or from a given point of view. In a non-comparative (or absolute) judgment no such comparison is expressed. It is a nice question of theory whether there is not always some comparison implicit or in the background, but we shall here keep that question in the background.

Moral judgments are made about different sorts of things: actions, kinds of actions, persons, and institutions; and a moral judgment is a judgment about the morality or moral status of an action, or a general kind of action, a person, or an institution. Thus an action can be judged right or wrong, as what ought or ought not to be done, as what someone has or has not a right to do; a person may be judged a good or a bad person—as kind or cruel, considerate or inconsiderate, trustworthy or untrustworthy, generous or selfish; and an institution may be judged just or unjust, harmful or beneficial, as monstrous (slavery), difficult (marriage), or essential (language). One proviso should be inserted immediately: we judge an action on the supposition that it is (or was) voluntary, we judge a person on the supposition that the person is sane. But the claim that some person is irresponsible is a moral judgment, not a withdrawal of judgment.

I have spoken about what moral judgments are in fact made about. The question 'What *ought* moral judgments to be made about?' is not easy to attach any definite sense to. The following might provide a case. We judge conduct on the supposition that it is voluntary and that the person in question is not insane, and on a showing to the contrary we tend to withdraw the judgment. Now one might claim that we ought not to pass moral judgments on the behaviour of people not responsible for their actions or that we ought not to condemn such people, and some sense can be made of this—certainly enough to generate controversy on the nature reality and limits of responsibility.

A moral judgment, in the primary sense, is an answer to a moral question, a proposed solution to a moral problem. When the question is one of practice, a judgment is a hypothesis to be carried out in conduct.

To understand what a moral judgment is, then, we must understand what a moral problem is. A moral problem arises out of conflicting moral considerations, considerations of what is right or wrong or ought to or may rightfully be done, about what would be equitable, just, fair, decent, or rotten in the way of conduct or the treatment of persons. A moral problem arises in a social context, where one already has some realization of and to some extent accepts the standards of conduct out of which the problem arises. One who has no moral beliefs can have no moral problems, probably could not even grasp the concept; and that is a heavy price to pay for the elimination of perplexity. Something is a moral problem if it calls for action of some kind to resolve it, if it substantially affects the interest of others, and if one ought to take those interests into account in deciding what to do. This last provision makes

149

the determination of whether some problem is a moral problem itself in part a moral problem, but this circularity, if such it is, is not serious. And it is not necessary that a moral problem involve the interests of others. One can have a moral problem where one feels that one's self-respect or sense of self-worth or self-esteem is somehow at stake, whether the interests of another are involved or not. But even though in some given situation the interests of others may not be materially affected, one can acquire a sense of self-respect or self-esteem only in a social setting in which one has acquired a moral code and developed a moral sense, a sense of right and wrong.[3]

None the less, the notion of a moral problem is a peculiar one because of the complexities of the notion of 'solving' one. What is it to *solve* a moral problem? One thing is obvious. If the problem is a practical one, and not a theoretical problem about some past happening, it calls for action to resolve it. No practical problem can be solved *merely* by thinking about it, though many call for thought beforehand. If my problem is to determine what to do with a sum of money at my disposal, which fund, say, to invest it in, my problem is not solved if I merely work the thing out on paper, conclude 'There—that's the solution', and leave the money in my current account or under my mattress. I have to *do* the thing I decided ought to be done, and without the doing the problem has not been solved. What may have been solved was some intellectual enterprise, but not a practical problem. Similarly, if my problem is what to do with my elderly, ill, and increasingly senile mother, since having her in the house is causing problems with my marriage and for my children, this will no doubt take careful considera-tion and consultation. But if after I contemplate and consult and make up my mind about what the best course of action would be, I then do nothing but simply continue as before, although I may have arrived at a correct answer to the question 'What would be the best thing to do?', I certainly have not solved my problem. This would be analogous to W. C. Fields' recipe for curing insomnia: 'Get plenty of sleep!' The last problem mentioned is both a practical and a moral problem. Does it have a *solution* in any ordinary sense? Certainly scientific problems have solutions, as do mathematical and logical problems. And presum-ably so do social and ecological problems (the latter being a subclass of the former). And some practical problems do, though some may not.

John Dewey once said that 'intellectual progress usually occurs through sheer abandonment of questions together with . . . the alter-natives they assume—an abandonment that results from their decreas-ing vitality and a change of urgent interest. We do not solve them: we get over them.'[4] Surely something similar occurs with moral problems. Yet this is not altogether accurate. Some we do not get over, and some disappear or simply become less urgent. But in the main the way to solve moral and social problems is by *dealing with them*, in the light of intelligence and informed thought and an enlightened moral sense and a developed sense of values.

A moral problem may not have a solution in the same sense as a problem of science, mathematics, or logic, or in the same sense as a problem of cookery or a military or chess problem. But a moral problem does call for action of some kind, even though the action might go astray. It might be ill-calculated to deal with the problem in question, or unforeseen events might intervene. John Passmore manifests on this matter a curious combination of acuity and absent-mindedness. 'To solve any sort of social problem', he says,

> is to describe a satisfactory way of reducing the incidence or the severity of the phenomenon stigmatized as a problem. To solve the problem of alcoholism is to describe a satisfactory way of reducing the number of alcoholics; to solve the problem of traffic accidents is to describe a satisfactory way of reducing the number and the severity of such accidents . . . 'Satisfactory way' is, of course, vague. The conclusion that a social problem has been solved . . . involves an evaluation just as much as does the decision that the problem exists.[5]

This last point is a significant one, and applies as well to moral problems. The conclusion that a moral problem has been solved involves evaluation just as much as the judgment that the problem exists. Hence value judgments are involved in the very being of moral problems. However, in saying that 'to solve' such a problem is merely 'to describe' something, Passmore goes curiously off the mark. This may do so far as the work of an expert brought in for consultation goes. It does not for the society or official concerned. Merely 'to describe a satisfactory way of reducing the number of alcoholics', though no doubt a considerable achievement in itself, is not to solve the problem of alcoholism, even if it is thought to do so by some consulting expert. The 'solution' has to be carried out in practice, and here is where it may be discovered that the 'solution', which seemed so reasonable on paper, will not work. This is why I earlier referred to moral judgments as hypotheses to be tested. An 'intellectual solution', though no doubt very important, cannot be regarded as identical with a *solution*; it may even be some distance from it.

II

Now to the distinction between consequentialist and deontological theories. A consequentialist theory maintains that the morality of an action depends solely on the value of its consequences: if the consequences are good, the act is right; if the consequences are bad, the act is wrong. Utilitarianism is a form of consequentialism, and a fairly rigorous formulation of the principle of utility was first provided by Sidgwick in 1874 (*Methods of Ethics*, 7th edn (1907), Bk IV, Ch. 1, p. 411): 'the conduct which, under any given circumstances, is objectively right, is that which will produce the greatest amount of happiness on the whole . . . taking into account all whose happiness is affected by the conduct'. Mill, in his *Utilitarianism* (1863), provides a looser formulation which none the less brings out the point that is of moment here. Mill says that 'actions are right in proportion as they tend to promote happiness, wrong as they tend to produce the reverse of happiness. By happiness is intended pleasure, and the absence of pain; by unhappiness, pain, and the privation of pleasure' (Ch. 2, para. 2, Everyman edn, p. 6). And Mill goes on to distinguish from 'this theory of morality' what he calls 'the theory of life on which [it] is grounded— namely, that pleasure and freedom from pain are the only things desirable as ends'. What Mill here calls a 'theory of life' is a theory of value, and the theory of value Mill here is presenting is Hedonism: pleasure is the only thing intrinsically desirable, good in and for itself. Non-hedonistic varieties of utilitarianism have been developed since Mill's and even Sidgwick's time, by Moore (1903) and Rashdall (1907), and later multifarious varieties by numerous writers.[6] But the essential point for our purpose is that on Utilitarianism, and on any form of consequentialism, all moral judgments are taken to rest on value judgments, so that moral theory presupposes value theory, 'axiology' as it is called in Germany and America, in some sort of alliance against English. If pleasure is the good, whatever produces pleasure is good and ought to be done; if pain is bad, whatever produces pain is bad and ought to be avoided. The intramural disputes among utilitarians are not now on our agenda, so I am content to leave the statement as it is, even though it is capable of indefinite refinement. If we do not specify what utility is, or take it as something other than pleasure, the principle will tell us that whatever produces or maximizes utility is right and ought to be done; that whatever fails to produce or maximize utility is bad and ought not to be done. Utility can be measured by the satisfaction of desires, or by the satisfaction of persons, interests or needs; it is all one. And this is true for all consequentialist theories.

Teleological theories, which emphasize purposes rather than results, do not usually take a maximizing form, place aiming at good ends in paramount position. Aristotle's *Nicomachean Ethics* opens thus:

> Every art and every inquiry, and similarly every action and pursuit, is thought to aim at some good; and for this reason the good has rightly been declared to be that at which all things aim. But a certain difference is found among ends; some are activities, others are

products apart from the activities which produce them. Where there are ends apart from the actions, it is the nature of the products to be better than the activities . . .

And continues:

If then, there is some end of the things we do, which we desire for its own sake (everything else being desired for the sake of this), and if we do not choose everything for the sake of something else (for at that rate the process would go on to infinity, so that our desire would be empty and vain), clearly this must be the good and the chief good.[7]

Although it is not absolutely brought out by these opening passages, Aristotle's ethics, though teleological, is not a form of consequentialism, nor does it require any maximizing formula. The basic idea is that the realization of some good end is the criterion of whether an action is virtuous or not, so that value judgments, judgments of the worth of the end, are prior to the moral judgment of the conduct. But for Aristotle the manner of the action and the disposition of the agent play a role in the evaluation of the action, another reason why teleological theories are not necessarily consequentialist.

In Bentham's version, ethics is even thought of as a science. Since the morality of acts, individual, governmental and legislative, depends solely on the consequences, and since the consequences have their value determined, in Bentham's view, by the hedonic calcus for determining the value of 'a lot of pleasure or pain'—which is, at least in principle, a semi-mathematical operation—the question whether some proposed act would be right or wrong is the question of what its consequences are likely to be compared with the consequences of the available alternatives and the value of those compared consequences. On a maximizing interpretation of the principle of utility, that act will be right that maximizes utility (pleasure, happiness, good, satisfaction) and the question whether an act is right or wrong turns out to be a matter of fact, in principle if not always in practice answerable by appeal to scientific procedures for predicting consequences and measuring their value. Value theory—axiology—thus becomes prior to moral theory, which is thus, and not in any mysterious way, amenable to scientific treatment.[8]

Another form of consequentialism that is not a form of utilitarianism has been presented by Dewey. Thus Dewey says:

. . . the moral issue concerns the future. It is prospective. To content ourselves with pronouncing judgments of merit and demerit without reference to the fact that our judgments are themselves facts which have consequences, is complacently to dodge the moral issue . . . The moral problem is that of modifying the facts which now influence future results (HNC, 19).

Again:

> ... consequences fix the moral quality of an act ... In the long run but not unqualifiedly, consequences are what they are because of the nature of desire and disposition (HNC, 44–45).

And again:

> Consequences include effects upon character, upon confirming and weakening habits, as well as tangibly obvious results (HNC, 46).

And in reporting on one aspect of a view that he ultimately regards as one-sided, Dewey says:

> Morality is found in consequences; and consequences are definite, observable facts which the individual can be made responsible for noting and for employing in the direction of his further behavior. The theory gives morality an objective, a tangible guarantee and sanction. Moreover, results are something objective, common to different individuals because outside them all ... (*Ethics*, 1st edn, 234).[9]

It is manifest that Dewey is a consequentialist, of a sort that has not been adequately understood because it is so thoroughgoing. Dewey includes under consequences effects on character, habits, dispositions, and even motives, much in the manner of Mill in some passages in *Utilitarianism* (Ch. 2, paras 23–25) that are often overlooked, in which Mill talks about secondary or remote consequences, such as the effects on the character of the agent, on habits, and on social expectations and institutions.

But the theory that morality depends solely on consequences runs into both difficulties and opposition. The opposition is provided by so-called deontological theories which maintain in various forms that the morality of a line of conduct depends either on the motive or disposition or intent of the agent, or on the character of the agent, or on something in the nature of the action—and either not at all or only to some degree on consequences. Theories of this sort tend to emphasize general rules or principles of conduct, which can be applied to an action in virtue of the kind of action it is, and independently of consequences. Such theories range from various forms of Intuitionism, to Will of God theories that make right and wrong depend on Divine Commands, to Will of the State theories that make it depend on the commands or rules of the state or sovereign (Hobbes, Austin), to a theory of the complexity of Kant's.

Kant certainly holds that the morality of an action is not a function of its consequences. Instead, Kant tells us, whether an action has moral worth—a conception that has no parallel with anything mentioned so far—depends on whether it is done from duty, that is, out of the sincere belief that it is morally right and for no other reason. This is the meaning of the famous opening sentence of the *Groundwork of the Metaphysics of Morals*: 'It is impossible to conceive anything at all in the world, or even out of it, which can be taken as good without qualification, except a *good will*'.[10] This introduces the conception of *moral* value or *moral* worth, and it also introduces the unprecedented concept of being good unconditionally or without qualification, which is not the same as having value as an end. The Good Will does not play the same role for Kant as happiness or utility does for utilitarian theories—it is not the end towards which everything else is to be accounted a means; and Kant does not accept the standard means-end model of action according to which all actions are to be understood as means to ends other than themselves and as deriving their value from the end to which they are subservient. Kant is saying that in order for an action to have moral worth it is not enough for it merely to correspond to what duty requires, it must be done for the sake of *duty*. One consequence of this famous first proposition is that only a good will, and those persons and actions that manifest a good will, can be *morally* good, have *moral* worth or value. A good will is the settled determination to do what is morally right simply because it is morally right; another word for this is 'conscientiousness'; still another is 'character'. Thus Kant is drawing a distinction between an act's being morally right and its having moral value. Kant is saying that an act has moral worth only if it is right (in accordance with duty) and done for that reason (done from duty).

The principle on which a person of good will acts is called the Categorical Imperative, and Kant provides us with a number of statements of it, which, though they are intended to be at bottom one and the same, do not give that appearance. One formulation is: Act only on that maxim you can at the same time will to be universal law. Another is: Act always so as to treat humanity, whether in your own person or in that of another, always as an end in itself, never merely as a means. A third is: Every rational being is subject only to laws that are self-given and are at the same time the same laws for all. This is the Principle of Autonomy, the basis of Kant's concept that rational beings have dignity, a value beyond price. If something 'has a price', Kant says, 'something else can be put in its place as an *equivalent*; if it is exalted above all price and so admits of no equivalent, then it has a *dignity*' (Gr., 434).

Nothing can have a value other than that determined for it by the law. But the law-making which determines all value must for this reason have a dignity—that is, an unconditioned and incomparable

155

worth—for the appreciation of which, as necessarily given by a rational being, the word *'reverence'* [or 'respect'] is the only becoming expression. *Autonomy* is therefore the ground of the dignity of human nature . . . (Gr., 436).

This is clearly not consequentialism or any form of utilitarianism. For Kant the moral law determines the morality, in the sense of the rightness or wrongness, of an action, and some actions are ruled out as immoral in advance irrespective of any advantage or happiness thay may bring to no matter how many people. Kant's theory also provides us with another conception of value, that of *moral* value, which is held to be so far superior to any other form of value (such as economic value, aesthetic value, literary value, scientific value, entertainment value, nutritional value, hedonic value and so on) that no comparison is possible or even permissible. This is I think the origin of the idea, often stated through not well defended, that moral considerations necessarily take priority for a moral person over all other considerations, that *moral* values are pre-eminent.

Not everyone of course accepts this estimate. I once heard a television interview with Edward Teller, in which he first responded to some question of the interviewer (whose name and question I do not recall) by saying, 'What? What was that?', and then, when the question had been clarified, said, 'Oh, I see—merely moral objections'. Again, at the time of the Watergate scandal, Warren Burger, then Chief Justice of the United States, is reported to have said: 'Apart from the morality, I can't see what they did wrong'.

Kant defends his principles by arguing that they are presupposed in the common ordinary moral judgments of the ordinary good person, such that one cannot engage in moral thinking or make any moral judgment without presupposing them. Kant also thinks that an 'ought' cannot be derived from an 'is'; but his way of dealing with the is/ought problem is to maintain that these principles of morality and moral worth are presupposed in the moral judgments that all who make moral judgments actually make. This would bypass the need for any such demonstration.[11]

There is another difficulty with maintaining that only consequences have moral relevance, and that therefore antecedents have none, which is what consequentialism has been taken, quite properly, as maintaining. Some actions cannot be understood or conceived of apart from the intention of the agent. One example is lying, which involves the intention of deceiving, otherwise would be indistinguishable from honest error, which is not a moral fault. Sophisticated forms of consequentialism will have ways of getting around of attempting to get around this apparently minor obstacle. But motives, so important in Kant's ethics, are also held importantly by other thinkers. Thus Bishop Whately held that 'It is entirely on the motives and dispositions of the mind that the *moral* character of any one's conduct depends'.[12] Another point of consequence is that since only voluntary actions are the objects of moral judgment, this necessarily brings the matter of intent. Even a cursory survey of human actions and reactions brings out that intent can in some situations make all the difference. Whether one has been tripped accidently or on purpose is of vital import. 'Even a dog distinguishes between being stumbled over and being kicked';[13] and so, of course, do human beings. The purely physical damage may be the same, but the hurt to feelings—and the moral import—is much greater if the hurt was intended or is felt to be. A theory that ignores the role of intentions in determining what an action is, what actually was done, is in no position to determine or assess the consequences, and consequently in no position to assess the morality of the action.

'Tis a pity that Mill, who so unqualifiedly held that 'the motive has nothing to do with the morality of the action, though much with the worth of the agent' (*Utilitarianism*, Ch. 2, par. 19, Everyman edn, p. 17), did not face up to this and give greater consideration to the nature of actions in relation to agents. And it is especially surprising, since Mill's forerunner Hume, regarded so widely as a utilitarian, emphasizes the essential importance of character and motives in morality. Thus Hume held that

> when we praise any actions, we regard only the motives that produced them, and consider the actions as signs or indications of certain principles in the mind and temper. The external performance has no merit. We must look within to find the moral quality . . . (*Treatise*, Bk III, Pt II, sec. i, p. 478).

The conflict between consequentialist and deontological views of ethics, though an instance of a perennial dialectic of thought, is not really necessary, and a balanced view would select the meritorious elements in each. Because for each there is a great deal to be said—as one side of the story. Adlai Stevenson was given to saying 'We judge ouselves by our motives, others by their actions'.[14] As a statement of a perennial human tendency, I have no doubt that this is true, and there would have been no point in the remark—and Stevenson's remarks always had point—if it was something he was advocating. I take the point to be that we *ought* to judge ourselves and others by a consistent standard: if we judge ourselves by our motives, we ought to judge others by theirs: if we judge others by their actions, we ought to judge ourselves by ours. This is but a version of the Golden Rule, so widely accepted but so seldom practised. And we have here found a point where we can move from an 'is' to an 'ought'. All it required is a little reverse English.

III

All right, then, how are facts and values related? Can morals or values be derived from facts or otherwise established by them? I cannot do more here than provide a few hints and clues, but provide a few hints and clues I will.

First to the distinction, and the connection, between facts and values. The terms of the problem, in my judgment, have been distorted, partly by a confusion about facts, partly by confusion about values.

The concept of a 'fact' is both elastic and chameleon-like. What is a fact varies with the context and with what it is being compared with. A statement of fact in one context can be in another, or in comparison to something else, a statement of law, of morals, of values, of opinion, of theory, of interpretation, of logic, or of convention. And the term 'fact' has a multiple ambiguity. It can mean: (a) something that exists in reality; (b) a true proposition (as in 'It is a fact that . . .'); (c) a state of affairs; (d) what 'is the case'; or even (e) testimony (in legal usage the testimony of a witness is referred to as fact, with no implication that the 'facts' so related are true; an attorney in summing up might say 'The facts related by this witness have been shown totally false').[15]

In law a distinction is normally drawn between questions of fact and questions of law, with questions of law said to be for the judge, questions of fact for the jury. But what is a question of law in one case or context can be settled fact in another. John Lucas, in a brilliant paper of thirty years ago, pointed out that what are taken to be and referred to as the facts of some matter are what are not in dispute but are accepted by both sides to a dispute, and I think he is essentially right, though I do not think that that is all there is to *facts*.[16]

> A fact is a fact relative to a given dispute, or relative to two or more persons at a given time arguing about a given point. The points that both sides accept as true, each side will describe by the word 'fact' . . . The word 'fact' is an incomplete symbol; the complete locution being 'facts in respect of such and such a dispute' . . . (p. 146).

And on values as well as Lucas makes some very telling points:

> A similar variableness appears in value-judgments. Very seldom is the distinction between facts and values either as sharp as [supposed], or drawn where [it is thought] it ought to be drawn. Often the facts which we adduce to support an evaluative conclusion, are not absolutely non-evaluative themselves. In a dispute about a man's

moral worth we claim, and it will be conceded to us, that at least *this* action was generous and that just, and it will be claimed againt us, and we shall concede, that some other deed was inexcusable and yet another difficult to defend . . . (p. 147).

Two parties may agree that *it is a fact* that one ought not to lie, as a general thing, but disagree on the evaluative or normative judgment to be derived from that 'fact' on some specific occasion. Here what is supposedly a moral matter is taken as a 'fact', and no one has any problems with that. Is the theory of evolution a fact? When then-candidate Ronald Reagan was asked this question back in 1980, he said—and I paraphrase—Well, it's called a theory, isn't it, so it can't be a fact. Brilliant deduction, of course. Is it a fact that the earth revolves around the sun. Well, in one context, yes; in another, it is a theory or hypothesis.

A. E. Murphy more than once observed that every attempt to state the problem of the separation between facts and values 'is at once a distinction and a connection between' them.

> And it is only as the distinction is kept clear that the connection can be understood. If 'fact' is used broadly to cover everything that is discoverably the case, then it is a fact that there are some things we ought, and others we ought not, to do.[17]

A similar variation affects values. What is a value in one situation is a fact in another.

IV

A distinction is sometimes made between 'absolute versus relativist theories of value'. A relativist theory of value is one that maintains that values are relative to persons or to cultures, that nothing is good for or to everyone or in every setting. There is much sense in this, but generalization into a universal theory makes it so refined as to evaporate. Milk may be good for you; it is very bad for me, since I lack the enzyme required to digest it. This shows no more about the relativity of values than it does about the relativity of enzymes. If I did not lack lactase milk would be good for me, and there is nothing relative about that, though it may be somewhat speculative.

Sometimes by the relativity of values is meant no more than whether something is good or bad is relative to the situation in which it is performed. Customs, expectations, and traditions vary from place to place and time to time; therefore, since whether something is right or good depends so much on custom and tradition and the way it is received and interpreted in the place it occurs, it is held that morals and values are relative. 'In Rome', we are sagely told, 'do as the Romans do.'

But that, though sagely said, is not such sage advice. It depends upon what the Romans are doing. Though Caligula was a Roman that is no reason for doing as Caligula did, in Rome or anywhere else; and if you are in Rome, hard luck!—you had better get out before you become someone Caligula does it to.

The sensible interpretation of this idea is that 'the character of every act depends upon the circumstances in which it is done'.[18] Under certain circumstances one may be justified in telling a lie or taking a life, although in general one is not. And it may be right for me to do something, because of certain traits or skills I possess, that would not be right for another. If this were the sole content of relativism there would be nothing wrong with relativism.

Relativism is usually taken as the polar opposite of Absolutism, and if one is ill-defined, so is the other. In one meaning of the term, Absolutism is the idea that certain selected moral rules hold absolutely, no matter what the circumstances or consequences. Something akin to this can on occasion be defended. For instance, rape is always wrong, no matter what the circumstances or consequences. But not many act-types—indeed, very few—match this description, and, as Mill has pointed out, 'rules of conduct cannot be so framed as to require no exceptions, and . . . hardly any kind of action can safely be laid down as either always obligatory or always condemnable' (*Utilitarianism*, Ch. 2, para. 25, Everyman edn, p. 23). But it is certainly more comfortable, though not more reasonable, to latch upon some rule that seems agreeably easy, or difficult, to abide by absolutely, and maintain it as holding absolutely. This sometimes takes the form of maintaining that the standards and practices of one's own time or community are inherently right, while others are wrong, simply because they differ. Another term for this is *parochialism*, and it is put out of court by the fact that conflicts occur among the rules and standards so enshrined, and the selection of one over another in a case of conflict is bound to be arbitrary. The opposite of parochialism is another form of relativism, which holds—if 'holds' is the appropriate term—that there are no valid standards, because there are so many. This often leads to the *avant-garde* view that no one ought ever to make any moral judgments, because it is unfair for one to impose one's values on others. The incoherence of this should be obvious. No doubt it is unfair to impose one's own values on others—though this might depend on the nature of the imposition. But this claim itself presupposes a normative standard. Merely to make a judgment is not to impose anything on anyone. Both these views confuse mores with morality—what is or is thought to be with what ought to be—which of course makes them perennially up to date.[19]

V

In a letter to one of his correspondents, Miss Pauline Goldmark, written in September 1901 from Silver Lake, New Hampshire, William James said: 'Dear Pauline,—your kind letter . . .', and then interrupts himself with '(excuse pencil—pen won't write)'. Now what was wrong with that pen of William James? Was it merely out of ink, with no supply on hand? Or was it broken? Was it a defective pen to begin with? If so, why did James attempt to use it? Indeed why did he buy it in the first place?

I am not really about to embark on a historical inquiry along these lines, and now that I have introduced my next topic by means of this example, I leave James's letter to Miss Goldmark in midstream, as it were [and to the readers of *The Letters of William James* (Boston: The Atlantic Monthly Press, 1920, Vol. II, p. 162)], and go on to point out that value judgments, at least of certain kinds, are capable of being verified hence established beyond doubt. The judgment that a pen is a good one can be verified by empirical facts. If a pen holds ink without leaking, will write, does not splatter ink all across the page and the writer's hands, holds a plentiful supply so that it does not need refilling too frequently, lets the ink flow in a relatively uniform way, and is a comfortable fit in the hand—all of which can be discovered by trying it out—then it is a good pen. On the other hand, a pen that will not hold ink, or won't write, splatters ink, leaks or is too heavy to hold is a bad one.[20]

Similarly with evaluations of watches and knives. A watch that won't tell time or tell it accurately, is not a good one, no matter how pretty it is or how much it cost. It might be a nice piece of jewellery; it is not a good watch. A knife that won't cut meat and cannot be sharpened so as to do so, or whose handle starts to detach itself from the blade, is not a good knife, no matter what the ads said about it, no matter how much it cost, and no matter how much its diamond and silver handle impresses the dinner guests. Once the meal starts and they try using it to cut their food their 'oohs' and 'ahs' might change to uh-ohs, ouches and curses (expressed more silently of course). Similarly with hosts of other things or activities or persons. We need not restrict ourselves to functional or manufactured articles. We have criteria for whether someone is a good tennis player, a good philosopher, a good teacher, or a good student, even though some of these evaluations, such as 'good teacher' and 'good father', involve some measure of moral judgment, are not morally neutral evaluations. There are standards or criteria of evaluation involved in such evaluations, which are what connect the facts with the value judgment. A word or two about these.

First, something about the relations between objectivity and truth. Objectivity is a matter of degree; it is an achievement; not something one starts with but something one aims at. This means that one's personal predilections and prejudices must be kept to a minimum. For we are here talking about evaluation, which is a matter of judgment, not a matter of taste or preference. Objectivity is dependent on reasons and is a function of impersonality; hence it is independent of the person, since it is meant to be the same for all who would use or evaluate the thing or make the judgments in question. However, a judgment can be objective and not be true and can be true without being objective, just as a belief can be probable and not be true and true without being probable.

Second, a value judgment can be made intelligently only on the basis of appropriate and relevant standards or criteria, standards appropriate to the thing being evaluated and also within the range of human possibility. (Someone who says that no human being ever has run a good mile because to run a good mile one would have to travel faster than sound, may be drinking good whisky but is not exercising good judgment.) A value judgment is objective when related to and made consciously and deliberately in the light of criteria or standards of value which are sensibly judged relevant and appropriate to the kind of thing being judged and to the human purposes such a judgment can sensibly be supposed relevant to. In judging the standards relevant and appropriate, and determining and judging the relevant facts in the light of them, one is claiming that the standards are the same for all who would evaluate the thing in question. In this way, then, the standard is supposed to be and is regarded as impersonal, hence objective, and the standard in turn rests on a judgment, not merely a preference.

There can of course, be discussion and disagreement, sometimes fruitful, about the standards themselves, whether *these* are the appropriate ones or whether *those* are, or what are the relevant and appropriate standards. Sometimes we simply don't know, or else the topic is inherently controversial, as in at least the more rarified air of aesthetics. But someone who thinks that 'Roses are red/violets are blue/sugar is sweet/and so are you' is a better poem than any of Shakespeare's Sonnets, say Sonnet 129, someone who genuinely thinks that is, in Bradley's marvellous phrase, either a fool or an advanced thinker, and in either case is in need of a brain transplant. Just to heat up a cold January evening I shall declaim it to you:

> The expense of spirit in a waste of shame
> Is lust in action, and till action, lust
> Is perjur'd, murd'rous, bloody, full of blame,
> Savage, extreme, rude, cruel, not to trust,

> Enjoy'd no sooner but despised straight,
> Past reason hunted, and no sooner had,
> Past reason hated, as in swallowed bait,
> On purpose laid to make the taker mad;
> Mad in pursuit, and in possession so,
> Had, having, and in quest to have, extreme,
> A bliss in proof, and prov'd, a very woe,
> Before, a joy propos'd; behind, a dream.
>> All this the world well knows, yet none knows well
>> To shun the heaven that leads men to this hell.

When I read such a poem as that and experience its searing beauty, I think that talk of criteria and standards is out of place. We do not grade poems as we grade apples, nor should we. One must read it and reread it and understand it and feel it—and perhaps have had some experiences of the sort emblazed in it to appreciate it.

Yet consideration of the quality, the merit, the exquisite beauty of at least some poetry is also part of value theory, and is what is discussed in literary criticism or poetic aesthetics. A theory of value is a theory of the nature and basis of value and value judgments, for distinguishing good from bad and better from worse, and for determining how such judgments can be sustained in difficult or controversial cases. This can get immensely complicated, especially since there are so many different forms of value, moral value being just one type. That is why we should not let ourselves forget the obvious cases. Not everything is controversial here, or there could be no controversy; not everything is doubtful, or doubt could have no meaning.

Instances of manifestly fallacious reasoning to normative claims are not hard to find. I give the following because of its quaintness. You remember the famous 'Checkers' speech in 1952 when the Senator Nixon was running for Vice-President on the ticket with General Eisenhower; he saved his place on the ticket, and in political life, with that speech. Well,

> Mr Clark C. Thompson . . . chairman of the executive committee of the American Spaniel Club, heard the celebrated Nixon speech over the radio. 'When Nixon mentioned his cocker spaniel, it made me prick up my ears', he said. 'I liked his little touch when he said he was going to keep the dog, regardless. Anybody who feels that way about cocker spaniels must be a good man' (*The New Yorker*, 11, Oct. 1952, p. 26).

With hindsight we can see how accurate Mr Thompson's conclusion was, but the fallaciousness of the reasoning was evident *a priori*, with hindsight irrelevant to that. Now if some reasoning to normative claims can be judged poor, as can this, then some can be judged good, and there are standards for such determinations whether we can make them out or not.

VI

Do values exist? What are values? Talk about 'a value', which often goes along with talk about 'creating' or 'discovering' or 'changing' values, is difficult to decipher. Surely there are values, for a person's values are what that person thinks important, but this does not somehow embed value in the universe or give warrant for talking of values as somehow 'there' somewhere independent of us; and such talk, it has always seemed to me, is either nonsense or elliptical for something sensible but much more complex. (This may be why in Anglo-American philosophy the tradition has been more to talk about 'value-judgments' than about 'values'.) Values are not objects, and it does no good to talk of them as though they are. Values are relations, albeit complex relations, and are related to persons and purposes. This does not mean that a person's sense or scale of values cannot be objective, that values are ineradicably and essentially subjective. What was already said about objectivity applies immediately here. What a person thinks important can be actually and objectively and truly so, and a discussion about values is not and need not be merely a trading of prejudices—though of course that is often what in fact it is.

Do we choose values? Can we? People talk this way. Such talk needs interpretation. The new Dean of Students at my university has been quoted as saying that students 'have to make choices about careers, ethics and values'. Certainly they have to make choices about careers. But choices about ethics and values? All this can mean is that they have to make choices of fundamental kinds that will develop or stunt their ethics and values, that will require them to think in ethical and value terms in ways they never had to think before when they lived in the cocoon of the home. But to talk of literally choosing one's ethics is literally nonsense, as though one can choose one's values as one can choose what shoes to wear or whether to have sex tonight. One's values will be manifested in the latter choice, one's taste in the first. Given that a person's values are what a person thinks important, to choose one's values is to choose what to think, and this is impossible for anyone, no matter how high the degree to which one aspires and no matter how hard one studies.

So we can interpret what the Dean has said and make sense of it, though we cannot interpret it literally and make sense of it. To 'choose values' means to make choices that will reflect one's values and perhaps give one's values a chance to change in a better direction, which is in turn a value judgment about values.

I have seen it said, with great assurance, that 'An individual can espouse any morality he chooses'.[21] This is nonsense; not even the most devout believer in free will can believe that. The most it can mean is that an individual can do whatever he or she chooses (and even that is hyperbole). But no one can *choose* a morality. One's choices are guided by the morality one has—just as sometimes they are stimulated by rebellion against it. With morality and values we reach the limits of the commodities available in the marketing or consumer society. They are not for sale or even selection. One can choose to try to change the principles on which one acts, but this means no more than that one can try to change how one acts—it involves no change in the principles themselves, except that what were once one's principles are one's principles no longer. But one can no more choose a morality than one can choose one's beliefs or choose to make principles true.

VII

Certain confusions which are plentiful in this area can be avoided by taking seriously certain essential distinctions.

(1) First is the distinction between 'I want it' and 'It's in my interest'. The fact that one wants something does not prove that it's in one's interest; we have all had sufficiently painful experiences to make us aware of this. One may want that last drink for the road; that doesn't mean that it's in one's interest to have it, or in anyone else's for that matter. A few years ago in the US there was a television ad that was very clever in bringing this out. A man sitting on edge of bed, looking ill and awful, says: 'I can't believe I ate the whole thing! Did I eat the whole thing, Alice?' Wife, disgusted resigned look on face, says, 'You ate the whole thing, Ralph'. This (I think) was supposed to be an ad for Alka-seltzer, or maybe it was Bromo-seltzer. You see why as an ad it might not have been so good. But in bringing out the difference between what one wanted and what was in one's interest it was superb, though of course that was hardly its object.

Just recognizing this distinction is sufficient to establish a basis for certain judgments of value, namely, judgments of prudence. One can recognize 'I want that, but it wouldn't be good for me. I shouldn't have it.' This brings out the distinction we all must in sanity recognize between what we want and what is good, at least good for us. This in turn establishes a basis for some value judgments, judgments of prudence, which rest on a conception of what is one's own best interest on the whole. It is not easy to recognize, in particular situations or in general, what is in one's own best interest or for one's own good. It is in fact one of the hardest yet one of the most important tasks of life. Yet the simple distinction mentioned is sufficient to bring out that there is such a conception, that we all recognize it, and that there are occasions on which in practice we can make it out. Just how one's good on the whole is related to what one wants is a philosophical question of great difficulty, but the difficulty of the question is no reason for denying the reality of the distinction.[22]

(2) Closely related to this first distinction is that between preference (aversion, liking, disliking) and opinion or judgment. To like something or prefer one thing over another is a matter of taste. In the gustatory which is the primary sense of taste this is manifestly an individual matter about which disputes are silly (though they do go on). If something tastes salty to me, it is salty to me, even if it is 'just right' for you. Salt tastes salty, sugar tastes sweet, lemons taste sour, pepper tastes sharp. These are facts about taste about which few would disagree. But preferences—in that sense, tastes—vary, and there is really no occasion for argument (though they do go on). Where there are differences they are not, usually, over whether something in being sugared tastes sweet, or in being salted tastes salty, but over whether, as salty, or sweet, or sour, it tastes *good*. This is a matter of preference in the primary sense, over which there can be no sensible disputing, though there can be discussions and proposed trials that might lead to a change in taste. (I here put to one side the question whether something salty or sweet is good for one, in some medical sense, as irrelevant to the present point. I put to another side the sort of tasting engaged in by professional wine tasters, as too *recherché*.)

One can have a preference without having an opinion, and one can have an opinion without having a preference; further, where one has both they do not have to coincide. Plenty of people have been of opinion that sex was a bad thing and still enjoyed it. Newspaper item: 'What is your favourite Christmas song? You can call in your opinion [it says] between 6 tonight and 2 p.m. tomorrow.' Actually, that is not so; you cannot call in your opinion on what is your *favourite*, since you cannot have an opinion on which is your favourite. 'Opinion' here is out of place. The item illustrates how the two are often confused. Another newspaper item: 'We are interested in your opinion of which columnist would be of more help to you before we make our decision. So who would you prefer?' But the one I prefer might not be the one who in my opinion would be of most help to me. What am I being asked? No doubt those who bothered to phone in their—what was it, their preference or their opinions?—were not bothered by the nicety of usage that I have here singled out an abuse of. It is none the less abuse and confusion.

An opinion is something that is capable of being true or false, correct or incorrect. It contrasts on the one side with preference, which cannot be correct or incorrect, and on the other side with fact. Another word for opinion in this context is 'judgment'; a matter of judgment is not a matter of preference, taste, or liking, though someone's judgment can be corrupted by preference, taste, liking or aversion.

(3) The third distinction is between approving of something and liking it. To approve of something or someone is to make a favourable judgment of it, him or her; to disapprove is to make an unfavourable judgment. Approval and disapproval rest on reasons, though one may not always be able to make one's reasons explicit. Liking or disliking need not rest on reasons. I can dislike someone without being aware of my reasons for doing so, and I can like someone even though I disapprove of him, that is to say, take an unfavourable view of his behaviour, judge it bad or wicked or indecent or scandalous. To disapprove is to make a moral judgment, to regard as wrong, and a judgment must rest on reasons; if it does not, it is only a disguised expression of liking or disliking. Now one may have reasons for liking something or someone, but one need not; and on some matters, such as liking the taste of chocolate, it would make no sense to ask for one's reasons.

(4) Related to these others, though subsidiary to them, is the distinction between a matter of opinion and a *mere* matter of opinion. A matter of opinion is a matter on which all the evidence is not in and different people can hold different views, in the light of different interpretations of the evidence and different weights placed on them. God is incapable of having opinions; God knows. Sometimes a second physician is called in for another opinion, sometimes a third, though the process must end sometime. When judges disagree they issue conflicting opinions. But none of these people, if they are genuinely professionals, can think that the opinions issued are a *mere* opinion, that is to say, not something capable of being correct or incorrect. The way in which a medical opinion is shown correct or incorrect differs from the way in which a legal opinion is; none the less neither party to the dispute believes for a moment that neither opinion has any claim to correctness. Justice Holmes held a sceptical metaethics. 'Our system of morality', he held, 'is a body of imperfect social generalizations expressed in terms of emotion.'[23] None the less, when he was not expressing a metaethical view but was making moral judgments for himself—when, in other words, he was in the context of moral judgment, as he often was in his position on the Supreme Court—he took a different view, and necessarily so. This is brought out by the concluding words of his dissent in *Abrams* v. *United States* (250 US (1919) 616, 624): 'I regret that I cannot put into more impressive words my belief that in their conviction upon this indictment the defendants were deprived of their rights under the Constitution of the United States'. The words are pretty impressive; they simply failed to convince the majority. And the fact that Holmes speaks of his 'belief', not his 'opinion', solidifies the point.

A *mere* matter of opinion would be one on which no evidence one way or the other is available, no arguments, no reasons except spurious ones; but then the alleged opinions put forward are preferences under an alias.

VIII

We use the term 'ethics' to speak of a person's character, as honest, reliable, trustworthy, kind, generous, just and their opposites, either absolutely or in various degrees, and in sum good or bad. An ethical person, in this sense, is one who has in noticeable degree a good moral character, and who (usually) has this not accidentally but deliberately, because concerned with the moral character of comtemplated behaviour. Thus an ethical person is one who, completely by instinct or training and without reflection on the consequences of his or her actions, does the right thing, or else one whose conduct is governed by the concern to do what is right. An unethical person, on the other hand—and there are many about—is either one who pays no attention whatever to the ethical ramifications of his conduct, or else one who, knowing the moral dimension of his conduct, is not moved by it. Thus an unethical person is one who is prepared to lie, to cheat, to steal, to cause pain to others, on the slightest provocation or simply because he feels like it.

Character and conduct are by no means independent of each other. A person's conduct if informed, influenced, determined, by that person's character, and a person's character is formed, affected, modified by, can on certain occasions even be drastically changed by, the felt and observed nature and consequence of his conduct.

A person's values also enter into this equation. A person's values—what that person thinks important—are those standards, principles, ends, aims, and ideals that affect that person's conduct. They are consequently part of and enter into the composition of that person's character.

By reflection and the experience of life, either first- or second-hand, one can modify one's values, come to think that what was before thought important no longer is or perhaps never was, or that what was before not valued should be or should have been. In this process one's character is modified, for better or worse, and this has effects on the person's conduct, sense of self-respect, and relations with others.

Thus one who by such reflection comes to think it a horrible and unacceptable thing that there are people in the community—or in the world at large—who are starving or suffering or homeless through no fault of their own but by the action of thoughtless or heartless or careless social agencies, may set out on a course of social reform and realign his or her values accordingly. Things that seemed important before no longer seem so, but seem rather trivial or worse, while things that were never thought of before—the sufferings of people three blocks away or across the world—loom large as top priorities for action and for changes in social policy. The psychology of character studies the psychological mechanisms by which this process works. Ethics concerns itself with the standards by which it can itself be appraised as good or bad, wise or foolish, right or wrong. And one's own ethical philosophy, so far as one has one or has snatches or glimpses of one read about or studied in school, also plays a role in this process. This gives an especially prominent role to the teaching of ethics and morals and values. It is itself a moral responsibility, not just another academic subject.

Notes

[1] Imagine that there are just five trees in the world. Match up each tree with the number of leaves it has, and name each tree by that number. Then tree one will have 1 leaf, tree two will have 2 leaves, tree three will have 3 leaves, and tree four will have 4 leaves. What about tree number five? By hypothesis it cannot have no leaves, and it cannot have five or more leaves because of the hypothesis that there are more trees in the world than there are leaves on any one tree. It follows, then, that it must have either 1 leaf or 2 leaves or 3 or 4; we don't know which, but it doesn't matter, since no matter which there will be two trees with the same number of leaves. Now nothing in this reasoning depends on our initial assumption that there are just five trees in the world; it holds for any number. Hence if there are n leaves in the world, on the conditions of the problem no tree will have more than $n-1$ leaves, no matter what n is. And there is nothing in the reasoning restricting us to trees and leaves, we could have spoken instead of books and pages, *und so weiter*.

[2] In general, any theory that maintains that there can be no good and sufficient reason for a normative claim, that there are no sound normative or evaluative arguments, that ultimate normative principles cannot be proved, that normative claims cannot be true or false or correct or incorrect, that normative claims have no rational basis, or that the difference between right and wrong, good and bad, better and worse, is merely a matter of custom, convention, taste, feeling, preference, opinion, or tradition, is a form of moral scepticism; but moral scepticism can take still other forms. The present writer, whose name at the moment escapes me, has discussed this matter in 'Moral Scepticism', *Skepticism and Moral Principles*, Curtis L. Carter (ed.) (Evanston: New University Press, 1973), 77–108.

[3] I have here used and modified somewhat some ideas earlier presented in *Philosophy* (January 1985), 11–12. Let me add that there are at least three types of moral problems. Type (a) occurs when two moral beliefs clash, and one then has the problem of determining what or which is right in this instance. Type (b) occurs when a moral belief (about which one really has not much doubt) conflicts with a desire or aversion, and the problem then is

169

not—or not so much—to determine what is the right thing to do, as to *do* it—or get oneself to do it. Type (c) occurs when, as sometimes happens, the second type merges into the first, when our desire or aversion is so strong it leads us to question or doubt the original belief; this can sometimes be enlightening; it can also be corrupting.

[4] John Dewey, *The Influence of Darwin on Philosophy* (New York: Henry Holt and Company, 1910), 19.

[5] John Passmore, *Man's Responsibility for Nature* (New York: Charles Scribner's Sons, 1971), 44.

[6] G. E. Moore, *Principia Ethica* (Cambridge University Press, 1903) and *Ethics* (London: Oxford University Press, 1912); Hastings Rashdall, *The Theory of Good and Evil*, 2 vols (London: Oxford University Press, 1907)—see esp. Vol. I, Ch. vii, entitled 'Ideal Utilitarianism', the name that came to be adopted generally. An excellent account of utilitarian ethics is Anthony Quinton's book of that title—*Utilitarian Ethics* (New York: St Martin's Press, 1973).

[7] *Nicomachean Ethics*, transl. by W. D. Ross, Bk. I, Chs 1 & 2, 1904a. For the sake of comparison, consider the translation provided by Welldon:

> Every art and every scientific inquiry, and similarly every action and purpose, may be said to aim at some good. Hence the good has been well defined as that at which all things aim. But it is clear that there is a difference in the ends; for the ends are sometimes activities, and sometimes results beyond the mere activities. Also, where there are certain ends beyond the actions, the results are naturally superior to the activities. [This offhand remark by Aristotle is by no means self-evident, as Aristotle evidently takes it to be—MGS.]
>
> If it is true that in the sphere of action there is an end which we wish for its own sake, and for the sake of which we wish everything else, and that we do not desire all things for the sake of something else (for, if that is so, the process will go on *ad infinitum*, and our desire will be idle and futile) it is clear that this will be the good or the supreme good [*The Nicomachean Ethics of Aristotle,* transl. by J. E. C. Welldon (London: Macmillan and Co., 1892), 1 & 2].

[8] The most sophisticated account of this procedure is in a book apparently little known to moral philosophers or to philosophers in Britain, Felix Cohen's *Ethical Systems and Legal Ideals* (New York: Harcourt Brace and Company, 1933), Ch. III, Sec. 1 and passim, esp. pp. 115–126. The idea that was distinctive of Bentham—and, through Bentham, later utilitarianism—is the dictum that each is to count for one, none for more than one. In Hutcheson's prior version of a hedonic calculus, the importance or status of persons could give their pleasures or pains greater or lesser weight. See Francis Hutcheson, *Inquiry Concerning Moral Good and Evil* (1725), Sect. III, esp. pp. viii and xi, in Selby-Bigge (ed.), *British Moralists* (Oxford: Clarendon Press, 1897), Vol. I, 98–117, esp. 107 and 110.

[9] J. Dewey, *Human Nature and Conduct* (HNC) (1st edn, 1922; Modern Library edn, 1930, from which passages quoted are taken); John Dewey and

James H. Tufts, *Ethics* (New York: Henry Holt and Company, 1908; 2nd edn, 1932, thoroughly rewritten); passage quoted is taken from 1st edn.

[10] Kant, *Grundlegung zur Metaphysik der Sitten* (1785, Prussian Akademy edition), Vol. 4, 393; Paton translation, abbreviated in text as Gr., with page number given thereafter. Beck's translation is: 'Nothing in the world—indeed nothing even beyond the world—can possibly be conceived which could be called good except a *good will*'. And Abbott: 'Nothing can possibly be conceived in the world, or even out of it, which can be called good, without qualification, except a Good Will'. The German is relatively simple: 'Es ist überall nichts in der Welt, ja überhaupt auch ausser derselben zu denken möglich, was ohne Einschränkung für gut könnte gehalten werden, als allein ein *Guter Wille*'. It is the next sentences that are hard.

[11] Kant's other line of argument on this score is contained in his basic supposition that what a perfectly rational being *would* do, out of necessity, is what an imperfectly rational—therefore a human—being *ought* to do. Cf. pp. 28–29 of Paton's 'Analysis of the Argument' prefixed to his translation of the *Groundwork*, entitled *The Moral Law* (London: Hutchinson's University Library, 1948), and Gr., 412–414. A more detailed account of Kant's ethics is contained in 'Morality and Universality', Ch. 25 in *An Encyclopaedia of Philosophy*, G. H. R. Parkinson (ed.) (London: Routledge, 1988), 568–586. An excellent account is *Kant's Moral Philosophy*, by H. B. Acton (London: Macmillan, 1970). As mentioned, Kant's ethics is not the only form of deontological ethics. It is only (until recently, at any rate) the most difficult and complex. Another main form of deontological ethics is represented by the views of Butler (*Sermons Upon Human Nature*, 1726; 'Of The Nature of Virtue', 1736), Richard Price (*Review of the Principal Questions in Morals*, 1758), Thomas Reid (*Essays on the Active Powers of Man*, 1788), W. D. Ross (*The Right and the Good*, Oxford: The Clarendon Press, 1930; and *Foundations of Ethics*, Oxford: The Clarendon Press, 1939), and H. A. Prichard (*Moral Obligation*, Oxford: The Clarendon Press, 1949). More recent versions of note—though with them the notion of 'deontological' begins to get very slippery—are John Rawls, *A Theory of Justice* (Cambridge: Harvard University Press, 1971—see esp. pp. 3–4), and Alan Gewirth, *Reason and Morality* (Chicago University Press, 1978).

[12] Richard Whately, *Paley's Moral Philosophy* (London: I. W. Parker and Son, 1859), 14. Cf. Jean Piaget: 'All morality consists in a system of rules, and the essence of all morality is to be sought for in the respect which the individual acquires for these rules' [*The Moral Judgment of the Child* (London: Routledge & Kegan Paul, 1932) 1].

[13] Oliver Wendell Holmes, Jr, *The Common Law* (Boston: Little, Brown and Company, 1881), 3.

[14] Quoted in *Adlai Stevenson: A Study in Values*, by Herbert J. Muller (New York: Harper & Row, 1967), 277.

[15] Consider the famous opening sentences of the *Tractatus*: 'The world is everything that is the case. The world is the totality of facts, not of things . . . [L. Wittgenstein, *Tractatus Logico-Philosophicus*, Ogden transl. (London: Routledge & Kegan Paul, 1922), 31]. There is an intriguing account of 'facts' in M. Cohen and E. Nagel, *An Introduction to Logic and Scientific Method*

(New York: Harcourt, Brace and Company, 1934): 'It denotes at least four distinct things. 1. We sometimes mean by "facts" certain discriminated elements in sense perception. . . . 2. "Fact" sometimes denotes the propositions which *interpret* what is given to us in sense perception. . . . 3. "Fact" also denotes propositions which truly assert an invariable sequence or conjunction of characters. . . . What is *believed* to be a fact in this (or even in the second) sense depends clearly upon the evidence we have been able to accumulate; ultimately, upon facts in the first sense noted, together with certain assumed universal connections between them. Hence, whether a proposition shall be called a fact or a hypothesis depends upon the state of our evidence. . . . 4. Finally, "fact" denote those things existing in space or time, together with the relations between them, in virtue of which a proposition is true. Facts in this sense are neither true nor false, they simply *are* . . . Facts in this fourth sense are distinct from the hypotheses we make about them. A hypothesis is true, and is a fact in the second or third sense, when it does state *what* the fact in this fourth sense is. . . . Consequently, the distinction between fact and hypothesis is never sharp when by "fact" is understood a proposition which may indeed be true, but for which the evidence can never be complete . . .' (pp. 217–219).

[16] J. R. Lucas, 'On Not Worshipping Facts', *Philosophical Quarterly* **8** (April 1958), 144–156.

[17] Arthur E. Murphy, *The Theory of Practical Reason* (La Salle, Ill.: Open Court, 1965), 265. Cf. p. 267; indeed, the whole of Ch. 10.

[18] Cf. *Generalization in Ethics* (New York: Alfred A. Knopf, 1961), 13 *et seq.*

[19] Some of these points have been borrowed from 'Metaetyka a istota etyki', published in Polish in *Etyka*, Vol. 11 (1973) 121ff.; translated into Polish by Ija Lazari-Pawlowska and here untranslated into English by the author.

[20] It is hard to improve on what Kurt Baier has said on this matter in the chapter on 'Value Judgments' in *The Moral Point of View* (Ithaca: Cornell University Press, 1958). Another key work is J. O. Urmson, 'On Grading', *Mind* **59,** No. 234 (April 1950), 145–169. A brief earlier effort of the present writer's is in a review in *Ethics* **70,** No. 4 (July 1960), 330–332, of Alan Montefiore's *A Modern Introduction to Moral Philosophy* (New York: Frederick A. Praeger, 1959); the book seems to have survived the review.

[21] By Carll Tucker, in the *Saturday Review* (11.26.77), 5. For the antidote, G. J. Warnock's 'On Choosing Values' (*Midwest Studies in Philosophy* **III** (1978), 28–34) can be recommended as choice. On the matter of the existence of values a recent book that has given me pause is Hans Reiner's *Duty and Inclination* (The Hague: Martinus Nijhoff, 1983); my review of it, *Philosophical Review* **96,** No. 2 (April 1987), at 300–301, will provide the requisite references.

[22] There is considerable wisdom on this matter in A. E. Murphy's *The Uses of Reason* (New York: The Macmillan Company, 1943), Part II, Ch. I, 'The Context of Moral Judgment'.

[23] *Collected Legal Papers* (New York: Harcourt, Brace and Company, 1921), 306.

How to Reason About Value Judgments

I

When opinion polls are conducted on some urgent matter of the day (the character of Colonel Qaddafi, or the compatibility of some soon-to-be-married royal couple) those polled are permitted to declare themselves 'Don't Knows'.[1] It is usually a minority who are so ill-disposed as to forget their civic duty to have an opinion on each and every subject, and they can usually expect to be rebuked as fence-sitters or slugabeds. People confronted by the demand that they take sides can generally produce a 'view' which they maintain against all-comers without the slightest attempt to seek out confirmation or counter-evidence. Sometimes, no doubt, this view 'bubbles up' from the speaker's entrenched evaluations and opinions; sometimes it has simply been selected, off the cuff, from the available alternatives and entered in the speaker's 'axiom set', the things she'll say when asked, or which she may even 'act on' in some more material way—without any implication that the alternative opinion would not once have done as well.

People choose sides in civil, fashionable, moral or metaphysical questions very much as children choose which local football team they will (notionally) support. 'I'm the sort of person who supports Everton rather than Liverpool, pretends to adore the Queen Mother and detest Princess Anne, thinks that Qaddafi is insane and Gorbachev is a nicer chap than Brezhnev, and votes for Mrs Tiggywinkle while expressing cautious disapproval of her policies.' Or in other circles: 'I'm the sort that was born under Aquarius, thinks the military–industrial complex controls the Western world, and that the "scientists" are only not revealing their solutions to death, UFOs and telepathy bacause they're in league with the Freemasons'. Taking a position, like wearing a particular dress or choosing to drink lager, is expressing loyalty to a group, an image of oneself, a particular rhetoric.

Those of us who honestly don't know (and don't much care) which team or party or celebrity to claim to 'like' suffer from more than pollsters. Hesse's description of the Age of the Feuilleton, in *The Glass Bead Game*, comes to mind:

> Noted chemists or piano virtuosos would be queried about politics, for example, or popular actors, dancers, gymnasts, aviators or even

Stephen R. L. Clark

poets would be drawn out on the benefits and drawbacks of being a bachelor, or on the presumptive causes of financial crises.[2]

Those who possess some genuine expertise in one profession or craft may even believe that they have superior insights to offer about some other craft, but in many cases 'stating a position' is only to represent oneself as a certain kind of person, claiming the affection of others of that kind, expressing a particular but unexamined loyalty. The world of letters is awash with ignorant assertion and self-dramatization.

Can anything be said for this practice? Sensible people like myself, of course, would shrink from making ill-informed and impertinent comments on royal marriages. We might even have learnt, by middle age, sufficient prudence not to write to newspapers in instant judgment, one way or another, on the manifest misdoings of momentarily celebrated social workers, journalists or engineers. But even sensible people like me, or you, will swing one way or another on great civil or metaphysical questions. We do not invariably suspend our judgment on such matters, and perhaps we could not. William James, at any rate, observed that, 'if we believe that no bell in us tolls for certain to let us know when truth lies in our grasp, it seems a piece of idle fantasticality to preach so solemnly our duty of waiting for the bell'.[3] Of course we must sometimes 'make our minds up': never to do so would be to abandon all attempt to rule our own lives, would amount to a surrender to the judgment of those less humble or less cautious than ourselves.

Public-spirited persons must have a view, must join the game, because democracy itself requires us to make judgments on the rights and wrongs of public issues: the processing of nuclear waste, the likely general effects of increasing personal taxation, the right of Argentinians to claim to 'own' certain offshore islands.

> Seeing that, although the *polis* was frequently subject to *stasis*, some of the citizens were so apathetic as to be happy to accept any outcome of it, Solon laid down a law with precisely such people in mind: it stated that anyone who in a time of *stasis* in the *polis* failed to join in the struggle on one side or another should be deprived of his citizen rights and shut out from the life of the *polis*.[4]

In most such cases, we do not know what may befall, or what was done a century and more ago, or which paper to believe (and may suspect that neither does anyone else). Even if some promoter of opinions seems to us to have a good argument going we are uncomfortably aware, if we have any residual loyalty to right reason, that in civil matters any argument is defeasible. In logic or mathematics, what follows from true premises must itself be true, no matter what else is true. In civil questions (and indeed in practical engineering) what 'follows' from true premises may still be false. It may be true, for example, that the

174

increase of learning is a good thing, and that to experiment destructively on orphan children will increase learning: to that extent such experiments are demonstrably good, but other premises as indubitably declare them bad. What sounds like a good idea may not be, because other factors that the promoter has not mentioned must be taken into account. And how shall we ever know that no other factors are important? Perhaps that is one reason why there are infant prodigies in mathematics, but not in practical politics or moral thought: that such debates are never finally formalized. So democratic procedure requires us to take sides on wholly inadequate information, that we trust our lives and futures to bridges built by committee, and by committees who are never sure that they have all the information that they would need for rational choice.

In the absence of any firm and rationally incontrovertible argument for their favoured programme, the opinionated are likely to label their preferred opponents as irrational or wicked. We do not need to attend to any particular thesis, speech or would-be argument (and could not rationally assess them if we did), because we have already decided to reject everything that our opponents 'stand for'. Civil argument becomes the exchange of personal abuse; victory goes to the sermonizer with the thickest skin and the most strings to pull. 'No case', as the (no doubt) apocryphal advice to young barristers runs, 'abuse opponent's attorney.' Having no argument—strictly so called—for our opinions, it will also be psychologically tempting to suppose that no one could ever be in any better case. All civil argument must be uncivil, since disagreement must always be of the nature of personal abuse! To say that such and such an opinion is false, misleading, ambiguous or ill-defended is only to say that I don't like it, only because I don't like, do not choose to be thought to like, the sort of person who would say that sort of thing. As MacIntyre has pointed out,[5] when it is assumed that no arguments are available for any given civil opinion, disagreement must become a power-play, a rhetorical attempt to put one's opponent down.

Not everyone is ready to join in that game: despite Solon, and the need for citizens of a democracy to take a stand, many of us may prefer to mind our own affairs, and suspect that civil peace owes a lot to those who don't much mind how things are settled. But drop-outs and the domestically inclined forgo the chance of rising in society: most of those who get as far as university have been caused to think that they must 'have opinions' and must take a stand. What they often lack is any conception that the stands they take might be subject to more than abusive or admiring judgment. So when first-year undergraduates are asked to consider some civil question, they generally offer an opinion, at any rate if they can be brought to feel confident that this opinion will not type them as 'the wrong sort of person', in their tutor's or their fellow-students' eyes. Asked actually to think about the opinions they proclaim, they usually only tense their muscles. Pressed to justify them, they may feel justifiably annoyed: who is this fellow impertinent enough to criticize their chosen selfhood? If it had been an opinion about engineering or astronomy or disease, then maybe it could be questioned or corrected, but 'civil questions' are precisely ones that anyone has as good a claim to understand and answer as anyone else, since they are only answered at all so as to signal to observers what sort of person we are.

'His own thinking is of all things the dearest to every man of liberal thinking and a philosophical tendency', remarked Peacock sardonically.[6] Questioning that thinking is like criticizing someone's taste in indoor decoration, or her child. 'A person who arbitrarily chooses the propositions that he will adopt can use the word "truth" only to emphasize the expression of his determination to hold on to his choice'.[7] Holding on to that choice is to persevere in one's own being, and conversion to another creed would be destruction, and an unimaginable birth. Those who have yet done little with their lives may have little but those opinions, slogans, party manifestoes to define themselves, and be the more impervious to doubt the less they seriously think that what they say has claims to being 'true'. Those who are older have more secure identities, merely because they have past histories and possessions, and can afford a looser grip upon their chosen 'philosophies' of life. The vocal young are far less tolerant of subversive or disagreeable opinion than the old, though both classes may reject the possibility of serious reasoned argument.

> All empty souls tend to extreme opinion. It is only in those who have built up a rich world of memories and habits of thought that extreme opinions affront the sense of probability. Propositions, for instance, which set all the truth upon one side can only enter rich minds to dislocate and strain, if they can enter at all, and sooner or later the mind expels them by instinct.[8]

Though not everyone would choose Yeats as their example of a balanced thinker!

II

The complex situation I have described is part of the reason that A-level and undergraduate questions on Contemporary (and chiefly moral) Issues are so poorly answered. Another, no doubt, is just that the students are, as Aristotle thought, too young, inexperienced and over-emotional.[9] But all of us are coached to think that answering such questions is a matter of offering an opinion, presenting a 'good face' to the world, joining a particular party. In most cases we know ourselves to lack the concrete detail we would need in matters of immediate moment. We have also been caused to suppose that we should not concede the existence of any experts in such moral matters: if there are such experts, after all, we ought not to question nor anticipate their diagnosis. But without the possibility of expert analysis and criticism, all opinions, groundlessly accepted, are expressions only of personal endeavour. Moral judgment may occasionally be a sincere expression of personal emotion; more often it must be an arbitrary choice to be a certain kind of person, the sort that goes with those friends and not these. Where such judgments are made, as they so often must be, in a time of civil stasis, they amount to attempts upon the souls of others, trials to command. Emotivism, existentialism and imperativism, in short, are theories descriptive of contemporary practice. Asking students to say whether or how they would justify experimentation on human embryos, eating dogs, discriminating against foreigners or females, is an invitation to rhetorical indulgence. Even if the student suspects that reasons are being asked for, she hardly knows how one might reason on such subjects, and instead (at best) portrays herself as 'someone interesting to know', or (at worst) offers stale slogans from her chosen party.

One further feature of modernity deserves a mention before I discuss possible solutions to this problem. Even if the answers we propound to civil questions are arbitrarily devised, or merely expressive of individual emotion, nothing is to say that we should not propound such answers. Those who think that there is no objective element in our judgment of value may still make such judgments. Some of those who do so even imagine that we might all agree upon some shared list of really important values, rules that must be enjoined on all if any of us are to achieve anything at all of what we want. The rules of justice, on that account, are only those laws that desperate brigands might enforce upon each other for their safety's sake[10]—though why such regulations should have any moral force at all Mackie does not convincingly explain. Others, more sceptical of such a possibility, and still more confused, fiercely condemn all moral condemnations, all attempts to 'force one's own morality on someone else', forgetting that this is what they themselves are doing!

Even these (especially these) make moral judgments, and feel bound by them. But some students of these matters have concluded instead that all civil answers are bound to be ideological, bound to express class interest at whatever level. From this they conclude not merely that nothing is to be counted as 'objectively' right or wrong, but that they will support or reject nothing, that they will dissociate themselves from whole-hearted love of any cause, even while they support it. Such nihilism must in practice be eroded, sometimes quite easily by the mere reminder of what enormities are possible in human life. There are few people who can easily endorse (or not denounce) the torture and rape of children, necklace murders, violent theft from eighty-year-olds, or embezzlement of public funds. That there are some—or these events would never happen—is unfortunately obvious. Such nihilists, practising what modern philosophers seem to preach, who would do anything at all to serve the ends of their own arbitrarily chosen class, and profess to admire no one, must be the terror even of their present allies. After all, they have no argument to say that anyone, least of all themselves, should serve those ends for ever. They live above the law, and will betray.

But how can the great mass of half-way decent students hope to answer civil questions? Or contrariwise: how can those who set or mark the exams expect to get sensible or philosophically assessable answers? After all, there are some answers it is insane or morally corrupt to question, in real life: 'People who are puzzled to know whether one ought to honour the gods and love one's parents or not need punishment, not argument!'[11] Or if you prefer more modern cases: what should be done with someone who seriously advocated the murder of political opponents, the obliteration bombing of refugee camps, or the breeding of imbeciles for the use of experimentalists and licensed pederasts? Do we rely on people's cowardice or laziness to keep them from the acts they advocate? Can we concede any intellectual credit in such advocacy of dishonourable causes, or honourably distinguish 'academic' virtue from common decency? As Chomsky mourned, 'By accepting the presumption of legitimacy of debate on certain issues, one has already lost one's humanity'.[12] If, on the other hand, we ask candidates to solve some genuine moral crux, where there are many angles and possible solutions, to be distinguished, if at all, only in anguished confrontation of the concrete cases, how can we possible expect a sensible, abstract answer (it may be, of course, that the case Chomsky himself had in mind should really fall into this latter category)? If the case has a clear answer ('should you kill your mother to avenge an insult to your father?'), who needs to examine 'reasons' that will invariably be less clear than that one simple judgment ('No')? If there is no clear answer, can candidates be judged for not providing it?

One solution to the problem is familiar from our recent history: we could concede that philosophers have no special expertise in answering civil questions, and claim instead to worry at the metaethical domain. Civil questions, after all, are analysable into the technical and the ideological. Technical questions, about the cost or feasibility of bridges, kidney transplants or cuts in income tax are not to be solved by philosophic reason. Ideological questions are answered as well or ill by anyone. Philosophers should have no special views upon the great questions—or if it turns out that they do, we should be suspected of class interest. This option, however, has had its day. It was never very plausible as an account of how those people called philosophers have reasoned in the past, or what the would-be-philosopher expects to study. And plausible or not, it is now out of date. Plenty of contemporary philosophers purport to reason upon civil questions, and set examination papers on 'applied philosophy'. Indeed, it seems that we are expected to.

Granted that we ask our students to respond to questions about what to do, how do we expect them to respond? Another option would be to grant the claim of a Gorgias or Protagoras: the name of the game is 'Persuasion'. The sophist skilled in speeches, *logoi*, offers lessons in persuasiveness. How can we get our slogans and hypotheses entered in the public consciousness? To get anywhere at all we need, as Aristotle said, to understand what motivates our hearers. We need to tailor our speeches so that our hearers will acknowledge them as their own, so that they create the new identities for which such speeches will be natural. Handbooks on the art of rhetoric are relatively unchanged since ancient days. Even where modern psychological research is invoked to buttress this or that rhetorical technique, we are not surprised to find that the technique is one long known: tricolon structure, movement from familiar themes to unfamiliar, pretended innocence of oratorical technique.[13]

On this account, what students now are asked to do is very much what Roman schoolboys did: the preparation of persuasive speeches on absurd or melodramatic topics. In 'Sophistopolis'[14] and its environs we debate whether or not to keep a ransom promise made to pirates, whether to kill a wrongfully arrested Amerindian to secure the promised release of several, or kill oneself lest one betray one's friends. May I honourably threaten what I may not honourably perform? My favourite absurd example runs: granted that love is a sickness, persuade the draft board to excuse you, being an infatuated lover, on the ground of ill health. No one need suppose that what we imagine to be said in play is what we would say or do in concrete situations vaguely resembling those we imagine. No one need suppose that we could not change sides—indeed, the very point of these declamatory exercises would be that the students did change sides. No one need suppose that speakers should be limited to strictly logical arguments: on the contrary, such speeches, *logoi*, should be used as might persuade the hearers, not merely those arguments, *logoi*, as would convince a critical dialectician. The idea that only those 'arguments' are sound or serviceable as would convince 'just anyone' is one of those rhetorical devices, after all, brought into play to denigrate opposing theories, and carefully forgotten when we seek to 'prove' our own. We do not need to prove our opponent incoherent, if we can show that she is absurd; nor yet prove

179

she is absurd, if we can only convince people that she is subversive. Doing that much may only need the subtlest redescriptions of her thought or actions, or verbal association with some mistrusted cause. Teaching people how to do these things will make them more competent at their own speaking, and give them some immunity against the wiles of others.

A-level general papers, and perhaps some others, could well be treated as examinations in such rhetoric. The art is plainly useful, and not only to those destined for public administration. Rhetoric is not the cynical or frivolous embellishment of speech or writing, but the art of persuasion through the use of words. To show a cause to its best advantage requires us to tailor what we say to our audience, to make clear the advantage of our own thesis, and our opponent's failings, to make good use of a well-stocked memory of examples, to distinguish the questions asked at any given stage. It is no dishonourable craft. Essayists, like barristers and statesmen, should learn to ask the four separate questions: did it happen, what was it that happened, what quality was the happening, what should we do about it?[15] As it might be: did the accused take the money; was it theft; was the theft infamous; what should be done with her? Such rhetorical distinctions are the stuff of ordered argument.

But of course the enmity of rhetoric and 'true philosophy' goes back to our own rhetorical beginnings. Is it an appropriate response to philosophical examination to devise appropriate declamations upon this side or that? Perhaps it is: at any rate, the standard of response might well be drastically improved if candidates could be induced to argue against their own 'true' theories, against their instinct or approved commitment. This is not a frivolous suggestion: candidates who tried the task would really have to think, and might discover that the theory they had abominated was not quite what they'd thought. It might even be that they would learn the profound truth in Bohr's aphorism, that a profound truth is one whose opposite is also profoundly true.

Rhetoricians can point in their turn to the rhetoric of philosophy, the tricks and redescriptions by which we have distinguished between the speeches that persuade the masses, and the real arguments that persuade the wise. Part of our self-identity as philosophers has been the conviction that we will not be taken in, that we will follow the argument only where it leads, that we will not be caught out with ungrounded premises or credulous of received opinion. But it is obvious to us all that not even philosophy can be conducted on this basis. We have to start from our received opinions, from the world of common day, and cannot ground all argument upon strictly indubitable dicta. In one sense, there are no such indubitabilia (not even that I exist); in another, there are far more than Descartes allowed (as that I have two hands, and that some acts are sins). 'The attempt to think without presuppositions is unreasonable and vain'.[16] It is also true that some of the greatest of our philosophical texts are not strictly composed of arguments at all, moving by strict logic from clear premises to their conclusions: many of the texts we read with profit amount to rhetorical redescriptions of the world, attempts to make the conclusion for which the writer sometimes argues one that someone 'sensible' might entertain. All arguments strictly so called, after all, can be taken as refuting their own premises instead of establishing the preferred conclusions.

The gap between 'mere rhetoric' and 'true philosophy' is not so great. Rhetoricians and philosophers use speech to explore the human landscape, to tell stories, to make unexpected links, and open forgotten pathways. Rhetoricians do not need to think that what they say is 'true', whereas philosophers—at some level—scorn such make-believe. But once philosophers have abandoned the Platonic vision, given up the optimistic claim to see things 'as they are', not simply as they seem, how does philosophy differ from rhetoric? Modern philosophy, as it is professed by 'modern minds', is only concerned with our descriptions of the world, and with redescribing it. 'Interpreting the world' means only 'telling a fresh story', or 'telling some story that will fit in with other approved stories'. On this account, a 'philosophical discussion' of some vital topic must be assimilated to an artistic one. A candidate who is asked 'whether she would judge it right to betray her friends for personal gain if part of the bargain were that she were assisted to forget her act' is being asked to tell a story about herself that she could bear to live with. 'Truth is that which a man troweth . . . (and) thus the truth of one man is not the truth of another'.[17] To answer the question 'truthfully' is to tell the story of the one's would-be life, to offer 'the picture of the world which was born at a man's birth . . . that which he does not invent but rather discovers within himself, (that) is himself over again: his being expressed in words; the meaning of his personality formed into a doctrine'.[18] Obviously, A-level candidates cannot usually be expected to do this well—though it may turn out that they will have done it better than they thought, that the true and abiding outline of their personality will have been there. But their contributions could, at a pinch, be judged as self-expressive, Self-creative, essays. Examiners should not necessarily expect that these effusions will be more exciting than the laborious reporting of received opinion, but they might be more fun to write.

You will notice that this suggestion is the opposite of an earlier one: before, candidates were asked to speak on their opponent's side; here, they are asked to expound their Selves in words. It would take me far too far afield to offer reasons for my intuition that although the strategies advised are opposite, the actual results would be the same. Let them stand simply as diverse strategies, employed by scholars well past the examination stage!

III

But something is still missing. Even philosophers who admit their use of rhetoric, even those whose professed theories make it doubtful, or at least unnecessary, that we ever speak 'real truth', expect a certain style of argument in philosophical attempts at the great civil questions. Rhetoricians may explore what speeches, images, examples would in fact persuade an audience to disconnect or reconnect a life-support machine. Novelists or poets may seek to unfold what sort of person one would have to be to do the one thing or the other. Any of us may try to spell out what at least we'd like to think we'd do, and some of us will have to act in earnest—though we may doubt that any special argument will sway us then. But none of this is quite what the philosopher desires. Even if we lack the Platonic faith in absolutes, we model ourselves on Socrates.

> I'm a midwife's son and practise the art myself. When I ask a question, set about answering it to the best of your ability. And if on examination I find that some thought of yours is illusory and untrue, and if I then draw it out of you and discard it, don't rant and rave at me, as a first-time mother might if her baby was involved . . . I do what I do because it is my moral duty not to connive at falsehood and cover up truth.[19]

It matters to us that the stories that are told make sense, that the real implications of the theories are unfolded and do not contradict each other. There may be (almost certainly is) no one finite rule of action or belief, that guarantees a creditable or bearable result, but all the rules and images we use should mesh. If people say that terrorists who take children hostage and torture them to death deserve no quarter, it is up to them to explain why nuclear assault on civilian targets is permissible. If it would be wrong to serve 'roast sucking coolie', it is up to objectors to explain why piglets deserve no better. Those who reply that it is 'obvious' that the cases differ must dig a little deeper: who is it obvious to, and why?

Another image of philosophy to stand beside the academic rhetorician (who need not stoop to merely popular persuasive speech), or the self-dramatizing novelist, is the shaman.[20] Doubtless the thought is shocking, and I do not imply that all shamanic practices have analogues in universities. The point I mean to emphasize is that the shaman and the philosopher alike submit to radical dismemberment, to being torn apart and reconstructed, to the death of easy certainty and unfocused 'being at home'. 'Profound philosophy must come from terror. An abyss opens beneath our feet; inherited convictions, the presuppositions of our thoughts . . . drop into the abyss.'[21] We may relapse, like David Hume,[22] upon the certainties born of beef and backgammon, but at any rate in 'philosophical' mode we are intended to tease apart the tangled web of doctrine, habit, mood and inspiration. Doing this demands a willingness to be refuted in our most basic being, to find that we've been talking incoherent nonsense, that our life till now (and afterwards) has been (will be) a 'dream and a delirium'.[23]

This governing image, no doubt, is often as distinct from the reality of life for us professionals as corresponding images of 'scientific neutrality' are from the actual conduct of laboratory research. Fortunately, individual scholars and scientists do not need to be quite so self-effacing: our colleagues will do the destructive criticism for us (as we for them)! We are also fortunate that there are already great machines in place to check our reasonings and rebuke our pride: I refer not only to formal calculi (propositional, predicate, modal or deontic), but also to the great moralizing systems. These are the final topic of this paper.

The two such systems whose ramifications have been most thoroughly explored of late are the Utilitarian and the (so to call it) Libertarian. The former has as its central concept, happiness; the latter, liberty or natural right. Both are at once collectivist, universalist and egoistic; both have an uneasy association with liberal principle; both can sound overwhelmingly plausible; neither catches the whole, or any crucial part, of practical wisdom. Both, in the end, are either vacuous or obviously biased towards a particular, late Western concept of human nature and the universe. Their usefulness is as machines: systems that generate imaginable strategies in more or less orderly form, which no one but an abstract theorist could think of applying exactly. As Vico said, to bring the geometric method into the matter of how to run one's life is as if one were to take trouble to go mad by rule.[24] Just as physical theories may provide usable approximations, secure within a margin of error and circumstances, and still be only 'models', not pictures of reality, so the great moral systems are models too. Understanding what imaginably we might do if we were guided only by Libertarian or by Utilitarian policy, we adjust our action to historical reality, and sometimes correct our standing rules of action, sometimes stick by them none the less.

To amplify my somewhat gnomic characterizations, I must digress. The simplest of all moral rules is 'do good, and eschew evil'. Utilitarianism takes the first half of that rule and tries to give it a more concrete meaning: so act that more happiness is created than unhappiness, more pleasure than pain. Seek to bring it about that more of what is wanted is produced at as small a cost as possible of what is abhorred. What actually is wanted, or is likely to be wanted, must be discerned by present observation and biological probability. No such want is, of itself, of any higher standing than any other—though such humane utilitarians as J. S. Mill attempted, after Plato,[25] to suggest that anyone with experience would in fact prefer the so-called 'higher pleasures' (not necessarily at the cost of losing all the 'lower' ones forever). Sensible utilitarians acknowledge that we cannot, as individuals, ever be quite sure what consequences any act chosen from infinity would have. In practice, we must follow maxims, rules and laws that seem to have served well; in practice, our own moral satisfaction or distress will alter the simply hedonistic calculation; in practice, we should very rarely break established rules upon the pretext of a greater happiness. But the system does tend to erode local or family loyalties, deny sacred significance to promises or cultural taboos, and make all values simply commensurable. Which is why *The Times* Religious Affairs correspondent, Clifford Longley, was not, in my view, wholly wrong to describe (practical) utilitarianism as a moral disease. All peoples have their price, and must in the end be forced to accept what then they will reckon happiness, even if they hate the prospect now. What Amazonian Indians think is 'theirs', the land of their ancestors, the only home for them, is only a resource that might or will bring greater happiness if colonized. Imperial action does not 'violate rights', for 'natural rights' are 'nonsense upon stilts', and positive legal rights are to be accorded only when by doing so we increase happiness.

Libertarians, by contrast, expand upon the second half of the first moral maxim: eschew evil. It is not the business of any one of us to engineer the whole world into shape. We must concede to others the same liberty to act and live as we require for ouselves. The best available society is one that protects for each the greatest liberty compatible with an equal liberty for all. Each of us must be allowed an area of unfettered choice, and a real, effective share in the decision-making processes of all such groups as now contain our lives. That is the only sort of bargain, 'social contract', I could rationally be thought to have made, one that gave me protection from oppression and help in some extremities. Even if the bureaucrats, or aristocrats, or a majority of the electorate suppose that they, and I, would be far happier if they took my liberty away, they have no right to do so, they ought not. Happiness, considered as a collective good, is nugatory: my happiness, and yours, resides in actually living out our choices, and that liberty is not to be removed upon the plea that someone else knows better. Even less than utilitarians can libertarians conceive that there are moral rules binding even on solitaries: Crusoe had no rights to violate till Friday came, so needed no morality. Historically libertarians have restricted the class of rights-holders to the human species, and utilitarians have generally allowed much greater weight to the moral claims of sentients. But there seems no good reason why libertarian principle could not be extended; and it is unfortunately true that utilitarians need not, in practice, allow sentients so much moral weight as to stand in the way of anything we want to do.

These systems can be used to justify both liberal and illiberal action. Both tend to disregard the actual historical and personal setting as mere matters-of-fact without much moral weight. Neither can easily concede that some particular plans are right or wrong regardless of utilitarian calculation or value-neutral law. Both take it for granted that the fundamental goods are things 'good for' (i.e. desired by) individuals, and differ chiefly on how these multiple goods, enjoyed by different individuals, should be aggregated. Both seek in effect to be neutral about desires: on the libertarian view no one should be stopped from doing what they choose unless that action violates another's rights; on the utilitarian no one should be stopped unless by act or omission this diminishes (or fails vitally to enlarge) the sum of happiness. The law should make no primary moral differences between desires. So utilitarians should only object to gang rape if it is clear that it brings less pleasure for a greater cost in pain than currently available alternatives. And libertarians should not object to miserly or self-destructive action. It is not clear how long people merely raised to 'increase happiness' or 'not violate rights' could retain the virtues of courage, loyalty, temperance and common prudence, or any sense of a life well-lived.

Considered as machines or models, in short, these systems do have virtues: they serve to remind us of particular features that we might forget, of dreadful possibilities that we might realize. But it is not laws nor principles nor systems that take action in the end: it is we that act. We act as members of an historically grounded community, having ways of seeing, talking, doing that we could not create *de novo*. Our notions of happiness, and of liberty, are ones that make sense only in that history. Any duty we may have to universal happiness is a wild abstraction compared with our given duties to sustain the lives and welfare of our family, friends and fellow citizens. Our obligation to respect the 'natural rights' of all is of far less effect than our understanding of each individual soul as having her own duty. We do not have one rule only ('Increase Happiness' or 'Respect Rights'), but manifold associated rules that spring from careful virtues needed for our living well, in whatever way it is one lives. Crusoe needed virtue before Friday came: none more. Whether he could have had it if he had not first grown into a particular historical community, if he had begun *de novo* as an abstract intellect, seems moot.

The sort of philosophical sceptic who purports to reject all presuppositions is, pedagogically, a menace. In Vico's words:

> Scepticism, putting in doubt the truth that unites men, disposes them to follow their own sense, each according to his own pleasure and advantage, and thus recalls them from civil community to the state of solitude—and not the solitude of the gentle animals, which are able to live together peacefully in flocks and herds, but that of the huge fierce ones, which live scattered and alone in their dens and lairs; and the reflective wisdom of the educated, which is supposed to guide the vulgar wisdom of the masses, gives them instead the cruellest shove so that they rush headlong forward and perish.[26]

IV

So to bring my paper round again to concrete cases: how should two British girls sent back into 'forced' marriages in the Yemen now be regarded? How is the case even to be described? The Yemeni father doubtless thinks that he has done his duty, that his daughters are the momentary carriers of racial value, that they are lawfully married, with the appropriate bride-price, to men to whom they have borne children. If they are unhappy that is their error, their unfortunate infection by an alien creed which he had sought to obviate by early action. Their 'liberties' are not in question: it is only the deracinated West that ever imagined that mere individuals were sovereign over 'their' own lives, and even in the West the 'self' is being deconstructed by psychologists, sociologists, literary critics and philosophers. Who are you, alone, yourself and nameless? Is it not more reasonable, or as reasonable, to think of family lines, or tribes, as sovereign over the short lives that compose them? To suppose that a wife, mother, daughter could or should defy the patriarch is like supposing that the foot should not obey the head. Do even liberals really wish that parents have no authority to determine their child's future? Who else does?

It is necessary no doubt to emphasize that this is not my view. My point is merely that neither utilitarian nor libertarian doctrine, as long as they attempt to be genuinely abstract, unhistorical or value-free, can really answer the case. We need to admit to ourselves that what we here oppose is a form of slavery of which our own society has been guilty too; what we oppose is now an alien vision precisely because our liberties, as free-born Britons, have been hardly won. Asking what abstract individuals 'behind a veil of ignorance' would have chosen, is vacuous: such intelligences could actually choose nothing, or (if they could) we don't know what it would be.

All we have of freedom, all we use or know—
This our fathers bought for us long and long ago.
Ancient Right unnoticed as the breath we draw—
Leave to live by no man's leave, underneath the Law.[27]

The questions that must underlie a serious, philosophical discussion of the Yemeni case include at least the following. What sort of community do we desire or think demanded? What sort of creatures are to be thought of as decision-makers? Who or what owns a life? The Yemeni case can only be a cue for such a discussion: who among us can claim the expertise and particular knowledge that would make expressions of particular opinion more than impertinent rhetoric? Perhaps, after all, the case has been flagrantly misreported. Perhaps, as the Yemeni government is said to have declared, it is 'a family matter', which that family must sort out itself (but who sorts out family matters?). Neither liberal nor counter-liberal effusions would count as a sound answer to the philosophical question, which is instead an invitation to discover what presuppositions lie behind the different answers possible, to identify our own historical community as one human experiment among many, without thence drawing the illegitimate and incoherent conclusion that we somehow 'ought not' to judge the common practices of other cultures.

All good people agree,
and all good people say,
all nice people, like Us, are We
and everyone else is They;
but if you cross over the sea
instead of over the way,
you may end by (think of it) looking on We
as only a sort of They.[28]

But Kipling did not himself conclude to a deracinated relativism, but rather to the underlying force of the common law of humanity, the 'Gods of the Copybook Headings', the 'Law of the Jungle'—which is not the law of selfishness. Customs differ, and the narrow-minded mistake all such difference for wickedness or stupidity. But it does not follow that there are no such real things as wickedness or stupidity. The question is, what can we identify as these, and how purge our minds and characters of prejudice without thereby emptying them of what we should still know?

I remarked a short while ago that any reasons adduced for certain simple judgments (as that it would obviously be wrong to kill one's mother to avenge an insult offered to one's father) are almost bound to be less clear and less convincing. A similar suggestion led philosophers earlier in the century to conclude that 'moral philosophy was founded on a mistake'. Anyone who needs an argument to 'act morally' cannot be very moral; anyone who needs to discover whether or not to betray her friends will never do so by working out the implications of the Categorical Imperative or the Utilitarian Principle. Nor will any serious moral crux be settled merely by appeal to any theoretical system: obviously not, if a system does deliver one particular answer it will always be moot whether the system proves the answer right, or the answer proves the system wrong!

But the truth is that this is simply a feature of the human intellectual condition. The principles that explain why simple mathematical or physical facts are as they are will themselves be less immediately convincing than those facts. Sometimes it will be difficult to decide whether a theory's predictions falsify the theory, or the observational methodology we employ. Sometimes the point of a proof, in mathematics, is not to establish a conclusion, but to suggest areas of doubt.[29] It is very rare to find, in any area of life, that there are simple, incontrovertible principles from which we could systematically deduce all lesser truths. It does not follow that it is pointless to try to systematize our knowledge, check our observations and our theories against each other, ask what would have to have been different for another judgment to be plausible. Similarly in the philosophical examination of moral cases: the aim is to explore the might-have-beens, the yet-might-bes, of human life. Those who seriously attempt the task must end by being fiercer with themselves, gentler with others.

And even if they do find themselves adrift, and quite unable to give snappy answers to those curious people who suppose that moral philosophers must be moral experts, called in to unravel moral tangles, they will insist—if they continue in the moral enterprise at all—that there is something that it is to be just, that it is just to be just, that justice itself is not a matter of degree even if some acts, some people, some nations, some laws are more or less what justice demands they be. They will be confident, that is, of earlier, less systemized versions of the Platonic Theory of Forms. Further meditation on what the being of those Forms might rest in, so it seems to me, may lead them gradually toward the theory that served Europe well for two millennia. The Forms, the patterns of ideal activity and character, are the lineaments of the divine intellect, and true philosophy is the inevitably incomplete attempt to think like God, or (better) to submit our thought and action to the rigours of objective truth. But that, for the moment, is another story.

Notes

[1] Some of the material in this first section was first published as 'Having Opinions' in *Chronicles of Culture* (April 1987), 13–15.

[2] H. Hesse, *The Glass Bead Game*, trans. R. and C. Winston (Harmondsworth: Penguin, 1972) (first published 1943; translated 1960), 23.

[3] W. James, *The Will to Believe* (New York: Longman, Green & Co., 1897), 30.

[4] Aristotle, *Athenaion Politeia* 8: M. Crawford and D. Whitehead, *Archaic and Classical Greece: Selected Readings* (Cambridge University Press, 1983), 139. I owe this reference, and many others, to Dr Gillian Clark.

[5] A. Macintyre, *After Virtue* (London: Duckworth, 1981), 16f.

[6] T. L. Peacock, *Headlong Hall*, Ch. 14.

[7] C. S. Peirce, 'How to Make Our Ideas Clear', *Collected Papers*, C. H. Hartshorne, P. Weiss and A. W. Burks (eds) (Cambridge, Mass.: Harvard University Press, 1931–60).

[8] W. B. Yeats, *Autobiographies* (London: Macmillan, 1955), 469.

[9] Aristotle, *Nicomachean Ethics* 1.1095a2ff.

[10] J. L. Mackie, *Ethics: Inventing Right and Wrong* (Harmondsworth: Pelican, 1976), 10; see S. R. L. Clark, 'Mackie and the Moral Order', *Philosophical Quarterly* **39** (1989), 98ff.

[11] Aristotle, *Topics* 2.105a5f; see C. S. Lewis, *The Abolition of Man* (London: Bles, 1943) for what is still one of the best dissections of an unthinking and dangerous subjectivism.

[12] N. Chomsky, *American Power and the New Mandarins* (Harmondsworth: Pelican, 1969), 11.

[13] See J. C. McCroskey, *An Introduction to Rhetorical Communication* (Englewood Cliffs: Prentice-Hall, 1978, 3rd edn); M. Atkinson, *Our Masters' Voices* (London: Methuen, 1984).

[14] D. A. Russell, *Greek Declamation* (Cambridge University Press, 1983), 21f.

[15] McCroskey, op. cit., n. 13, pp. 47f.

[16] J. Weinsheimer, *Imitation* (London: Routledge & Kegan Paul, 1984), 27, after Peirce, op. cit., n. 7, 5.265.

[17] Peacock, op. cit., n. 6, Ch. 7.

[18] O. Spengler, *The Decline of the West*, trans. C. F. Atkinson (New York: Knopf, 1926), I, xiii.

[19] Plato, *Theaetetus* 151cff, trans. R. A. H. Waterfield (Harmondsworth: Penguin, 1987), 29.

[20] J. M. Glass, 'The Philosopher and the Shaman', *Political Theory* **2** (1974), 181ff. see S. R. L. Clark, *From Athens to Jerusalem* (Oxford: Clarendon Press, 1984), 208.

[21] W. B. Yeats, *Essays and Introductions* (London: Macmillan, 1961), 502f.

[22] D. Hume, *Treatise of Human Nature*, L. A. Selby-Bigge (ed.) (Oxford: Clarendon Press, 1888), I.4.7.

[23] Marcus Aurelius, *Meditations* 2.17.1.

[24] Vico, *De Italorum Sapientia* 1.75; *Vico: Selected Writings*, L. Pompa (ed.) (Cambridge University Press, 1982), 71; see M. Mooney, *Vico in the Tradition of Rhetoric* (New Jersey: Princeton University Press, 1985), 122ff.

[25] J. S. Mill, *Utilitarianism*; Plato, *Republic*.

[26] Vico, 12 January 1729: cited by Mooney, op. cit., n. 24, p. 101.

[27] R. Kipling, 'The Old Issue' (1899), *Collected Verse* (London: Hodder & Stoughton, 1927), 294.

[28] Kipling, 'We and They', op. cit., n. 27, p. 710.

[29] H. G. Forder, *The Foundations of Euclidean Geometry* (Cambridge University Press, 1927), viii; see I. Lakatos, *Proofs and Refutations*, J. Worrall and E. Zaher (eds) (Cambridge University Press, 1976), 48.

Freedom, Law and Authority

I: NORMAN BARRY

The State and Legitimacy

I

Despite the emphasis on the state in the history of political philosophy, the twentieth century has been characterized by a remarkable lack of philosophical reflection on the concept. Until recently analytical philosophy had eschewed those evaluative arguments about political obligation and the limits of state authority that were typical of political theory in the past in favour of the explication of the meaning of the concept. However, even here the results have been disappointing. Logical Positivist attempts to locate some unique empirical phenomenon which the word state described proved unsuccessful, and indeed led to the odd conclusion that there was nothing about the state that distinguished it from some other social institutions.[1] For example, its coercive power was said to be not unique: in some circumstances trade unions and Churches exercised similar power over their members. Ordinary language philosophers were far more interested in the complexities that surround words such as law, authority and power than in the state. In all this there was perhaps the fear that to concentrate attention on the *state* was implicitly to give credence to the discredited doctrine that it stood for some metaphysical entity; propositions about which could not be translated into propositions about the actions of *individuals*, and which represented higher values than those of ordinary human agents.

In all this, political philosophy was in an unconscious alliance with empirical political science: a discipline which has been obsessively anxious to dissolve political phenomena into readily observable 'facts' about groups, parties and other agencies whose behaviour was thought to be explicable, in principle, by testable theories. Yet to do so is surely to drain modern politics of its most salient features, since our understanding of it is not exhausted by a mere description of the actions of particular authorities. For authorities, governments and officials act under rules of an association, the state, which is quite different from other associations and hence there is a task for political philosophy to unravel the meaning of such rules. Thus although in the notorious Clive Ponting case[2] the court ruled that, in the context of the Official

Secrets Act, government actions should be treated as the actions of the state, this was merely a legal convenience. It prevented the defence arguing that a betrayal of government secret information was not an action against the state, but it did not, of course, tell us anything about the state.

Despite the absence of any philosophical guidance we do in normal speech, and in political argument especially, refer to the state as if it were an institution, or perhaps complex of institutions, qualitatively different from others in society. The existence of a state is not self-justifying, as is perhaps the case with a system of law. Although one can obviously protest at *particular* laws on the ground that they are not consonant with certain moral principles, it would be odd to suggest that man could do without a system of rules of some kind. The briefest reflections on the human condition suggest the necessity for some form of regulation: indeed, the concept of society implies a distinction between rule-governed, and hence more or less predictable action, and haphazard, unco-ordinated and *asocial* behaviour. The unalterable 'facts' of scarcity, ignorance, vulnerability and so on dictate the necessity for some rules[3] (whatever their substantive content); for example, laws that allocate property titles (though this does not in any way imply that they should be private, public or any particular mix of these two models of ownership) and restrictions on the use of violence. But do those 'facts' dictate the necessity of a *state*?

Thus the most casual observation of the features of the modern state, such as determinate boundaries, centralized authority, the claim (not always successful) to a monopoly of coercion, and the assumption of the power of law creation (or sovereignty) suggests an *artifice* or contrivance which stands in need of some external justification (from ethics and perhaps political economy) rather than something intrinsic to the nature of man. The very fact that most states are a product of force, as Hume argued, suggests this. Indeed, historically in Western Europe the state is a comparative latecomer, not really emerging until the sixteenth and seventeenth centuries. Prior to that, social relationships were regulated by customary law, the remnants of Roman law and Christian natural law. The idea that *law* could be deliberately created by a centralized agency was alien to the medieval mind; as indeed was the notion even of a 'country'. Again, anthropologists have vividly described 'stateless' societies:[4] communities regulated by law, and even characterized by rudimentary forms of 'government', yet lacking those specific features of statehood I have just adumbrated.

For what is so characteristic of empirical states is political *inequality*, the existence of a public set of rules that authorize some individuals to perform actions not permitted to others, the authority to tax, conscript individuals into an army and so on, but perhaps more significantly, to make law. The philosophical anarchist, R. P. Wolff,[5] argues that the state must be illegitimate since its existence implies the authority to give commands and orders simply because it is the state. Yet obedience to such orders cannot be a moral action (although it is presumably prudential) because it would necessarily be an attenuation of personal autonomy; to submit to authority merely because it is the state's is to eliminate moral freedom in the Kantian sense.

It is the recognition that the state stands in need of some extra-political justification that suffuses Nozick's *Anarchy, State and Utopia*.[6] For it is argued here that if one takes a rights-based view of morality, an institution with a claim to a *monopoly* of coercion must possess rights not available to ordinary citizens and thereby be immoral. Hence the philosophically interesting aspect of *Anarchy, State and Utopia* is not so much his justification for a strictly limited state (against the claims of a redistributive conception) but his attempt to show that such an institution can (logically) emerge by an 'Invisible Hand' process, in the way that, say, the 'money good' has been said to emerge in a free exchange system, without violating anyone's rights. Only then would it be legitimate.

However, the above reflections on the problems of the state may be said to be seriously deficient in that they illicitly pose the question of legitimacy in terms favourable to an individualistic methodology, i.e. the state appears as an alien entity, the justification for which depends on it being consonant with traditional liberal values of choice and freedom. Thus, so far from an account of the modern state in terms of the public nature of its rules, determinate nature of its boundaries, sovereignty and so on, being a 'neutral' definition, which leaves us free to evaluate its actions by reference to other principles, such as economic efficiency or human rights, it is actually already loaded with contentious assumptions about the nature of man, law and morality. There are surely other equally plausible accounts of its meaning.

If the state is then an 'essentially contested concept',[7] about which there are rival and incommensurable theories (theories which need not necessarily differ in terms of substantive moral and political values), at least two such claimants may be distinguished. I shall label them, for convenience, the *agency* theory and the *organic* theory. What is significant about each is not so much what they imply for practical politics but the accounts of legitimacy that they contain. From a consideration of these two rival theories I shall develop in a rudimentary way, a third notion of the state, not a hybrid but rather an extension of the agency theory which avoids some of its more obvious inadequacies. This third theory attempts to explain how that plurality of ends and purposes that characterizes all societies may be accommodated: a point obscured by the agency theory and denied by the organic theory.

193

The agency theory takes a purely subjectivist view of the state: it is a device or contrivance for transmitting individual choices into collective outcomes. If it is assumed that any society will require some public delivery of goods and services, the contention of the agency theory is that the state should be no more than a conduit for the transmission of individual preferences for these goods and services. The state has no prior validity independently of choice and its rationale is a function of its ability to solve the familiar co-ordination problems that confront individuals defined purely in maximizing terms. If all ends are subjective then it must follow that public institutions can have no validity prior to individual ends. A state does not have any authority or legitimacy by virtue of its objective features but only if it is successful in meeting individual demands. It matters little whether the state is understood as an agency to solve co-ordination problems (as in welfare economics) or a contrivance to protect rights (as in traditional liberal political theory). In both versions it can have no validity apart from that derived from the choices of individuals. Each is peculiarly 'modernistic' in that it presupposes that every social institution has to be justified by reference to human reason, irrespective of the 'non-rational' claims of history and tradition. It should be apparent here that a distinction (if only conceptual) between law and state is germane to the agency theory: for the invocation of the state as a contrivance which is useful for fulfilling specific purposes presupposes that the rules of ordinary *private* law for the facilitating of exchange already exist. However, the explanation of these rules in terms of individual choice is a problem for some versions of the agency theory, as we shall see below.

In the organic theory this distinction is rejected and the description of legitimacy in terms of the state fulfilling the demands of abstract individuals detached from any communal moorings specifically denied. Indeed it is claimed that the identity of the individual cannot be established by reference to his choices: these are transient, ephemeral and incapable of describing a person fitted for political order. The concept of the state must be located in an ongoing form of the political life which itself is the depository of authority and legitimacy. Hegel argued that: 'Since the state is mind objectified, it is only as one of its members that the individual himself has genuine individuality and an ethical life'.[8]

It is to be noted here that the proponents of this view do not have to assert (as Hegel does) the somewhat bizarre ontological doctrine that states and other social objects are real persons that 'act' independently of the volitions of empirical individuals, but merely that individuality itself only has *meaning* in the context of given social and legal forms. Thus political orders, and the moral foundations on which they rest, are received, not chosen: indeed it is claimed that the individual so

194

described in the agency theory, a soulless maximizer of utilities or a bearer of abstract and universal rights, is incapable of generating those rules upon which a permanent political order depends. *Government* may perhaps be treated as an agency charged with specific functions, but its authority is derived from pre-existing political forms. The state and law therefore are co-terminus since they constitute a total objective social order. The state, in this theory, cannot be treated as a mere contrivance, logically detached from a form of life and, in the popular parlance, 'rolled backwards' (or forward) according to a calculus derived from the transient preferences of abstract and fragmented individuals. It is not there just to solve co-ordination problems that arise in exchange relationships between individuals but a necessary condition for co-ordination to take place at all.

II

It should be clear that the agency theory of the state is not a theory of the state as such, i.e. an explanation of some unique political phenomenon, but rather a theory of any institution which performs those limited 'public' functions which essentially private individuals may require. In an important sense, then, it denies the *primacy of the political*. Thus there is no real distinction between state and government, since the defining characteristic of the agency is what it does rather than its institutional form. It is, then, a purely normative theory; indeed its lack of an explanatory component constitutes its great weakness.

In conventional welfare economics, various outcomes (or 'states of affairs') that emerge from the exchange process are compared in accordance with how each generates efficiency, where this refers to the satisfaction of individual desires, *whatever these may be*. These are the subjectively determined desires of the fragmented, liberal-individualist self. If the state imposes some state of affairs which is not co-terminus with those desires it is *prima facie* illegitimate. In keeping with methodological individualism, it is argued that when the state does not respond to individual wants it is not representing some *objective* welfare function for the community but only the subjective choices of the officials of the organized state.

The market exchange system is said to generate desirable states of affairs since it reflects the voluntary choices of individuals. But this must be distinguished from the utilitarian tradition, or more specifically its Benthamite variety. In this, an efficient state of affairs represents a *sum ranking* of individual utilities. However, such a sum ranking can only be derived from an interpersonal comparison of utilities, i.e. an assessment, made perhaps by an 'ideal observer', of how a particular government policy affects each person and aggregating these effects into a measurable social utility function. This Benthamite justification for state action, which persists to this day, is classically exemplified by progressive income tax: on the (illicit) assumption that everyone's taste for money income is the same, it is claimed that as income rises its marginal utility to each person falls so that a transfer of income from the rich to poor would increase *total* utility. In other words, progressive income tax hurts the rich less than it pleases the poor. Under this utilitarianism individual desires are conflated into a collective entity called 'society'.[9]

This approach is explicitly denied by individualist political theorists. If they are of the ethical variety they argue that the legitimacy of the state cannot be established by its maximizing a sum of utilities since such a process destroys the 'separateness' of persons and uses them as mere counters in the aggregation of total satisfactions. The more scientifically inclined simply reject the notion of the measurability of utility; it is assumed to be a private experience which cannot be calibrated as if it were the temperature on a thermometer. Thus the authorization of the state to maximize a social utility function is no more than a disguised way of licensing the 'ideal observer' to impose his subjective preferences on others.

The prohibition on the interpersonal comparability of utilities, of course, may have counter-intuitive, even bizarre, implications. For it necessitates the illegitimacy of any transfer of resources without individual consent, even in cases of dire emergency. To illustrate the implausibility of unsullied individualism the economist Amartya Sen[10] has pointed to examples of avoidable famines: cases where sufficient food was available to relieve suffering but the redistribution of it would have violated individualistic principles. The difficulty is that many individualistic minimal state theorists do justify the market system on *indirect* utilitarian grounds, i.e. the states of affairs generated by decentralized systems are likely to be better than those of centralized economic planning, as judged by an ideal observer, without assuming that they represent some 'objective' social utility function. Yet if this is an empirical judgment, as surely it must be, it can be refuted by examples of the kind discussed by Sen. However, if the prohibition on interpersonal comparisons of utility and the violation of rights remains, then the individualist is disabled from any critical comment on such catastrophic outcomes. Only if individuals expressed a preference for state redistributive action in such circumstances (which they might well do) would it be legitimate.

To retain the purity of subjectivism, welfare economists who write about the state adopt the 'Pareto' criterion (originated by the Italian economist and sociologist, Vilfredo Pareto) to validate collective action. The Pareto criterion prohibits any change from a given *status quo* which makes one person worse off. To the limited extent that it is a moral judgment it entails that any improvement that benefits at least one person while others are unaffected makes society better off. However, society here has no ontological significance: it is not a conflation of individuals into one entity, as is the case with some versions of Utilitarianism. Two further points may be added: the individuals engaged in exchange have no social attributes but only *wants* (which could be for anything), and the criterion is silent on the distribution of resources from which trading begins. The latter point does not make the Pareto criterion *necessarily* conservative: the *status quo* is not valued (or disvalued), it is simply where we start from. Any state action to alter an existing distribution without consent is not excluded *per se*, it is just that it is not legitimated by the Pareto criterion.

Although normally market systems maximize subjective choice, and hence generate Pareto improvements, there are circumstances in which certain goods, which are desired by individuals, cannot, for technical reasons, be supplied by the market. The famous 'Invisible Hand', which (metaphorically) guides individuals to an end which is no part of anyone's intentions, does not always operate so felicitously and has to be supplemented by the state: self-interested action by rational individuals may produce outcomes not desired by these very same individuals. Only the state, because of the universality of its rules, the 'public' nature of its actions and its claim to sovereignty, can supply the familiar collective goods of defence, law and order, clean air and (possibly) welfare.

But even to admit the existence of such goods raises an immediate philosophical problem for the subjectivist, agency theory of the state. For the person in this theory is an entity defined solely by his choices: his wants are private to him and cannot be 'mistaken' without invoking an authority independently of consent, and his rationality is understood in terms of immediate calculation only. Yet we are now told that as a member of the public there are things that he wants which are not revealed by his preferences. Does it not follow that the subjectivist theory is guilty, just like Utilitarianism, of interpreting 'society' as an untenable conflation of individual wants, in its assumption that the 'public' wants some states of affairs which are not the results of the immediate calculations of rational individuals?

It is this apparent paradox that has been seized upon by those critics of Subjectivism who maintain that it is impossible to conceive of a state that is consistent with the minimal self of individualist theory and that its legitimacy cannot be established if it is seen to be merely a conduit for the transmission of individual wants. Furthermore, if the self is identified independently of any communal features, how can an essential loyalty to a political order be sustained? For if obligation is a product of immediate calculation, the fragmented self of individualist theory will disobey whenever it is convenient for him so to do. Not only that but individualist theory, at least in its economic variant, seems to be unable to distinguish between authoritarian and liberal states since, on Hobbesian grounds, any political regime is legitimate to the extent that its very existence is a form of some sort of consent. The only consistent position would appear to be that of the natural rights anarchist who, while obeying the moral law himself, asserts that the state by virtue of its defining characteristics can have no legitimacy—a somewhat precarious position to hold given the obvious prudential advantages of having some form of politically organized community.

The agency theorist of the state holds that these problems only occur because of the fact that certain technical features of public goods make co-operation and co-ordination difficult and that they can be solved without invoking a conception of the self different from that described by subjectivism. These features are non-rivalness in consumption (or jointness of supply) and non-excludability.[11]

Non-rivalness means that once supplied the consumption of a good by one person does not reduce the amount available to others (unlike in the case of an ordinary private good). The information transmitted by a light-house and the deterrence effect of national defence are the classic examples. If a good is non-excludable it means that it is not possible to charge individuals for its consumption. In addition to the previously cited examples, clean air is the most familiar case of a non-excludable good. The problem is that if such goods were to be supplied through voluntary transactions the difference each person's contribution makes (compared with the potential benefit received) to the financing of them is so infinitesimally small that no one would pay. In the case of clean air, *a fortiori*, in the absence of appropriate *public* rules no profit-maximizing producer has any incentive to refrain from using processes that pollute the atmosphere; even though it might make him worse off in his capacity as a member of the public. It is thus said that in such cases, especially those involving large numbers, individuals have no incentive to reveal their *true* preferences: a potentially devastating implication for the subjectivist theory of the self and one, furthermore, which has Rousseauistic overtones. If coercion is to be used to supply public goods then on the agency theory the legitimacy of the state can only be a function of it satisfying the 'real' wants of individuals: a strange position for a classical liberal to adopt. For how can those 'real' wants be known if they are not revealed by subjective choice?

The problem of public goods derives from the familiar 'Prisoners' Dilemma' of game theory. Two criminal suspects have been arrested and are interrogated *separately* by the district attorney. If no one confesses then they are both likely to get off; if *only* one confesses and implicates the other then he will get off lightly while the other will be heavily punished; if both confess they will be punished. Rational self-interest drives them both to confess whereas the best solution is for neither to confess. But in the absence of a binding agreement to this effect rational self-interest cannot generate this outcome. It makes little difference if individuals can communicate with each other since the problem is one of ensuring that no one defects from the deal. It is easy to show that the familiar public good problems, such as pollution, despoliation of the natural environment and the rapid depletion of scarce resources, and even voluntary 'social contracts' between trade unions and government to keep wages down, are all exemplifications of the dilemma. Of course, the problem was originally diagnosed by Hobbes and his solution was a unanimous agreement to the creation of absolute sovereignty.

It is well known that in repeated plays of the Prisoners' Dilemma game (the iterated or 'Supergame') between small numbers of players, solutions can emerge and voluntary co-operation can get going without the state.[12] But in these circumstances co-operation is a function of the players knowing that the desired outcome depends on their individual contributions: if they defect no benefit occurs. However, what is characteristic of the social dilemmas described above is the fact of large numbers: one person's contribution makes such a small difference to the supply of good that he will have no incentive to co-operate.

All the agency theory shows is that there is a need for a state to solve such dilemmas but it does not solve the problem of legitimacy. For no explanation is given of how the state arose or in what form consent to it was granted. In Paretian welfare economics it is a 'given', an exogenous institution that somehow automatically satisfies individuals' wants for public goods. But how can it know what these wants are if the only acceptable mechanism for registering wants, the exchange system, is conceded to fail? If it is to sustain its claim to establish legitimacy on subjectivist foundations the agency theory requires some surrogate for the market if it is to function properly as a conduit for the expression of preferences. Otherwise, no distinction can be made between liberal and authoritarian states since they both rest on the same foundations, i.e. 'imaginary' consent.

It is also the case that the distinction between state and law which is crucial to the agency theory is difficult to sustain in the face of Prisoners' Dilemmas. Since a market system requires two essential features, the protection of legitimately acquired property and rules to enforce contracts, for it to be viable, it surely follows that a system of law is therefore a public good to be supplied by, and totally dependent on, the state? If this is so, then 'politics' precedes exchange and the claim that

199

legitimacy can be established on subjectivist foundations looks dubious.

III

The organic theory of the state seeks to establish legitimacy by reference to authority rather than individual choice. The primary argument here is that the whole notion of authority must be rooted in specific historical experience and in traditional structures of rules: and these must precede the notion of individuality. What is specifically excluded is a criterion of legitimacy that has a pretence to a *universal* validity; whether such a purported validity is parasitic upon man as a utility-maximizer or the bearer of natural rights is immaterial. Rather than individuals delegating authority to the state to do certain things, the authority of the state is said to exist prior to the actions of its officials. An obvious implication of this is that the social contract, the device often recommended as a solution to the public good problem, cannot be a grounding for legitimacy since it attempts to derive authority from a moral vacuum. The organic theory trades heavily on the obvious fact that the description of a continuing political order (or any public institution) will be in terms of concepts not readily translatable into those describing individual volitions and intentions.[13] To suppose, then, that the legitimacy of a social institution is deliberately chosen or intended is a peculiar form of individualistic rationalism. The nature of political institutions is that they are essentially *public*, and the validity of them is not a function of subjective choice.

If the conditions and circumstances that determine the legitimacy of the state are neither chosen nor intended, how then are they understood? In Roger Scruton's political theory, men's obligations are defined by particular facts rather than any purportedly universal features of the human condition:

> Their very existence is burdened with a debt of love and gratitude, and it is in responding to that burden that they begin to recognize the power of 'ought'. This is not the abstract universal 'ought' of liberal theory . . . but the concrete, immediate 'ought' of family attachments. It is the 'ought' of piety, which recognizes local, transitory and historically conditioned social bonds.[14]

The origins of these thoughts lie, of course, in Hegel's idea of the 'ethical state': a form of political organization which unites the subjective self of whim and inclination with the objective self subject to concretized obligations. Obedience to this form of organization does not diminish freedom because the 'negative' freedom of liberal theory is illusory: it is a notion of liberty that is realized only in the satisfaction of momentary, ephemeral desires. It is these ephemeral desires that caused the problems of public goods.

It should be noted that the view of political authority here is not necessarily conservative in a *substantive sense*. In fact it can easily be made consistent with the features of a classical liberal order, private property, market exchange, the rule of law and so on, but the moral value of these phenomena is a function of a continuing tradition of authority rather than some notion of indefeasible individualistic claims. It is also the case that not dissimilar anti-individualistic theoretical views are espoused by left-wing thinkers. Alasdair Macintyre, for example, in *After Virtue* claims that: 'All attempts to elucidate the notion of personal identity independently of and in isolation from the notions of narrative, intelligibility and accountability are bound to fail'.[15] This in effect means that the 'abstract' individual is unintelligible and that the narrative structure of the self can only be established by reference to concrete communities.

On all of those views, political philosophy should be concerned with the investigation of forms of life and the *meanings* of rules, institutions and practices integral to them, of which politics is simply one aspect. One implication of such an investigation would be that the distinction between law and state (which is germane to the agency theory) is fallacious precisely because it fragments the self into private and public capacities when, it is claimed, all political and social life is necessarily public. Put more prosaically, this means that there never was a set of private rules which existed independently of some public authorization and, more precisely, *enforcement*. Thus, although it might look as if the Common Law preceded what we now think of the state, this is only because we tend to think of the state in modernistic (i.e. liberal) terms as a mere agency.

It does not follow necessarily from the organic theory that a critical attitude towards politics is excluded. The exploration of the meanings inherent in a form of life will itself reveal principles and values relevant to the evaluation of political action. In a familiar example, the imposition of a *laissez faire* economy on an ongoing form of political life may very well be condemnable. This would be so if it failed to inculcate a sense of community, by, for example, excluding sections of the population from political life because of their inability to survive in the market. A free market society which rejected any bonds other than those associated with the cash nexus would simply reproduce that alienation which the state exists to overcome. What is excluded is the limitation of the state's authority by abstract principles. We cannot stand outside a given, objective political order (and its history) and evaluate it by values external to it.

201

However persuasive this account of political order may be it is vulnerable to a crucially important criticism from the agency theory. It is that by refusing to separate out the various aspect of 'governing' into legal and political modes the organic theory disables itself from a sustained critical analysis of the actions of the officials of the state. For while it may make sense to describe the state in terms of an objective structure of rules, it is also the case that it is manned by individuals whose behaviour can be analysed (and indeed interpreted in predictive terms) with the utility-maximizing theory of liberal-individualist political economy. Decisions made by officials of the state, although they are authorized by pre-existing rules, are nevertheless, subjective decisions. States do not 'act'. It is claimed of course, by organic theorists that 'governments' can be criticized if they do not reproduce the 'ends' inherent in a political form of life, but what are those ends if they are not the subjective choices of individuals? Since no real distinction is made between state and law there can be no theoretical limits on state action in the organic theory. Thus this theory turns out to be merely an account of what the state *is*, rather than a normative theory of the legitimacy of its actions. Just because the state's actions are 'right', since they proceed from an objective authority, it does not follow that they are immune from criticism, or that the structure of authority is itself the sole depository of rationality.

IV

There is, however, a possibility of an account of the state that recognizes the deficiencies of both theories: a theory that accepts the necessity of understanding human action within the context of given rules and practices yet which tries to show that the actions of the state must in some way reflect individual wants if an uncritical authoritarianism is to be avoided.

The major difficulty with the agency theory is its attempt to locate the legitimacy of all political action only in some notion of 'efficiency', where this means the satisfaction of subjectively determined wants. However, it is impossible to explain the rationale of a legal system in these terms and the actions of the state (as an agency) in the delivery of public goods are hard to reconcile with the rigorous individualism that is implied by the theory.

Nevertheless, once the concept of efficiency in terms of (conscious) individual choice in the above sense is abandoned the main elements of the theory remain intact. As the critics of the agency theory have shown, social institutions do precede individual choice. However, this fact need not imply that they cannot be given a (methodological) individualistic explanation or that society is somehow superior to the individual. Many of our legal and social institutions can be explained hypothetically in an *evolutionary* manner as solutions to co-ordination problems. The prime example is the development of the Common Law: a body of rules that has emerged independently of the state. Though it is clearly not without its flaws, and is sometimes in need of correction by statute, the *meaning* of its rules is not a function of the state's coercive authority. It does represent an 'aggregate' structure characterized by regularity and some predictability; to that extent it is an 'objective' order even though it emerged as a consequence of the actions of innumerable individuals. It is not legitimate because it emerged as a total structure from some deliberate act of choice or out of a social contract, but because it has succeeded over a period of time in co-ordinating human activity. Whether or not it is 'efficient' in the technical sense used by welfare economists is immaterial.

Indeed, the very existence of such phenomena as equilibrating markets and Common Law systems attests to the fact that 'Prisoners' Dilemmas' are constantly being solved in the process of social development. The emergence of social rules as *conventions* in which individuals have a direct (or indirect) interest in following may be interpreted as an example of an iterated Prisoners' Dilemma game producing solutions to co-ordination problems.[16] This secures the individualistic foundation for order (at least in an ontological sense) without presupposing that it has to be efficient on the criterion of *abstract* choice. Thus the kernel of truth in the organic theory, that we inhabit social orders not directly of our own making, can be retained without committing ourselves to some of the other implications of that approach (especially the argument that the legitimacy of the state can *only* be derived from tradition).

The state itself can then be seen as a kind of superstructure imposed on a pre-existing set of rules. Whether its presence is originally a product of force (as Hume, and others, maintained) or evolved by some 'natural' process, its activities still require some rationale. While there is considerable truth in the welfare economist's claim that it is required to provide public goods because of the danger of free-riders, this alone cannot explain its legitimacy. This is because in the absence of a market it can never be known what the optimal supply of a public good is. The claim that the state acts to provide some *scientific* solution to the problem of market failure is fallacious: the absence of a device for the determination of the solution means that the state's actions are no more than the subjective preferences of its officials. A more plausible view of the legitimacy of state action would be one that retained the basic notion of the state as an agency but saw its role in *procedural* terms rather than in the production of 'efficient' states of affairs. Since it can never be known what the efficient outcome of a social and economic process is, a legitimate political order would be one which permitted a *variety* of outcomes or states of affairs to emerge from individuals interacting under common rules. In this 'constitutional state' private and public law are theoretically distinct and the structure of public rules, ideally, should be one that prevents no one conception of the 'good' predominating over others. If it is the case that we live in a world of incommensurable values, between which reason cannot adjudicate, then constitutionalism is necessarily required to prevent those who operate the machinery of the modern state from imposing their subjective conceptions of the good on others. It follows that the 'constitutional state' is a form of democracy, but its rules will be more complex than simple majority rule precisely because this latter, if restrained by no other rule, has the propensity to generate coalitions of groups that coagulate the naturally co-ordinating processes that occur under the rules of private law. One important feature of the constitutional state will be special procedures for the protection of private law, for in the absence of these the imposition of one particular conception of the good on others is more likely.

This concept of the state is not therefore the limited state of conventional classical liberal theory, a state confined to the 'efficient' production of public goods by reference to the rational principles of welfare economics, since these limits cannot be determined by abstract theory. It is quite permissible for its actions to be legitimate in such fields of, say, education, welfare and income redistribution, which go beyond the liberal's rationalist conception of public goods, so long as these actions are consonant with constitutional procedures.[17] Thus although the state, unlike a general system of law, can be, metaphorically, 'rolled back and forward', its movements are ultimately controlled by the demands of *consent* (albeit a more rigorous version of consent than obtains in most existing states). The activities of the state are not legitimate because of some 'outcome' that it may generate (as a surrogate for the market) but because they are consistent with a *procedure*. The specifically liberal aspect of this derives not from economics but from ethics, namely that the procedure should not be one which permits one economic and political philosophy (be it *laissez faire*, socialism or any other substantive political and economic creed) to dominate over others.

The difficulty with the organic theory of the state is that because it locates political morality in particular institutional forms, and relegates subjective choice to a secondary role in social life, it removes the possibility of rational criticism. If the state embodies objective morality, and private individuals merely express subjective preferences, then it clearly cannot be neutral between individuals. If we live in a world of incommensurable values, as the genuine liberal-individualist believes, then a state authorized to act because it claims a prior claim to moral knowledge, must be guarded against. Not only that, but there is always the objection that in reality such alleged objective knowledge is merely as official's or legislator's opinion. Only a 'constitutional state', limited by general rules, can be prevented from becoming a caste or interest in its own right: a fear shared by both liberals and Marxists. If there is such a thing as a 'neutral state', i.e. a form of political organization that recognizes the diversity of men's values and purposes, it can only be in this form.

The state thus described remains as a kind of artifice the rationale of which lies in the fact that it is required to service the inevitably 'public' aspects of social life. The ethical anarchist would no doubt remain unconvinced of its legitimacy since the essential inequality of power remains. But in the constitutional state it is mitigated by the fact that in principle its structure prevents the elevation of one set of values over all others. Indeed, its rule-governed mode of organization is a specific recognition of the plurality of men's goals: something absent from the 'ethical state'. Furthermore, the inequality of power is tempered by the equality of citizenship that the constitutional state exhibits, in contrast to the notions of *status* and *hierarchy* that characterize other forms of political organization.

Existing states display these features in a somewhat attenuated form but, nevertheless, it seems to me that they are implicit in the Western political tradition.

Notes

[1] T. D. Weldon, *The Vocabulary of Politics* (Harmondsworth: Penguin, 1953), 46–49.

[2] For a discussion of this case, see Gillian Peele, 'The State and Civil Liberties', in *Developments in British Politics 2*, H. Drucker, P. Dunleavy, A. Gamble and G. Peele (eds) (London: Macmillan, 1986), 163.

[3] H. L. A. Hart, *The Concept of Law* (Oxford: Clarendon Press, 1961).

[4] H. Krader, *The Formation of the State* (New Jersey: Prentice-Hall, 1968).

[5] *In Defence of Anarchism* (New York: Harper Colophan, 1976).

[6] New York: Basic Books, 1974.

[7] See J. Gray, 'Political Power, Social Theory and Essential Contestability', in *The Nature of Political Theory*, D. Miller and L. Siedentop (eds) (Oxford: Clarendon Press, 1983), 75–102.

[8] G. W. F. Hegel, *Philosophy of Right* (Oxford: Clarendon Press, 1952), 156.

[9] J. Rawls, *A Theory of Justice* (Oxford: Clarendon Press), 22–26.

[10] A. K. Sen, *Poverty and Famines: An Essay on Entitlement and Deprivation* (Oxford: Clarendon Press, 1981).

[11] See Yew-Kwang Ng, *Welfare Economics* (London: Macmillan, 1979), Ch. 8.

[12] See R. Sugden, *The Economics of Rights, Co-operation and Welfare* (Oxford: Blackwell, 1986).

[13] See M. Mandelbaum, 'Societal Facts', in *The Philosophy of Social Explanation*, Alan Ryan (ed.) (London: Oxford University Press, 1973), 105–118.

[14] R. Scruton, *The Meaning of Conservatism*, 2nd edn (London: Macmillan, 1980), 201–202.

[15] A. Macintyre, *After Virtue* (London: Duckworth, 1981), 195.

[16] R. Sugden, *The Economics of Rights, Co-operation and Welfare*, 31–33. This excellent book contains a technical explanation of how solutions to co-ordination problems can emerge in an evolutionary manner; and some splendid examples.

[17] For a contemporary statement of liberal constitutionalism, see J. Buchanan, *The Limits of Liberty* (Chicago: University of Chicago Press, 1975).

Liberalism and Liberty: the Fragility of a Tradition

My discussion in this lecture is structured as follows. In section 1 I consider the nature of philosophical enquiry and its affinity to liberalism. In section 2 I lay out some of the basic components of liberal theory and explore their interrelations. In section 3 I discuss two challenges to liberalism: one concerning the conception of liberty which it involves and one concerning the way in which it introduces the idea of legitimate political authority. In section 4 I suggest that these problems, to do with the values of liberalism, arise on the basis of a prior conception of individuals which is in need of modification. In a brief concluding section 5 I indicate the need for a post-liberal political theory.

1. Philosophical Enquiry and Liberalism

There are two contrasting images of the nature of philosophy which are sometimes encountered. According to the first image, the subect is essentially radical and subversive. It involves a probing and questioning of received wisdom, an upsetting of preconceived opinions. In that spirit we might be referred to the gadfly activities of Socrates, the father of our subject, and we might be reminded that he was put to death for, amongst other things, corrupting the minds of the young. If this image of the subject were accurate, then according to our own lights we might regard it as a providing either a refreshing challenge to existing orthodoxy or a dangerous attack on vital values and beliefs. In any event, we might then be induced to tread cautiously when it was a matter of teaching philosophy, and especially political philosophy, to pupils at school.

But is this first image accurate? Co-existing with it is the second image of the subject, which depicts it as being, on the contrary, essentially conservative. It involves contemplative study rather than practice, thought rather than action. In that spirit we might recall the remark of Wittgenstein's that philosophy 'leaves everything as it is' (Wittgenstein, 1953, para. 124), or a much-misunderstood observation of Karl Marx's: 'The philosophers have only *interpreted* the world in various ways; the point is, to *change* it' (Marx, 1845, 402). I am also reminded of a slogan which appeared on a blackboard in my own department in the days when students were more willing to express discontent than they are today: 'When everything's said and done, there's a lot more said than done'. If this second image were accurate, then again, according to our own lights, we might either deplore the existence of such a complacent subject or applaud it for its potential for clarifying claims and convictions which are themselves simply taken as read.

Now it could hardly fail to be of interest for the study of topics such as freedom, law and authority if philosophy turned out to be either essentially radical or essentially conservative. But of course the rather obvious truth is that neither of these images successfully depicts what philosophy essentially is, if such a depiction is intended to capture the factual, historical record. There are countless instances of philosophers who have put forward either radical or conservative views in their philosophy, but it would be another matter to show that *philosophy itself* required them to do one thing or the other. To put the point in a particular idiom, there have been philosophers who have practised *descriptive* metaphysics, content merely to describe the existing structure of our thought about the world, and other philosophers who have practised *revisionary* metaphysics, with the determination to provide a better structure.[1] It would be a harsh judgment to conclude that one or other group was not really doing philosophy.

Indeed, in many cases it will be far from clear whether a given philosophy is properly regarded as conservative or radical in the first place. Take an example which has particular relevance to the area of political philosophy. For a sizeable proportion of the early and middle part of this century, the prevailing orthodoxy held that when it comes to the values which people espouse, philosophy must be an entirely 'second-order' study. That is, on the one hand there is the first-order business of making normative or practical claims about what things are valuable, what actions are right, and so on; and on the other hand there is the possibility of second-order reflection on claims of the first kind, discussion of their meaning, the concepts they employ, and so on. And it has frequently been held that philosophy could not itself involve making any recommendations of the first-order, normative or practical kind.[2] Is that view of the scope of philosophy radical or conservative? It has radical implications for the efforts of philosophers as diverse as Plato and G. E. Moore, who certainly did make normative recommendations in the course of their philosophy. It is clear, however, whether its impact on our belief in certain values, prior to doing any philosophy, is to be regarded as radical or conservative. It does not in any straightforward way endorse them, but neither does it attempt to supersede them.

What we can say with rather greater certainty is that this way of restricting the subject, its confinement to a particular kind of enquiry, has itself often rested on highly contentious philosophical assumptions.

It has often been assumed that statements expressing convictions about values are in some way suspect, not capable of being given the kind of reasoned support which is possible for other statements, and indeed not strictly being genuine statements at all. They have been taken to resemble expressions of subjective feeling rather than coherent expressions of thought, so that they do not represent a claim about some state of affairs in the world which might be supported by evidence and judged to be either true or false.

To the extent that the restriction of the scope of philosophy was bound up with this view of the nature of thinking about values, the orthodoxy which sponsored that restriction was itself only as secure as the contentious philosophical assumptions on which it rested. The orthodoxy described here is now very much on the wane, a fact borne out by the very substantial body of work which has built up in the last fifteen years or so displaying first-order commitment to particular values. The decline of an orthodoxy does not in itself show that there was anything wrong with it, of course, and alongside this body of work debate continues on the second-order question of the objectivity or otherwise of statements about values.[3]

The fact of this continuing debate perhaps gives us a clue to a less contentious and more modest truth about what philosophy essentially is. By reason of its nature as a form of intellectual enquiry it involves a commitment simply to *following the argument wherever it leads*, whether that turns out to be in a radical or a conservative direction. That characterization would cover an immeasurably wider span of activities and texts than either the radical or the conservative one, and it would gain assent from practitioners of the subject who might disagree vehemently on many particular questions of doctrine. Philosophy on this construction would simply promote *reasoning*, as against hollow rhetoric, covert manipulation, wilful obscurantism and many other less thoughtful ways of proceeding.

Philosophy on this construction would also connect in an interesting way with the political tradition that surrounds us. That tradition is in a recognizable sense a liberal one. It involves placing a very high premium on the liberty and dignity of individual human beings, and acknowledging the importance of voluntarily given consent where imposition of social arrangements is concerned. This produces a special commitment to the use of reason, as opposed to violence, as a means of organizing human affairs and dealing with disputes.[4] The commitment to reasoning, therefore, is common to philosophy and the liberal tradition. But then by the same token it becomes equally important in evaluating the liberal tradition to be prepared to follow the argument wherever it leads. It becomes important to meet challenges to that tradition by the use of rational argument rather than anything else.

2. The Components of Liberalism

The liberal tradition consists both of a set of concrete political *institutions* and of a set of underlying *theories*. The institutions are informed by the theories and give practical expression to them. We might include among those institutions civil liberties such as legal provision for freedom of expression, periodic elections, religious tolerance, trial by jury, and the like. These institutions are fragile. In historical terms they are relatively new, in geographical terms they are less than universal, and their desirability is not a matter of unanimous agreement even in those parts of the world where they exist. However, it is primarily the fragility of the liberal theory underlying these institutions which is the subject of my discussion.

First, we must give a slightly fuller characterization of liberal theory. This is a project which has its own difficulties. When we speak of the theory underlying an entire tradition, we are referring to a complicated web of overlapping beliefs and attitudes, deriving from a large number of different sources and stretching over a considerable span of time. To reduce this to manageable proportions, what we can do is concentrate on a core of doctrine which is not necessarily attributable in its entirety to any one theorist, but which does represent an articulation of a set of beliefs which would receive common assent. In any case, there is at least an obvious textual starting point in the writings of John Stuart Mill, described by another extremely influential theorist as the founder of modern liberalism (Berlin, 1969, 173).

In what must be one of the most widely quoted passages in the history of modern political theory, Mill asserts in his *Essay on Liberty* that 'the sole end for which mankind are warranted, individually or collectively, in interfering with the liberty of action of any of their number is self-protection. That the only purpose for which power can be rightfully exercised over any member of a civilized community, against his will, is to prevent harm to others. His own good, either physical or moral, is not a sufficient warrant.' To justify interference in someone's behaviour, that behaviour 'must be calculated to produce evil to some one else . . . Over himself, over his own body and mind, the individual is sovereign' (Mill, 1859, 72–73).

Freedom of action, then, is to be sustained over the widest possible area, such freedom being curtailed only when it threatens to harm someone other than the person exercising it. Interference on any other grounds is not justified, and this would exclude interference on two sorts of grounds in particular: *paternalistic* grounds, where intervention occurs in someone's life against their will but for their own good; and what we might call *purely moralistic* grounds, where action is taken to prevent someone from behaving in a way which is thought morally undesirable though not actually harmful to anyone else.

Traditional debate over Mill's principle has centred around the questions whether any acceptable definition of *harm* can be given so as to enable us to operate Mill's principle in a clear and acceptable way, and (relatedly) whether it is possible to distinguish a sphere of action where people are liable to harm only themselves from one where they run the risk of harming others as well. My own purpose is not to pursue this traditional debate directly, but simply to use Mill as a starting point.[5]

Implicit in his remarks is an indication both of the degree of importance attached in the liberal tradition to freedom or liberty (I use the two terms interchangeably), and of the particular conception of freedom employed in that tradition. As an illustration of the relative importance attached to liberty, suppose that some group of people live in very deprived conditions, as compared with others. It might be thought important that the non-deprived should help the deprived. Well and good if they can be persuaded to do so, but on the principle enunciated here[6] there would be no justification for actually compelling them to do so—at least not unless their failure to help could itself be characterized as a form of harm which they were inflicting on the deprived people. Otherwise, that one condition is not fulfilled which licenses interference with the liberty of the non-deprived group.

The particular conception of freedom implicit here has come to be known since Mill's time as negative liberty. In this conception, freedom is essentially a matter of simply being left alone by other human beings, of not being interfered with. This is distinct from an alternative, positive conception of freedom, according to which freedom consists in having the capacity and the opportunity to act in certain ways. The difference between the negative and positive conceptions can be brought out in this way. Suppose that no one is preventing me from dining at the Ritz but that because of a lack of money I am unable to do so. Then according to the negative conception I am free to dine at the Ritz, but according to the positive conception I am not. This is a consequence generally recognized in liberal theory, which preserves a distance between what I am free to do and what I am fully able to do.[7]

The consequence of combining the negative conception of freedom with a commitment to its preservation except where it threatens harm to others is a division of individuals' lives into, as it were, two spheres. There is a private sphere—private, not in the sense of being hidden or confidential, but in the sense of being a sphere where I am entitled to erect Keep Out notices to protect myself from the intrusion of others if I do not desire it. And there is a public sphere where my actions are subject to possible interference precisely because they may impinge in harmful ways on others.

What other values will be associated with liberty on this view of things? Plainly, *toleration* will receive heavy emphasis. I may find the behaviour of other individuals offensive, or wrong-headed, but the principle of preserving liberty to the maximum extent will enjoin me to tolerate such behaviour and respect the privacy, in the sense mentioned a moment ago, of those perpetrating it. To put it one way, liberalism requires me to combine commitment to the particular customs or practices which I value with a commitment to respecting what may be quite different commitments to quite distinct sets of customs and practices on the part of other people. And that, in a sense, is all it requires of me. On the face of it, at least, it appears to be remarkably neutral on the substantive question how people ought to live their lives. So far as that goes, all that liberalism seems to require of me is that I should tolerate *any* way of living as long as it does not harm anyone other than those living it.

The connection with *democracy* is more complicated. A large part of the reason why Mill insists on the importance of individual liberty is his fear of the tyranny of the majority, and Berlin argues that an individual may have more individual liberty under an easy-going despot than in an intolerant democracy (Berlin, 1969, lvii). But this caution about the link between freedom and democracy proceeds from a too-ready identification of democracy with majority rule. It is natural to make such an identification because systems of majority rule are the most familiar embodiment of democratic principle at the institutional level. But at the theoretical level there are grounds for resisting the identification and seeking an elaboration of the idea of democracy more in terms of consensus than of conflictual politics.[8] When that is done, it enables us to see how the notions of freedom, law and authority combine in liberal theory.

Let us grant the primacy of liberty. The problem then is that individuals' lives intersect in such a way that they do on occasion threaten harm, and indeed inflict it on one another. What is to be done about that? Intervention is as necessary here as it is unjustified in any other circumstances. Free agents can recognize this, and *decide* to set up an agency whose role it is to prevent or deter incursions on their own liberty. In this way, the law can be seen not as a constraint but as a protector and facilitator of freedom,[9] and authority can be acknowledged as residing in the body appointed to settle disputes over infringements of freedom.

In other words, we can tell a plausible story about how we recognize the danger of incursions in our lives, and agree to the setting up of an authority to settle disputes which arise in the course of human interaction, in accordance with general laws which are acknowledged and determined in advance. Along these lines a justification can be worked out, not, to be sure, for the actions of *any* state, but specifically for those of the liberal democratic state. For in this state, it can be argued, individual citizens themselves provide the input which determines what laws are to bind them. Nothing is being forced on them, therefore, and the resulting system of authority is justified not merely by its results but because it has been chosen by those it affects.

If my surmise is correct, then these thoughts about the background to freedom, law and authority will be familiar to anyone brought up in our political culture. They set the parameters, as it were, within which argument about equality, justice, penal policy and much else are conducted. It is therefore important to subject them to further examination, in order to judge whether they are defensible as starting points for these other questions, or whether, on the contrary, we need to revise them and construct our political philosophy on some different basis.

3. Is Liberalism Self-refuting?

Having given this sketch of liberal theory, I now want to consider the suggestion that at two points it is in danger of becoming self-refuting. This is a charge not just that the theory is under-defended, nor that it contains superficial inconsistencies which can be removed, but that it undercuts itself in some more serious way. Given some of the premises on which the theory is built, so it may be said, then the conclusions which it purports to reach become unattainable. (Obviously this claim will hold interest only if I have managed to invest the theory as I have described it with antecedent plausibility.) The two points at which this may be thought to happen concern the conception of liberty, and the setting up of law and authority.

Liberal theory, and arguably any political theory, presupposes a particular conception of human nature. This can be brought out if we ask why freedom, as defined in liberal theory, should be thought to hold any importance. What exactly is *wrong* with major interference in people's lives in any of the ways which liberal theory disallows? The answer, I suggest, is that there is an ideal of personal autonomy underlying the liberal emphasis on freedom.[10] People are capable of living their lives for themselves—of forming their own goals, making their own decisions about the best means to reach them, and acting in accordance with their own conception of how their life should be. And gross interference is wrong because it is wrong to take this capability away from them. This helps to explain, amongst other things, the importance attached to civil liberties when it comes to the concrete embodiment of liberal principles. The exercise of autonomy requires a readiness to reason, to open up one's ideas to the criticisms of others, to be guided by the weight of evidence, and so on. The provision of freedom of speech and expression, freedom of assembly and association with others serves this end at the level of institutional safeguards.

Is this notion of human beings as rational, autonomous agents to be understood as expressing a factual claim about what they *are* like, or a normative claim about how they *should* be? I suspect that it functions as both in the context of liberal theory, and is none the worse for that. It denotes a state of affairs to which actual human behaviour approximates, but it is a normatively charged state of affairs. Nor is it an implausible description of how human beings can be, although I shall suggest in section 4 that it is in need of modification and supplementation. For the moment, however, the question is what follows if something like this is taken as a premise about how human beings can be, sometimes are and should be.

Consider, therefore, the impact of these considerations on the liberal conception of freedom. If other individuals do not leave me alone, that may well have undesirable consequences for the plans I make as a reasoning, autonomous creature. But if the point in forming the concept of freedom is to bring under one heading the factors which may threaten my autonomous status, there is no reason to construct a conception as confined as the negative conception of freedom. Other factors than those to do with the actions of human beings, for example factors relating to my environment or my circumstances, may equally constrain what I can achieve as a reasoning, autonomous creature.

Concretely, imagine that a young person conceives the project of achieving a given level of proficiency on a musical instrument. He or she may have the requisite talent for this and there may be no direct interference by another human being to prevent it. Yet they may be thwarted in this autonomously chosen project because they lack money to buy tuition or an instrument. There is, therefore, as much reason to bring these too within the scope of the concept of freedom. The very point which the negative conception is meant to serve actually undermines that conception. The idea of the preservation of autonomy, which motivates the construction of a concept of freedom in the first place, is more accurately brought out when the interference of others is integrated with considerations such as the presence or absence of material resources or of appropriate knowledge, and so on, which may equally be prerequisites for autonomous action as the forbearance of fellow creatures.

Many critics of liberalism have taken issue with the negative conception of liberty. They have also been critical of the division of human social life into two spheres which is associated with that conception: the public sphere of citizenship, where the law can be expected to preserve negative freedom, and the private sphere of economic relations where different standards and expectations apply.[11] I endorse those criticisms. It seems to me arbitrary, for example, to deny that penury or limited horizons arising from lack of knowledge may curtail someone's freedom just as surely as the threat of an assassin's bullet. Equally, whilst the importance attached to civil liberties in the liberal tradition seems to me a point of immense value, it seems arbitrary to place emphasis on the need for legal provision and none on the material conditions which must also be fulfilled if there is to be any realistic possibility of particular agents' taking advantage of the liberties guaranteed them by law. But my point here is not merely to disagree with this aspect of liberal theory but to argue that the premises of liberalism itself suggest that we should be led away, to some extent, from the conventional wisdom of liberalism.

I turn now to the second charge that liberal theory stands in danger of self-refutation, which also proceeds from the underlying conception of human nature as that of autonomous, rational agents. Here, however, as I shall indicate, I believe that no straightforward endorsement of the charge is possible.

In contemporary society, one of the major sources of intervention in our lives is the state. It has a decisive influence in such matters as how and where we are born, what sort of houses we can live in and what we may do to them, how we educate our children, what sort of medical treatment we receive and how we are disposed of when dead. Where there is influence as striking as this there is also the possibility of harm, and the encroachments of the state therefore themselves stand in need of justification in the light of the importance attached to personal freedom. Moreover, a justification simply in terms of the good effects of state intervention will not suffice, given the general embargo on paternalism in liberal theory and the special status of autonomous beings. Given the presuppositions of our own historical era, we are likely to reject forms of argument which might have passed muster in earlier times. For example, we are unlikely to be receptive to lines of reasoning which might well ring true for people who accepted the Aristotelian belief that some human beings were by their nature born to be slaves. These considerations account for the stress laid on *consent* in justifying the demands of obedience which the state makes, as I indicated towards the end of section 2.

But why should that kind of justification of the authority of the liberal democratic state stand in any danger of self-refutation? We can begin to see why if we notice that the conception of autonomous agency which we have considered so far can be given a specifically moral tinge. I am capable not only of fashioning my own life in the way earlier described, but of doing so in accordance with notions of right and

215

wrong which I myself give assent to. I am capable of *conscientious moral action*. Moreover, there is a strong current of thought in the liberal tradition which holds moral action to be precisely that action which accords with an individual's conscience. I am behaving as a responsible moral agent when I act in what I sincerely believe is the right way after I have given the matter careful and serious consideration.

In sketching the justification for liberal state authority, we have assumed that the conscientious individual does assent to the existing arrangements for formulating and enforcing laws. But suppose that he or she does not. Suppose that they cannot find it in their conscience to allow curtailment of particular moral or non-moral plans which they have made, as is demanded by authority. And suppose that on that basis they claim a moral entitlement to resist it, and complain that the imposition of law in these circumstances would amount to coercion rather than facilitating freedom. What then are we to say?

The standard liberal response is to develop theories of civil disobedience and conscientious refusal at this point: to give a definition of these forms of resistance and an account of the circumstances in which they are themselves justified.[12] But this is to fail to appreciate the full force of the problem of conscientious disagreement with authority, and a far more thoroughgoing challenge to liberalism on that basis has been mounted by R. P. Wolff (1976). Wolff argues that the primacy of conscience is incompatible with the acceptance of *any* form of political authority. Because I am the originator of my actions, because I am in that sense responsible for them, I should *take* responsibility for them and retain wherever and whenever possible the discretion as to how I am to act (Wolff, 1976, 12–15). But, he argues, that is precisely what I relinquish if I recognize political authority.

Consider the liberal state, based as it is on principles of representative and loosely majority governed democracy. Representatives enact legislation which places me under constraints, but have no effective means of finding out what I, as an autonomous individual agent, would choose as legislation: I have elected them, if I elected them at all, simply on some very general programme, which they are in any case free to ignore when elected. Their decisions cannot therefore be taken as an expression of my will, any more than those of some benevolent dictator whose decisions happened to serve my interests or find my approval (ibid., 29–30). Similarly, while it may be true that liberal democratic systems reduce social friction, advance general welfare, or serve some other desirable end, such considerations can only function as reasons which I may choose to adopt as persuading me to co-operate with the state. They do not furnish a demonstration of the *authority* of the state, the right to demand my obedience to whatever it commands, for I could grant it that authority only at the cost of forfeiting my own autonomy (ibid., 40).

Many critics have taken the view that Wolff's arguments are easily disposed of. My own view is that they can be disposed of, but not easily.[13] They are directed against a genuinely held liberal position, rather than a man of straw: the position which holds that laws are not to be obeyed without exception, nor are they to be obeyed just because they are laws, but that we are under an obligation to obey the laws of a democracy and that obligation arises from weighty moral considerations which are not to be lightly overridden.

Wolff's challenge can be expressed in the form of the question 'Who decides?' If we say that I am under an obligation to obey laws only when they are just, or protect people from harm, or were democratically arrived at, that still leaves the problem what agency is designated as the one to decide when the appropriate condition is fulfilled. If I reserve that right to myself then I do appear to deny the authority of the state for, as I have argued elsewhere, it is a matter of legal fact that existing liberal democratic states do demand a greater degree of obedience and allow a lesser degree of autonomy than that, and it is a matter of plausible argument to say that they must do so (cf. Graham, 1982, 125–126). On the other hand, if I do not reserve that right to myself, then I am writing a blank cheque in a way which is arguably not the act of a conscientious moral agent. I am agreeing in advance to be bound in ways which I cannot yet specify and which I may well think to be, in the event, highly questionable.

Now it seems certain that this challenge must be capable of being met in some way or another. Even Wolff appears to be uncomfortable with the rather exiguous 'philosophical anarchism' which he is left with by elimination, and it is a ground for further confidence in the wrongness of his arguments that they would make it impossible for a conscientious moral agent to accept *any conceivable* form of political authority, not just those forms which happen to surround us in an imperfect world. Nevertheless, it is one thing to say that an argument is wrong and another thing actually to show what is wrong with it. We may feel disposed to react impatiently to Wolff's argument. After all, it may be said, though we may think highly of autonomy and conscience, philosophical niceties should not deter us from preventing wicked people from going around doing wicked things to innocent people. And that would be the result if the premium placed on conscience were allowed to loosen respect for the law. Perhaps that complaint is correct, but as I indicated earlier on, it is an important part of the liberal commitment to given an intellectual justification for our attitudes, and it will be unsatisfactory simply to assert that we have to do what we have to do.

217

4. Liberalism and the Individual

I described in section 1 the view that convictions about matters of value are suspiciously subjective and not capable of justification in the way that convictions about matters of fact are. Even someone (like me) who does not share that view would have to agree that there is certainly no available recipe for neatly resolving basic questions of value. That may lead us to suppose that we have now landed in very murky water indeed, for the two arguments about the self-refuting nature of liberal theory are essentially arguments about the acceptability of the values of freedom and authority as these are interpreted in that theory. But in this section I want to suggest that we should locate these questions about values in a wider (or deeper) context. I have already indicated how some particular conception of human nature is presupposed in a theory like liberal theory. It is a continuation of the same point to indicate how some conception of human *society* is also presupposed.

What presuppositions might appropriately be mentioned? Liberal theory has a very *atomistic* conception of both human nature and human society. The special place accorded to individual conscience will be apparent enough from our recent discussion; the individual human being is the locus of moral decision and subsequent moral action; the individual human being is the entity deserving of special protected status. The almost irresistible spread of democratic ideas in the West has, as de Tocqueville predicted, followed on from the idea, familiar since the Renaissance, that individual human beings as such are important. They are the building blocks of society, and social arrangements must be acceptable to them.

Several distinct forms of individualism can be discerned here: the *moral* individualism which allots protected status to human beings as such; the *psychological* individualism which rests on a picture of each human being forming ideas and plans and reaching decisions in relative isolation from the activities of other similar creatures; and the *ontological* individualism which holds that the moral and political realm which we are concerned with contains only these individual human beings or other entities which can be reduced to them.

Disentangling these forms of individualism is a complex business.[14] Without exploring the issue here in the detail which it deserves, my claim would be that the moral individualism rests in a complicated way on the other forms, rather than vice versa. If that is true, then we have not landed in the murk of a disagreement about values at bedrock. Rather we shall be able to progress in our assessment of liberalism if we can make an assessment of these more fundamental forms of individualism on which it rests. What I want to suggest is that they inadequately capture the significance of what it is like to live a human life in a human society. This is not a matter of calling attention to facts which liberals are unaware of or have forgotten: it is a matter of trying to ensure that these facts, unexceptional and commonplace in themselves, receive the kind of emphasis and significance which they deserve in the way we conceptualize our own situation.

First, the rational autonomous agent is not an isolated creature making up its own conception of the world or its own projects from scratch. On the contrary, our way of looking at things and our own aspirations will be at the very least deeply influenced by those around us. This is an obvious enough point[15] but an important one, which has implications for the notion of isolated agents as solely responsible, from a causal point of view, for what they do. Not only is the social input an indispensable part of the causal process which issues in subsequent behaviour, but human agents largely or wholly choose their plans and actions from a pre-existing stock, as it were. Consequently, causal responsibility for the outcome is spread well beyond their own choices and decisions. That is a particularly important consideration, it seems to me, for dismantling the challenge laid down in Wolff's critique of liberalism, but one which will not leave liberalism just as it was.

Secondly, the rational autonomous agent is also an *embodied* creature, with many material needs which must be met recurrently as a precondition of engaging in any further projects: we must eat, clothe ourselves and provide ourselves with adequate shelter. We do not live in a Garden of Eden, and generally speaking we are, individually, unable to make all these provisions for ourselves (both because of limited skills and knowledge and because of limited resources). In consequence, to aspire to any project whatever, including mere survival, is to aspire to a state of affairs which has large implications for large numbers of other people and the shape of *their* lives. That consideration seems to me to have serious implications for the two spheres view of human life.

Thirdly, individual human beings are not the only agents whose actions have significance for our understanding of our own social life. In many different contexts and at very different levels of generality we are members of collective entities: clubs, committees, juries, elector-ates, political parties, trade union movements, consciousness-raising groups, perhaps whole nations. Take a club as an example. In one sense, a club is reducible to individual human beings: it does not consist of anything but them and their relations to one another. Yet in another sense it is not so reducible: the club may be in a position to do certain things which its individual members are not (a fact which may be reflected in legal arrangements), and even though the club's acting in particular ways may require individual members doing something, we may precisely have to describe them as doing that thing *as members of that club* if we are to bring out the relevant significance of what they are up to.

The importance of collective entities in the modern world should not be underestimated. They may have resources at their disposal, powers of recall and powers of action which are entirely unavailable to individual human beings.[16] They may survive much longer than any collection of individual human beings who compose them at a given time, and they may have interests which are distinct from those of the individuals. All of this will make a difference to the reasoning which individuals will go through prior to selecting their goals and the means of achieving them if they are to live their lives sensibly and effectively.[17]

The upshot is this. The basic building blocks of liberal theory ought not to be thought of simply as active, conscious beings. They need to be thought of, from the beginning and consistently throughout our theorizing, as embodied, material entities, standing in ineliminable social relations to one another. Not only that, but it must be allowed that there are also other basic building blocks, entities which are not themselves individual human beings but which do possess some of the same characteristics (memories, resources, powers to decide and act) that are thought peculiarly apposite in liberal theory. If we gave these points the centrality they merit, the result would be a change of perspective which would be highly likely to result in a different theory from that provided in the traditional liberalism which I have been discussing. It might, in an important way, be some kind of *post*-liberal theory.

5. Conclusion

I said earlier that the liberal tradition consisted both of a body of theory and of a set of concrete institutions, and that my concern was with the theory. In conclusion, however, I want to turn briefly to the concrete context in which theorizing takes place.

It would, of course, be entirely naive to imagine that people sit down to think out some ideas of how to live together in society and then get up to design a set of arrangements which conform to the specifications of the ideas. The relation between theory and practice is far more complex and far less one-sided than that would imply. Besides, following the argument where it leads requires us already to direct our attention to one argument rather than another, and existing concrete circumstances are likely to have a considerable effect on that. This is clear in Berlin's case especially. His concern with liberal values was borne of an abhorrence of the totalitarian regimes which have given practical expression to *in*humane values in the twentieth century. A defence of liberal values on those grounds is entirely justified, even if those values are only incompletely realized in liberal institutions.

Our current concrete context is nothing if not fluid. Liberal institutions are probably no less under threat than they have been at earlier times (though it would be the subject of another and a different kind of enquiry to determine from what direction the greatest threat currently comes). There are glimmers, too, that some of the world's illiberal regimes may be becoming less so. But even if this were otherwise, we ought not to be dissuaded from further critical examination of liberal values merely because less desirable political institutions than those of liberalism exist, complete with their own apologetics. For, in the case both of political theories and of political institutions, it is arguable that the appropriate standard of comparison is not actually existing alternatives but *possible* alternatives.[18] If politics is the art of the possible, we should at least make sure that we explore the full range of what *is* possible. Liberalism is in more than one sense a Victorian doctrine. And whilst Victorian values may have much to recommend them, they are hardly likely to contain all the wisdom we need to see us safely through into the twenty-first century.[19]

Notes

[1] The terminology of descriptive and revisionary metaphysics is due to Strawson (1959), 9. Notice that even descriptive metaphysics is potentially subversive of received opinion. This is because philosophy rarely confines itself literally to description, as opposed to chains of reasoning. And chains of reasoning may lead us to places other than those we are familiar with or expect to arrive at. That, indeed, is the burden of some of my argument in what follows.

[2] The *locus classicus* for this view is Ayer (1936). In another place he says of a theory which he propounds: 'It . . . is an attempt to show what people are doing when they make moral judgments; it is not a set of suggestions as to what moral judgments they are to make. And this is true of all moral philosophy as I understand it. All moral theories . . . in so far as they are philosophical theories, are neutral as regards actual conduct' (Ayer, 1954, 245–246). This orthodoxy can be viewed as itself part of a wider orthodoxy, according to which the whole of philosophy was a second-order study, 'conceptual analysis', which did not itself imply any changes in the corpus of concepts it was concerned to analyse. For criticisms of this wider orthodoxy, see Gellner (1979) and Graham (1977).

[3] For a recent discussion, see Nagel (1986), 138–163.

[4] But for doubts about the adequacy of this dichotomy, see Edgley (1974).

[5] For the traditional debate, see for example, Hart (1963) and Devlin (1965).

[6] It is, of course, a matter of long controversy what exactly follows from this principle as it is enunciated by Mill himself. That question is complicated by the fact that he is a utilitarian and by the possibility that allotting primacy both to liberty and to utility places contradictory demands on a theory. (On the

other hand, it may be argued that any realistic conception of human beings' utility must include liberty itself as a major component.) The strategy of regarding failure to help as a species of harm also seems to me to threaten Mill's theory by leaving no potentially harmless activities. My disclaimer to be dealing with Mill's theory as such must be taken seriously, however. For sympathetic treatments of Mill which attempt to release him from some of these difficulties, see Gray (1983) and Ten (1980).

[7] Berlin, to whom the negative/positive distinction is due, says 'You lack political liberty or freedom only if you are prevented from attaining a goal by human beings. Mere incapacity to attain a goal is not lack of political freedom' (Berlin, 1969, 122). Consistently with this, he argues that having liberty is distinct from enjoying the conditions for its exercise (ibid., liii). Rawls similarly declines to count poverty or a lack of means generally among the constraints definitive of liberty: they affect the *worth* of liberty, its value to an individual, but they do not determine whether that individual has liberty (Rawls, 1972, 204).

[8] I argue this more fully in Graham (1986a, 101–114).

[9] I speak here, of course, at the level of theory. Actual laws can, and sometimes do, constitute a constraint on freedom in the negative, liberal sense.

[10] Gray notices that though the jargon of autonomy is absent from Mill's writing, the idea is of fundamental importance (Gray, 1983, 78). For a recent discussion of autonomy and its place in liberal theory, see Lindley (1986).

[11] For one such apposite criticism, see Macpherson (1973). The division of social life into two spheres is made explicitly by Rawls (1972, 61).

[12] Such an account is provided by Rawls (1972, 363–391) Towards the end of his account Rawls asserts that in a democratic society 'it is recognized that each citizen is responsible for his interpretation of the principles of justice and for his conduct in the light of them' (Rawls, 1972, 390). That is precisely the starting point for the challenge to liberal accounts of obedience to the state.

[13] For a discussion of Wolff's critics, see Graham (1982); and for successive attempts to dispose of his arguments, see Graham (1984 and 1986a, 75–116).

[14] For a more comprehensive account of forms of individualism, see Lukes (1973), and for some of the disentangling see Graham (1986a, 95–105).

[15] Mill recognizes it in saying of a 'person whose desires and impulses are his own' that they 'are the expression of his own nature, as it has been developed and modified by his own culture' (Mill, 1859, 118).

[16] This point is well brought out in O'Neill (1986).

[17] The difficulties either in doing this or in producing a theory which adequately exhibits how it is done should not be underestimated. I have considered some possible approaches and their drawbacks in Graham (1986b).

[18] I develop this point more fully in Graham (1986a, 239–242).

[19] I am greatly indebted to David Archard, Richard Lindley and Penny Wrout for critical comments on an earlier draft of this paper, which draws on ideas expressed in a number of my recent publications, listed under References.

References

Ayer, A. J. (1936) *Language, Truth and Logic* (London: Gollancz, 2nd edn, 1946).

Ayer, A. J. (1954) 'On the Analysis of Moral Judgments' in *Philosophical Essays* (London: Macmillan).

Berlin, I. (1969) *Four Essays on Liberty* (Oxford: Clarendon Press).

Devlin, P. (1965) *The Enforcement of Morals* (London: Oxford University Press).

Edgley, R. (1974) 'Reason and Violence' in Korner, S. (ed.), *Practical Reason* (Yale University Press).

Gellner, E. (1979) *Words and Things*, rev. edn (London: Routledge and Kegan Paul).

Graham, K. (1977) *J. L. Austin: A Critique of Ordinary Language Philosophy* (Sussex: Harvester).

Graham, K. (1982) 'Democracy and the Autonomous Moral Agent' in Graham, K. (ed.), *Contemporary Political Philosophy: Radical Studies* (Cambridge University Press).

Graham, K. (1984) 'Consensus in Social Decision-making: Why is it Utopian?', in P. Alexander and R. Gill (eds), *Utopias* (London: Duckworth).

Graham, K. (1986a) *The Battle of Democracy* (Sussex: Wheatsheaf).

Graham, K. (1986b) 'Morality and Abstract Individualism', *Proceedings of the Aristotelian Society,* **87**.

Gray, J. (1983) *Mill on Liberty: A Defence* (London: Routledge and Kegan Paul).

Hart, H. L. A. (1963) *Law, Liberty and Morality* (London: Oxford University Press).

Lindley, R. (1986) *Autonomy* (London: Macmillan).

Lukes, S. (1973) *Individualism* (Oxford: Blackwell).

Macpherson, C. B. (1973) 'Berlin's Division of Liberty' in *Democratic Theory* (New York: Oxford University Press).

Marx, K. (1845) *Theses on Feuerbach*, in L. D. Easton and K. H. Guddat, *Writings of the Young Marx on Philosophy and Society* (New York: Doubleday and Co., 1967).

Mill, J. S. (1859) *Essay on Liberty* (London: Dent, 1972).

Nagel, T. (1986) *The View from Nowhere* (New York: Oxford University Press).

O'Neill, O. (1986) *Faces of Hunger* (London: Allen and Unwin).

Rawls, J. (1972) *A Theory of Justice* (London: Oxford University Press).

Strawson, P. F. (1959) *Individuals* (London: Methuen).

Ten, C. L. (1980) *Mill on Liberty* (Oxford: Clarendon Press).

Wittgenstein, L. (1953) *Philosophical Investigations* (Oxford: Blackwell).

Wolff, R. P. (1976) *In Defense of Anarchism*, 2nd edn (New York: Harper and Row).

Notes on Contributors

D. C. Barrett, SJ, is Reader in Philosophy at the University of Warwick. He is editor of *Lectures and Conversations on Aesthetics, Psychology and Religious Belief by Ludwig Wittgenstein* and was a contributor to the 1987 Royal Institute Lectures *Contemporary French Philosophy*.

Norman Barry is the author of several books, including *On Classical Liberalism and Libertarianism* (1986) and *The New Right* (1987). He is Professor of Politics at the University of Buckingham.

Stephen R. L. Clark is Professor of Philosophy at the University of Liverpool. 'Slaves and Citizens' appeared in *Philosophy* (1985) and 'Abstract Morality, Concrete Cases' in the Institute volume *Moral Philosophy and Contemporary Problems* (1987). He is the author of several books, including *Civil Peace and Sacred Order*.

Kenneth Graham, Reader in Philosophy at the University of Bristol, is currently writing a book on Marx's philosophy. He published *The Battle of Democracy* in 1986, and his 'Morality, Individuals and Collectives' was contributed to the Institute volume *Moral Philosophy and Contemporary Problems* (1987).

A. Phillips Griffiths is Professor of Philosophy at the University of Warwick, where he has arranged a series of biennial conferences on philosophy for teachers in schools and colleges of further education. Director of the Royal Institute of Philosophy since 1979, he has edited five volumes of the Institute's lecture series, as he will (*DV*) the volume of the *Wittgenstein Centenary Lectures* which will be given at the Institute in 1989–90, and the *A. J. Ayer Memorial Lectures* to be given in 1990–91.

Professor D. W. Hamlyn recently retired as Professor of Philosophy at Birkbeck College, University of London. The latest of his many books is *A History of Western Philosophy* (1987). Most relevant to his lecture in this volume are *The Theory of Knowledge* (1971) and *Metaphysics* (1974). A member of the Council of the Royal Institute of Philosophy, he is a contributor to its journal, *Philosophy,* and to the Institute lecture series *Reason and Reality* (1971) and *Objectivity and Cultural Divergence* (1983).

Rom Harré is Fellow of Linacre College, Oxford, and the author of many books. Most relevant to his lecture in this volume is *Varieties of Realism* (1986).

Marcus G. Singer, Professor of Philosophy at the University of Wisconsin, edited the Royal Institute Lecture volume *American Philosophy* (1985) and has contributed a number of articles to *Philosophy*. His best known work is *Generalization in Ethics* (1961).

Notes on Contributors

Richard Swinburne is the Nolloth Professor of the Philosophy of Christian Religion at the University of Oxford. He is the author of many books, including *The Evolution of the Soul* (1986) and *Responsibility and Atonement* (1989), among which the most relevant to the present volume is *The Existence of God* (1979). He is a contributor to the Institute's journal, *Philosophy,* and edited the Institute volume *Space, Time and Causality* (1983).

J. E. Tiles was lecturer in philosophy at the University of Reading before his present appointment in the University of Hawaii. His article 'Techne and Moral Expertise' was published in *Philosophy* in 1984. He is the author of *Things that Happen* (1981) and *Dewey* (1988).

Mary E. Tiles was Secretary of the Royal Institute of Philosophy before her present appointment at the University of Hawaii. A contributor to *Philosophy*, her 'Epistemological History: the Legacy of Bachelard and Canguilhem' is in the Institute lecture series *Contemporary French Philosophy* (1987). She is the author of *Bachelard: Science and Objectivity* (1987) and of *The Philosophy of Set Theory* (1989).

Godfrey Vesey edited the companion volume to the present collection, *Philosophers Ancient and Modern* (1986), as well as eleven other volumes in the series including the lectures on *Philosophy in Christianity,* forthcoming next. He was Director of the Royal Institute of Philosophy for many years until 1979, and is now Deputy Chairman of its Council. He is the author of *The Embodied Mind* (1965), *Perception* (1971) *Personal Identity* (1974) and (with Anthony Flew) *Agency and Necessity* (1987). He is Emeritus Professor of Philosophy of the Open University.

K. V. Wilkes is Fellow of St Hilda's College, Oxford. Her *Physicalism* was published in 1978, and *Real People* in 1988. She is a contributor to the Institute's journal, *Philosophy,* and to past Institute lecture series. *Modelling the Mind,* of which she is co-editor, is forthcoming from the Oxford University Press.

Index of Names

Index of Names

Rashdall, H., 152
Rawls, J., 222 n.
Russell, B., 24–29
Ryle, G., 103

Schopenhauer, A., 8
Scruton, R., 200
Sen, A., 196
Sidgwick, H., 152
Skinner, B., 98
Socrates, 182, 207
Spinoza, B. de, 2
Stevenson, A., 157
Strawson, Sir P., 221 n.

Teller, E., 156
Tertullian, Q., 140, 143
Tocqueville, A. de, 218
Tucker, A., 95–98

Vesey, G., 101ff.
Vico, G., 183, 186

Whatley, R., 156
Wittgenstein, L., 141, 207
Wolff, R., 192, 216–218

Yeats, W., 176

Key themes in philosophy;
ed. by A. Phillips Griffiths.